D0789888

PENGUIN BOOKS

WHAT TO DO WHEN *HE* HAS A HEADACHE

Dr. Janet L. Wolfe, Executive Director of the Institute for Rational–Emotive Therapy in New York City, is a clinical psychologist and sex therapist with more than twenty years of experience in working with women and couples. She is a Diplomate of the American Board of Sexology and has conducted lectures and workshops worldwide, and written numerous articles on cognitive therapy and sexual behavior. She lives and works in New York City.

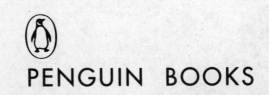

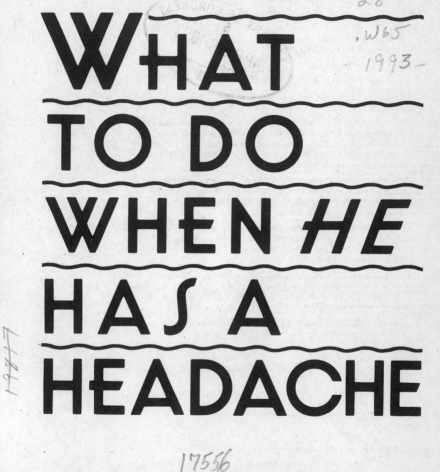

RENEWING DESIRE AND
INTIMACY IN YOUR
RELATIONSHIP

WHAT
TO DO
WHEN *HE*
HAS A
HEADACHE

JANET L. WOLFE, PH.D.

PENGUIN BOOKS
Published by the Penguin Group
Penguin Books USA Inc., 375 Hudson Street,
New York, New York 10014, U.S.A.
Penguin Books Ltd, 27 Wrights Lane, London W8 5TZ, England
Penguin Books Australia Ltd, Ringwood, Victoria, Australia
Penguin Books Canada Ltd, 10 Alcorn Avenue,
Toronto, Ontario, Canada M4V 3B2
Penguin Books (N.Z.) Ltd, 182–190 Wairau Road,
Auckland 10, New Zealand

Penguin Books Ltd, Registered Offices: Harmondsworth,
Middlesex, England

First published in the United States of America by Hyperion 1992
Published in Penguin Books 1993

10 9 8 7 6 5 4 3 2 1

Grateful acknowledgment is made for use of the following:

"Ten Commandments of Masculinity" from *The Liberated Man* by
Warren Farrell. Copyright © 1974 by Warren Farrell, published
by Random House, Inc., New York. (*The Liberated Man* is to be
republished by Berkley Books, N.Y., in 1992.) Reprinted by
permission of the author.

"Most Important Ingredients of a Mature Relationship" from *Why Love
Is Not Enough* by Sol Gordon. Copyright © 1988 by Sol Gordon,
published by Bob Adams, Inc., Holbrook, Mass. Reprinted by
permission of the author and publisher.

From *How to Stop Looking for Someone Perfect and Find Someone to Love*
by Judith Sills. Copyright © 1984 by Judith Sills, published by
St. Martin's Press, Inc., New York. Reprinted by permission
of the author and publisher.

From *Love and Marriage and Trading Stamps: On the Care and Feeding
of Marriage* by Richard Lessor. Copyright © 1971 by Richard Lessor,
published by Argus Communications, Chicago. Reprinted by
permission of the author.

From a Jules Feiffer cartoon in *The Village Voice*. Reprinted by permission
from Universal Press Syndicate.

THE LIBRARY OF CONGRESS HAS CATALOGUED THE HARDCOVER AS FOLLOWS:
Wolfe, Janet L.
What to do when he has a headache: creating renewed desire in your man/by Janet L. Wolfe.
p. cm.
ISBN 1-56282-973-4 (hc.)
ISBN 0 14 01.7899 6 (pbk.)
1. Men—Sexual behavior. 2. Hygiene, Sexual. I. Title.
HQ28.W65 1992
613.9′6—dc20   92–2809

Printed in the United States of America

To my parents

Sophia and Fred Wolfe

for their gifts of love and laughter
and for encouraging me
to pursue my dreams.

ACKNOWLEDGMENTS

To my exceptional friends who have provided an endless fount of love and support: Jill Sheinberg, literary critic, problem-solver, communicator *extraordinaire* and resurrector of my sense of humor, whose help has kept me anchored in even the roughest stages of writing this book. To Iris Fodor, mentor and friend, whose pioneering work in sex-role issues has been a major stimulus in my career path. And to Penelope Russianoff, my dear friend of over twenty-five years who, more than anyone, has helped me realize that deep, long-term female friendships are pure gold. I am also grateful for the inspiration provided by my brother and friend, Sidney Wolfe, who has influenced millions of people to mobilize their frustration over the health care system into constructive action.

To my colleagues at my clinic whose help was vital in many

ways, including commenting on drafts, giving examples from their own experience, and discussing ideas with me: Risa Breckman, Dom DiMattia, Bob Fried, Lisa Muran, and Gina Vega. Thanks as well to Betti Franceschi, Gloria Ren, Leon Russianoff, Malcolm Whyte, and Hannah Wolfe for their valuable suggestions; to Beth Free and Tim Runion for their tireless word-processing; and to Ashley Hoppin for her research assistance.

To the hundreds of men and women who have shared their stories and their lives with me. [I have altered the names and any identifying details in the cited case histories to maintain confidentiality while preserving the essential lesson of the case.]

This book could never have come to fruition were it not for my literary agent *par excellence,* Madeleine Morel, who encouraged me to write the book and cheered me on through every stage of the project with wisdom, humor, and grace. Thanks to my publisher, Bob Miller, for his unwavering support; and to my editor, Judith Riven, for her help in honing my copious first draft into a smoother and more compact form.

Finally, a very special thank you to Albert Ellis, my friend, colleague, and life partner: for providing the philosophical foundations for the book in his pioneering, self-empowering approach to therapy and for his longtime belief in my potential and constant support of my career. And most of all, for teaching me that silliness is next to godliness, and for making me giggle and sing more than anyone I know.

CONTENTS

INTRODUCTION

"I want you. I need you. Your body drives me wild." Heavy breathing and relentlessly seeking hands are all part of what we've been brought up to expect in men. As Tarzan beats his breast, Jane submits to his primordial sexual instincts and uncontrollable desires.

True? Well, it certainly seemed the standard when men were the providers and women stayed at home, when virginity was valued and women didn't discuss sex, at least not openly.

How things have changed! Women no longer "have headaches" or lie back and think of England, America, or their shopping lists while their mates do all the "work." Not only are women willing sexual partners, they are now frequently the ones complaining that their male partners are rejecting *their* overtures.

But complain to whom? Their therapist, if they have one, or perhaps a very close friend—provided they're not feeling too rejected or ashamed to expose their dark secret.

It takes tremendous courage to admit that your partner doesn't make love to you as often as you would like, or that you have sex only once or twice a month, or that when you go to bed he prefers to stay up to watch David Letterman.

Our upbringing has instilled in us the belief that we are the sex that, willingly or not, grants the sexual favors. Throughout adolescence and into the college years we were taught that it was the man who longed for our bodies. Several decades ago the most widely quoted sex book, Dr. William Acton's *Functions and Disorders of the Reproductive Organs* instructed readers that "the majority of women [happily for them] are not very much troubled with sexual feelings of any kind. What men are habitually, women are only exceptionally." Nowadays, however, it seems that it's the woman who, more and more, longs for her mate's sexual attentions. And if he doesn't respond, it may have devastating effects on her psyche.

Often the woman blames herself. "Am I too fat?" Aren't I sexy enough?" "Am I too old?" "Is it my spider veins?" She may worry that there's another woman. Or that her sexual technique is at fault— she's either not seductive enough or too seductive. Worst of all, she might be plagued by the fear that her mate no longer loves her. Millions of women today are wrestling with unprecedented feelings of hurt, anger, and rejection.

In my psychotherapy practice, and in the dozens of workshops I conduct each year throughout the country, I have found that 50 to 60 percent of the time the complaint that one's partner has fizzled out sexually comes from a *woman*. A *Redbook* magazine study of more than a hundred thousand married women revealed that almost four wives in ten, or 38 percent, felt they were not having sex often enough. Increasingly today's marriage dilemma is "*he* doesn't want to."

There are lots of variations on the theme. Tina and Sam—married for sixteen years—had sex four or five times a week for the first two years of their marriage. Now they make love once every two months—sometimes less. What would she optimally like? I asked. "Four times a week—minimum!" she responded. "Our relationship is great in a lot of respects. He's my best friend. But his libido seems to have dried up. And mine is at its peak! He hasn't shown any real sexual interest in me in *months*. And I'm getting sick of always being the one to initiate things. It makes me feel like I'm somehow defective as a woman."

On the occasions when Tina has attempted to talk about their sex life, Sam has gotten embarrassed and refused to discuss the situation. His avoidance and her hurt and anger over it have seriously eroded their relationship. "What am I supposed to do," she cried in desperation after their last fight, "go out and have an affair?"

Marsha burst into tears of embarrassment when she arrived at my office. "Last night I made Brad a beautiful candlelit dinner, then went out for a minute and came back with 'dessert': me, dressed in the sexy lingerie he bought me last Christmas. And guess what he said? That he just felt like spending the evening getting caught up on some reading! I felt so rejected and humiliated."

Although few women would wish a return to the old days of unfulfilling, dutiful sex, many are beginning to wonder if the so-called sexual revolution and women's liberation may have somehow done them in. At least sexually.

The old script was simple: dress seductively and act flirtatiously, but be demure and submissive. No one expected women to be active participants or openly interested in sex.

The main act was male-initiated intercourse leading to male orgasm. Sex was frequently associated with domination, power, and conquest. To have sex with a woman was "to score." The chase was vital to the process of male arousal. Women who were active participants were labeled "sluts," "whores," "castrating," or "nymphomaniacs."

The sexual revolution of the 1960s and early 1970s seemed to promise more sexual enjoyment for women. By demonstrating that the clitoris (and not the vaginal walls) was the primary source of arousal, Masters and Johnson helped women previously labeled "frigid" become orgasmic. The women's movement also helped women take charge of their sexuality, while the pill freed them from fears of pregnancy and the inconveniences of other birth control methods. Sex had progressed from a clunky encounter of foreplay–stop–insert diaphragm–intercourse to a more varied and imaginative set of possibilities. At last, it seemed, men and women could begin to be in sync with each other.

Sexual guilt was on the way out, while hot tubs, casual sex, and even masturbation training groups entered the scene. Our culture had finally caught on to the notion that sex could be good clean fun—for both men *and* women. The societal message was "Sex is good for you. And the more the better." (Or so it was before the age of AIDS and more information came out about the potential risks of the pill.)

Is sexual enjoyment on the rise between men and women? Lamentably, considerable distress exists for both men and women who assume that everyone else is having more sex than they. The most common complaint of partners seeking sex therapy today is a discrepancy between them in their desire for sex. How ironic that in this new era of sexual fulfillment women find their partners lagging behind.

After the sexual openness of the early 1970s, it's sad to see this new problem shrouded in shame and secrecy. Women feel hurt and humiliated when they can't rouse their husband's libido. Especially for women, being untouched and unnoticed can severely affect self-esteem and erode relationships. Men frequently don't even want to think about the implications of not being interested in sex, tied as that is to their sense of "manhood."

So, first of all, take heart. You are not the only couple to be suffering from desire discrepancy—you are not alone by far! With a moderate amount of goodwill and effort, the prospects of increasing the passion in your life are excellent!

WHERE, OH WHERE HAS HIS SEX DRIVE GONE . . . WHERE, OH WHERE CAN IT BE?

Why do so many men seem to be losing interest in sex?

Changing Sex-Role Scripts

Having been brought up with the old sexual script of man-the-pursuer and woman-the-pursued, it's not so easy to change. Men are now expected to relate sexually with a woman who works out, earns as much as or more than her mate, and expects participation from her partner in housework and child care. Having learned how enjoyable sex can be, she may now speak up about what she wants ("Ooh, just a smidgen to the left"), or she may even initiate sex.

One of my clients was told by her partner, "I think I'm intimidated by you sexually because you're so confident, so together." Many men blame women's assertiveness for their sexual avoidance and even for their impotence. One well-known male sexuality expert reports that as many as 30 to 50 percent of the men he encountered frequently felt that sex was a burden—especially now that men are "supposed to" give women orgasms. Many feel overwhelmed by the woman who truly *enjoys* sex: the time-consuming, voluptuous, more imaginative, demanding stuff. Feeling inadequate or threatened by a perceived loss of control, some men withhold sex as a means of restoring the "power balance." Other men may simply feel too lazy.

Is low sexual desire in men a side effect of the women's movement? In point of fact, clinicians have reported that many of the men with low sexual desire are in relationships with women who are not particularly involved in feminist groups. Much of the time, they are married to very traditional women. And Masters and Johnson report that male partners of women with full-time careers outside the home actually have *lower* rates of erectile problems than the male partners of traditional homemakers.

Fear of Closeness

Another offshoot of women's changing relationship expectations is their increasing expression of desire for more closeness. Intimacy can grow as partners get to know each other and accumulate a reservoir of shared experiences. While for most women emotional intimacy greatly enhances the sexual experience, for some men this kind of deep connecting can be "boring" or too much to handle. The resulting anxiety shuts down the desire circuits in their brain. Withholding themselves sexually may be a last-ditch effort to hold on to their individuality and to cope with fears of merging with their partner: "You've got me, but you ain't gonna get my body!"

Even in a fairly new relationship with someone he cares about, a man may begin avoiding sex out of fear of closeness, ambivalence about commitment, or terror of entrapment. So off he goes to the jogging track, the basement, the playing fields, or the ski slopes to avoid sex. It's as though a voice in his head says, "Don't get caught in bed: you'll have to relate to her, satisfy her sexually and emotionally, and she'll suck out your soul." And for good measure, he may convince himself something is wrong with *her:* she's not short enough, tall enough, blonde enough, docile enough, smart enough. Feeling him withdraw, she clutches more tightly—and he runs faster.

Overworked and Overstressed

Another cause of low sexual desire may be his intense involvement in work. This can result in a chronic stress level that prevents a man from switching off and relaxing, sexually or in any other way. One such workaholic, Stuart, a twenty-nine-year-old boyfriend of one of my clients, plops himself in front of the television only wanting to "veg out." Another, Hank, rushes from twelve-hour days at his law firm to two hours of squash, and then home to dive into his briefcase. "My entire life is a treadmill," he confided to me. "Sometimes all I want to do is shut myself in a closet and not be with anyone." Add children to the equation and the stress level can rise even higher.

Self-prescribed stress reducers such as drugs or alcohol may backfire by increasing depression and further causing him to switch off sexually. So, too, will prescription medications like tranquilizers or antihypertensive drugs.

Of course these days many women too are on the fast track careerwise while also juggling child care, household management, and the hundreds of other tasks needed to organize their lives and nurture others.

But while women see sex as a stress *reducer,* a means of connection and source of joy, too many men now view sex as still one *more* stressor, one more area in which they have to "perform."

"There's No Time"

With multiple activities tugging at both of you, from sick kids to business dinners and aerobics classes, sex is often one of the first things to be sacrificed. A major factor in sex getting squeezed out of busy lives is the simple failure to *schedule* it. We schedule workouts, interviews, kids' dance lessons, and dental appointments. If we don't set aside the time for intimate connecting, *it may simply not happen,* even in couples with active sex drives.

Rhoda and Bob both find themselves having sexual feelings and fantasies at various times during the workday. But by the time they get home, eat, and take care of assorted tasks, there's no time left to "do sex." If you don't get enough sleep or sex, sleep will usually take priority!

Basic Boredom

People who have lived together for some time often don't find sex or life in general as spontaneous and exciting as they were in the earliest days of their relationship. When people live together for many years, do their nerve endings change?

Many couples work at keeping their physical connection strong. It becomes a cement that helps them bond and remember, during difficult periods, their deep connection to each other. Or they may jointly make peace with their infrequent or relatively bland sex life, feeling that the many other things they share more than compensate for the sparseness of their sex life.

Others are less successful at keeping the fire alive. In the absence of intense, spontaneous psychological excitement a man may wrongly conclude he's just no longer "attracted" to his partner and there's no point in "forcing" himself. In fact, pushing himself past his boredom or inertia may merely require a little goodwill and effort. By thinking sexy thoughts and getting involved in some *physical* stimulation with his mate, in all probability he would become sexually aroused and proceed to have a quite satisfactory sexual experience with her.

Marital Conflict and Anger

Your man's feelings of anger can be a powerful antiaphrodisiac. They can cause him to withhold sex or even feel sexually repulsed. Anger generally starts in nonsexual areas, such as money, your children, or family chores. Less conscious sources may include a man's anger at his partner because she doesn't take care of him the way she used to or is more successful. Whether or not the anger has been verbally expressed, what better way to get back at his mate than by saying, in effect, "Unscrew you" (literally!).

A wife's anger, frequently caused by feeling ignored and hurt, can result in his becoming more turned off. One of my clients threw a tantrum because she was "sick of being treated like a roommate." Stomping up to bed, she expected her husband to "get the message" and follow her upstairs. Assuming she was still angry at him, he tiptoed up an hour later and timidly kept to his side of the bed. The next morning she angrily confronted him with his "callousness." "I can't believe how you could totally ignore me," she said indignantly, adding that her turning over to face him when he came to bed *"obviously* meant I wanted to make love!"

Fear of Sexual Dysfunction

If he's had problems with getting or maintaining erections or with quick ejaculation, he is likely to be anxious and ashamed and, rather than risk "failure as a man," may avoid sex altogether. This avoidance is no surprise since in our society performing in intercourse is seen by many as the only thing that really counts. Male sexuality expert Bernie Zilbergeld put it so well: his equipment is supposed to be "two feet long, hard as steel, and can go all night." Lovemaking is a sort of threesome: between him, you, and his penis.

Before the sexual revolution redefined women's sexuality, women often avoided close physical contact with their husbands so they wouldn't be pressured into unwanted sex. Now it's the man who might avoid any kind of physical contact—even hugs or kisses—lest it lead you to want more. The longer he goes without sexual or physical contact, the scarier it becomes and the more unlikely he will experiment with new kinds of sexual expression. Perhaps the saddest part is that, ultimately, he may even lose a sense of *himself* as a sexual or sensual person.

HOW DIFFERENT COUPLES REACT TO LEAN MALE LIBIDOS

In a basically good relationship, having little or no sex may not be a major problem. A couple just accepts it. "Sometimes we have it, most of the time we don't. Too bad, but hardly the end of the world. After all," confided Judith, "how many hours a week, even with the sexiest couples, do you spend having sex as opposed to doing other things?"

With some couples, however, the partner who feels deprived or neglected may begin to feel hurt, inadequate, or angry. And more often than not, it is her becoming extremely upset *over* this infrequent sex—rather than the lack of sex itself—that may begin to eat away at the fabric of an otherwise good relationship.

For other couples not only their sex life, but their relationship in general, may be problematic. For example, poor communication or very basic incompatibilities may exist. In these relationships, whether desire discrepancy is the cause or the *symptom* of trouble becomes difficult to determine.

The Male Ego and Desire Discrepancy

Those men who perceive their sexual energy ebbing may worry that their manhood is slipping away, thus compounding the problem. Some start blaming their mate. Others play musical beds, searching for that special woman with whom all will be well.

And many men give up sex altogether. They play ostrich—refusing to initiate, respond to, or even discuss sex. Perhaps they feel the way many women used to—wishing that they just didn't have to be bothered with it.

Women's Response? Why, Blame Yourself!

As we've all painfully come to know, women almost compulsively blame themselves for just about everything—including their mate's lack of desire.

"If no one wants to have sex with me, am I really a woman?" is a serious concern for some women with sexually inactive mates. They may conclude, "If he no longer finds me sexually attractive, he must not love me. And if he doesn't love (and lust for) me, I must not be a worthwhile person."

Ironically, this leads to the newly orgasmic woman who formerly denigrated herself for being "frigid" now blaming herself for her *partner's* lack of sexual interest. "Maybe I've put on too much weight," she might think, or "God, I'm looking so old—no wonder he's not attracted to me anymore." Or "I shouldn't have taken that job that pays more than his."

Some women withdraw into hurt silence, feeling sexually undesirable, unlovable, and inadequate. Others speculate that their mate has another woman and begin searching frantically for clues.

Because women traditionally see themselves as the "emotional administrators" of the relationship, many women jump in and try to "fix" things. They try to talk things over with their partner, and to understand his emotional pressures in order to figure out why his interest in sex has decreased. In many cases they get further rejected when he clams up and refuses to discuss the subject. One friend of mine reported that her mate actually locked himself in the study, he was so mortified by discussing what he viewed as his "sexual inadequacies."

Other women seek help from books and magazine articles on how to fan his sexual fires. They support a billion-dollar lingerie industry in an attempt to look like *Playboy* centerfolds or Parisian hookers. Despite the occasional bursts of flame induced by their frantic attempts to turn him on, women frequently are left with still more rejection, pain, humiliation, and frustration.

Eventually, many women begin to voice their frustrations in less helpful ways. They whine, sulk, or angrily attack their partner's apparent inadequacies—his low-paying job, lack of education, etc. Needless to say, these reactions only worsen the situation: anger, whining, and tears are not a turn-on.

Women need to put sex back in perspective. At its best, sex is a terrific relationship enhancer, a means of expressing love as well as a uniquely pleasurable form of recreation. It's cheaper than bowling—and you don't have to dress for it. But the amount of cultural hype about sex often makes it loom too large in our lives. Just as men have made sex into a do-or-die matter, women are now beginning to do so, using it, as men have, for many of the wrong reasons, such as to shore up sagging self-esteem, to create a closeness that is otherwise lacking, or to fill up a large hole in their lives.

Sex as a Metaphor

How a couple handles sex reflects how they deal with their overall relationship. This book will provide you with a guide not only to enhancing your sex life, but to improving your relationship as a whole. It will discuss how to deal with conflicting wants, excessive familiarity or sense of obligation, how to communicate and negotiate, and how to give and receive nurturance and pleasure.

The book will:

- help you identify and change your *own* overreactions to your partner's low interest so as not to exacerbate the situation;
- provide information on the psychological and physical conditions that interfere with your mate's functioning in both the sexual and nonsexual aspects of his life;
- detail concrete methods to help your partner relate and function better emotionally;
- provide a host of creative, proven sexual enhancement techniques that can be used not only to increase your sensual and sexual

enjoyment but also to improve the overall quality of your relationship; and

- show you how you can still be happy—with or without a scintillating sex life.

Case histories and step-by-step exercises will show you how to apply these guidelines to your own situation.

Low sexual desire is a problem shared by millions of people. It need not mean the end of your relationship. On the contrary, desire discrepancy can motivate couples to work on sparking up a partnership that's begun to feel stale. Those who can calmly acknowledge that things have slowed down and make an effort to communicate and experiment can revitalize not only their lovemaking but their entire lives together.

In this age of AIDS, herpes, and other sexually transmitted diseases, outside affairs no longer are a solution to sexual boredom. Rather, there is every reason to believe that with some education, goodwill, effort, and a rational approach to the problem, within a monogamous, long-term relationship, people can in fact keep their sex lives active and satisfying.

One final note: Although this book is aimed at heterosexual couples, it can be helpful to those in homosexual relationships as well. It will also help women not currently partnered in dealing with any feelings of inadequacy they may have if they are not being sexually "validated" by a man.

CHAPTER 1

HOW MUCH IS
TOO LITTLE, ANYWAY?

"I don't see much of Alfred anymore,
since he got so interested in sex."
—Mrs. Alfred Kinsey

HOW DO YOU KNOW IF YOUR SEX LIFE IS "NORMAL" OR "HEALTHY"?

Our era is so preoccupied with sex that almost all of us feel we have an inadequate sex life. We are bombarded daily by sexy ads, books, and steamy television or movie scenes of attractive men and women about to leap into bed. And often when we get around to having sex, it's not that great, it's over quickly, and we're left feeling, "So what?" One reason for this discrepancy between what we see depicted and what we experience is that the nearly perfect-looking faces and bodies in ads and films have little to do with ordinary, loving, tender, caring interactions between real people.

It's human to want to keep up with others in every way. However, in the sexual arena our standards of comparison are unrealistic. Even Carole Lombard supposedly said about husband Clark Gable's prowess as a lover, "Gable's no Gable." Unfortunately, when the reality fails to meet our expectations, we blame ourselves or our partner for the discrepancy.

Is there a "right" number of times to have sex each week?

Is there a "right" kind of sexual encounter to have? A certain number of orgasms? How long must the encounter go on to really count?

Must *both* partners have orgasms for sex to be OK? Or even genital contact?

Is nuzzling affectionately with each other in bed *not* sex as compared, say, to a "wham-bam, thank you, ma'am" episode of intercourse? Or does only an extended encounter involving intercourse and at least one orgasm each count?

To have a "good" sex life, should you be able to choreograph positions like Baryshnikov?

Is your sex life "normal" only if you both get easily and spontaneously aroused as opposed to making the effort to get each other in the mood?

Most people would probably agree that if one partner wants to have sex once every year or two, that partner is "undersexed." Or that a person who is preoccupied with sex, masturbating to orgasm a dozen or so times a day, is sexually overactive. The situation is seldom this extreme or clear-cut.

A wonderful scene in Woody Allen's film *Annie Hall* beautifully illustrates how the appraisal of "how much is enough" depends on who is doing the assessing. On the left half of a split screen, Allen complains to his therapist, "We hardly ever have sex. Maybe three times a week—tops," while on the right Annie laments to her therapist, "We are constantly having sex. My God, we must have it two or three times a week."

Many sex therapists use some variation on the following scenario to illustrate the same point:

Jeanne would be delighted to have sex with Richard three or

four times a week and considers sex once every couple of weeks starvation rations. Richard is quite content, however, to have sex once every week or two.

Suppose that Richard were now married to Kate, who prefers to have sex every three months or so. Can we now assume that Richard's desire is excessive? What if both partners want sex every six months?

To conclude that Richard or Kate has an inadequate or insufficient sex drive would require a sexual standard against which they could be compared. And guess what? Even among sex therapists there is no really clear standard for what is "right," "normal," or "healthy."

This chapter will help you better assess your own relationship in two ways:

1. It will teach you to "diagnose" the specific aspects of your sexual relationship that could use some work, from physiological aspects, misinformation or other problematic sexual attitudes, and emotional blocks to problems in the nonsexual aspects of your relationship.
2. It will help you pinpoint which of the various "prescriptions" offered in this book you need to try out in order to enhance your sex life. These "prescriptions" will fall into two basic categories: ways to help you and your partner be less upset about the current sexual and nonsexual problems in your relationship and specific techniques to enhance both the sexual and nonsexual aspects of your relationship.

Sexual "Primes" and Marital Declines: Fact or Fiction?

We all know men are "supposed to" begin to poop out when they're over thirty—or was that over eighteen—and that, in marriage, sex is "supposed to" slow down after the first year or two. If marriage dampens sexual desire, and if our husbands' sexual capacities begin to diminish when they hit their thirties, shouldn't we just accept the *status quo*?

First, let's take a look at the *trends* in sex through the life cycle that sex researchers have identified—so that we can get them out of the way, where they belong.

- Males are probably at their peak *orgasmic* capacities in their late teens; they're usually able to get aroused and erect in seconds or minutes and may even have a chain of ejaculations without fully losing their erection.
- The sexual potential of girls in their late teens is probably equally great. If they get effective stimulation and don't lose their sexual focus through emotional blocks or distracting thoughts, women are capable of a rapid sequence of orgasms.
- In their twenties men still get erections and orgasms easily.
- In their thirties men tend to be content with fewer orgasms and may be less preoccupied with sexual fantasies; and the period between orgasms begins to get longer.
- In their thirties women allegedly reach maximum responsiveness; however, now that the female orgasm is a much better understood and pursued phenomenon, it's conceivable that the period of "maximal" responsiveness could actually start in the teens and continue indefinitely.
- In their forties men tend to find the character of their sexual pleasure changing, with more direct stimulation required in order to become erect and orgasm becoming less important. Yet if they shift their main focus from orgasm to the total sensual experience, many men are able to be *just as sexually active as in their younger years*.
- For the majority of men between forty and fifty-five their testosterone level will slowly and gradually decline. Most men hardly notice. A minority—perhaps 15 percent—of men may have rapid, sharp declines or swings in testosterone or even mood swings; most of these symptoms disappear without treatment. Potency is really not a function of how much hormone you're secreting as long as you have enough, most experts agree.
- By a man's sixties, erections may be less firm and he may need a day or more to become fully erect again after an orgasm. Orgasmic contractions may be less intense, and he may feel less of a

need to ejaculate during each sex act. *But sex can be more exciting than ever.* With less need to focus on his orgasm, he can concentrate more on the overall sensual experience for himself and his partner. Even though his sexual *drive* may continue to diminish, however, *he still has the capacity for erection and orgasm* unless a specific medical condition precludes them.

- Women in their fifties and sixties will probably have less lubrication (in a sense, the equivalent of slower erections) and less elasticity of the vaginal walls, but need experience little change in sexual arousal, responsiveness, and activity. Even if they've had a hysterectomy, women can still have sexual interest. "In terms of frequency," according to Drs. Helen Singer Kaplan and Clifford Sager, "an 80-year-old woman apparently has the same physical potential for orgasm as she did at 20!"

But sexual behavior is much more complex than these rules of thumb indicate. Average *trends* in different life decades don't mean that people must inevitably be a certain way at age forty, any more than a person must die at an average age. Although the *quality* and *intensity* of sex may vary considerably in different situations and at different ages, sex needn't die. The potential for erotic pleasure begins at birth and doesn't stop for either men or women until death.

Sexual behavior is a result of three main influences: (1) *societal attitudes* and values, from ads to family sex education; (2) *psychological factors,* from guilt, anxiety and fetishes to the emotional climate between partners; (3) *physical factors,* from hormone levels to general health and energy.

A healthy man, as Helen Singer Kaplan and Clifford Sager note, "is able to enjoy sexual intercourse throughout life. Indeed, freed of the intense need for fast orgastic release and the inhibitions of his youth, more satisfying and imaginative love play is often enjoyed by the older man." A healthy woman—once she's learned about her body and what its pleasure triggers are—is also capable of enjoying sex more and more throughout her lifetime. Thus both sexes can be in harmony sexually as they move through their thirties, fifties, seventies, and beyond.

Changes in Sexual Response Do Not Mean the Death of Desire

While there's no denying that many things in life change, here are some reassuring truths:

- You can still play tennis at forty, fifty, sixty, or beyond although you may not be as fast on the court as when you were young. Maybe your game is even better!
- You still get up and go to work even though it takes you longer to get up in the morning.
- You're still very much in the game of life—even though a receding hairline, college tuition costs, and approaching retirement can provide special stresses at mid-life.
- You don't have to burn out sexually even though you may be feeling burned out at work.
- You can still experiment and find interests that turn you on even though some of your old interests no longer do.
- Plenty of men are married to Rubenesque women and are having outrageous, voluptuous sex. And many of these women were slender sylphs when the couple first met.

Your mid-life, your kid-life, your sex-life, and other crucial life conditions may undergo changes, but change doesn't equal *crisis*—unless you let it.

In other words, while some of the changes in your body or your life (or in those of your partner) may influence some of the ways you react physiologically and emotionally to sex, they don't inevitably *cause* a sexual falloff.

What Are Some Causes of His Sexual Falloff?

Chances are a man's attitudes and beliefs toward life's changes—as well as rigid expectations about how sex "should" be—are the main causes of his sexual desire and activity with you switching on or off. Self-fulfilling prophecies abound in sex:

- If he believes his seven years of marriage to you, plus your being his "buddy" and mother of his kids, means he can't have sexually exciting times with you, he can make that come true.
- If he thinks that now that he's fifty his life is over, it largely is. (It's not the men in your life that counts, it's the life in your men, according to Mae West.)
- If he thinks nothing will turn him on—physically or emotionally—he probably won't find anything that does.
- If he thinks having an affair with a younger woman will turn him on and make him feel young and virile, it probably will (at least temporarily).
- If he believes people have to be spontaneously aroused to have sex and he no longer gets spontaneously aroused with you, he *won't* initiate sex or respond to your overtures (thus, "proving" it to himself).

The same is true of you. If you believe that because your skin has slackened or your kids are in diapers you are no longer sexy, you can also create a self-fulfilling prophecy—and not get sexually turned on.

The important thing is to try to keep yourself going. If you let sex drop for long periods of time, you may have trouble restarting. "The old adage 'use it or lose it' is true," says sex therapist Dr. William Masters. "If you put your good right arm in a restraining cast for a few weeks, for example, you're not going to be able to use it right away without some practice."

So How Come Everybody Else Is Making Love More Often than We Are?

Surprise! They probably aren't! Four out of five people, according to a survey reported in *Forum Magazine,* were certain that other people were enjoying sex more than they were. Recent surveys show much *less* activity, even among young groups, than one would have thought from reading the popular reports:

- In a 1989 survey by the National Opinion Research Center at the University of Chicago, married people under forty reported having sex an average of only 78 times a year. Respondents in general had sex an average of 57 times a year, but there seemed to be some disagreement between the sexes on this point, with men's average being 66 and women's 51. (The researchers' suspicion was that men were overreporting and women underreporting.)

- A study by Ellen Frank reported in the *New England Journal of Medicine* revealed that 33 percent of 100 married couples were having intercourse *two to three times a month or less*. In a survey in *Men's Health* to which 1,600 readers responded, 38 percent of the men said they had sex three times a month or less. Another study by Drs. John Edwards and Alan Booth in the *American Journal of Psychiatry* indicated that one-third of 365 married men and women were not having sex for long periods of time—*with the average being once every eight weeks*. More than three-quarters of these couples were *under thirty-eight years old*.

If People Aren't Sexually Active, Doesn't That Mean They're Not *Interested*?

Not necessarily. Kinsey and other early sexologists who tried to quantify sex thought they could quantify desire by counting the frequency of sexual behaviors, such as the incidence of intercourse, masturbation, fantasies, and other activities leading to orgasm. The problem with this approach, as sex therapist Dr. Harold Lief points out, is that an individual could conceivably masturbate 20 times a week, but lack desire to have sex with a partner; or he or she could have sexual intercourse 20 times a month, but without any particular desire for it.

Today's sex researchers have found that a separate but equally important aspect of sexuality is *interest or desire*.

One reason that interest and activity may not always go together is that people's decisions to engage in sexual behavior come from motives *other* than active desire for a specific partner. They may initiate sex, for example, out of guilt over an extramarital affair, because of financial motives, to reduce anxiety, or to help them fall asleep. Others are hot to trot, but their mate can't seem to get wound up. Still others may have high levels of desire and get aroused by sexual fantasies, but choose not to engage in sexual *activity* with their mate because they don't automatically get an erection with her. Or they may have the old madonna/whore idea that it's not "proper" to have such a "dirty" activity as sex with the mother of one's children. Some of these men may have no sex, while others may have sex with *themselves*—accompanied, perhaps, by a *Playboy* magazine—or with a partner other than their mate.

Desire is a mental process. It involves a *thought* or *wish* about engaging in sexual activity, which you either act on or suppress. Desire and interest are not the same as arousal, which involves having actual erotic *sensations*—being physiologically excited or turned on. Desire can happen in one of two ways: it can *precede* arousal, or it may begin *after* there is actual physical stimulation or erotic fantasizing. People definitely can get aroused without spontaneous initial desire; who is to say that a sexual encounter that begins without strong feelings is any less valid than the encounter preceded by high levels of passion?

So What Is a Ballpark Estimate of Whether His Interest Level Is "Normal"?

Most sex experts agree on three basic issues: (1) It is very difficult to distinguish between "normal" and "abnormal"; (2) lack of *spontaneous arousal* or *instant erection* is often confused with lack of "interest" or "desire" or even love; (3) if you go for a long time without having sex, it becomes harder to get yourself revved up again—and to remember how delicious it can actually feel.

OK, then. Is it *common* for men to have a relatively low interest in sex? Yes! In a *Psychology Today* survey of 52,000 people, 39 percent of the men who responded admitted to occasional or regular lack of interest in sex, and 30 percent believed that sex was a "burden—more like work than play." (The respondents came from every economic group, all ages, single and married, homosexual and heterosexual.) In another study, of *happily married couples*, 16 percent of men reported a lack of interest in sex. And in *The Hite Report: A Study of Male Sexuality*, 65 percent responded "yes" to the question "Is sex overrated?"; 12 percent responded "somewhat"; and only 23 percent responded "no."

Drs. Joseph LoPiccolo and Jerry Friedman report an interesting trend. During 1974–1976, men accounted for approximately 30 percent of the "low desire" cases at their sex therapy clinic at the State University of New York at Stony Brook. By 1982–1983, men accounted for 55 percent of these cases. Some experts I've spoken to recently estimate that as many as 20 to 25 percent of the nation's fifty-three-million married men (roughly 10 to 13 million) have lower sexual desire than their mates.

Most sex therapists these days report that they see more clients complaining about lack of sexual desire than almost any other type of sexual disorder. A 1988 survey of 289 sex therapists found that the most common complaint of partners—in 31 percent of couples seeking sex therapy—was a discrepancy between partners in their desire for sex. The second most common complaint, reported by 28 percent, was being troubled by either too much or too little sexual desire. And according to various recent surveys of the general population, as many as half of all married or cohabiting respondents, male and female, mention their own or their partner's lack of sexual interest as one of the major difficulties in their sex lives or relationships!

The Best Approach: Sex as a Continuum

Probably the most useful way to look at sexual interest is to think of it as a continuum. On one end are men who have no wish for sex, and perhaps haven't for most of their lives. Those with this more generalized problem may be suffering from apathy or a biologically based low sex drive, and hardly any sexual stimulus, either real or fantasized, is likely to *arouse* them. In other cases they may begin to feel some desire and arousal in response to potentially arousing stimuli, but become so anxious or disgusted at the thought of genital contact that they quickly turn off.

On the other end of this spectrum we might put those who are highly interested in sex—with their spouse and perhaps nearly every attractive woman they see.

Much more typical, and probably accounting for the large middle section of our continuum, are men who experience a decline of sexual interest after a period of moderate or even high activity levels. An example would be the man who has little or no desire for his spouse, but is interested in or turned on by the thought of sex with outside women. Another example is the man who loses interest in sex during an unusually stressful life transition but resumes activity once things have calmed down.

But here's where the problem of defining someone as having "low desire" becomes tricky. Dave, for example, has little or no *desire* for sexual activity, and he rarely initiates it. Yet he does get physically and psychologically aroused and ultimately climaxes when his wife initiates sex. Is it "legitimate" for his wife to be distressed because even though Dave has sex 95 percent of the time *she* wants it, he rarely gets the ball rolling himself?

And then there's Kevin, who initiates sex every week or so with his live-in companion, Sharon, stimulates her manually and orally to orgasm, but only occasionally gets aroused and has intercourse with her perhaps six times a year. Is it appropriate for Sharon to see him and her sex life as "inadequate" or "abnormal"?

Sex, like love, is an inexact science and its quantity will vary from one person to the next. Perhaps the best approach is to look at the *frequency* of all sexual activities your mate engages in, as well as his *level of interest* and his degree of *arousal*. A possible fourth dimension would be the *quality* of the interactions; Godiva chocolate vs. Hershey bar—it's all good, but some are even better! With this approach, your man might be said to have more of a problem if he was lacking in four of these areas, less if only in one.

Your best approach to attempting to improve your overall sex life is first to accept that for now it's not where you'd like it to be. To accomplish this, try to stop worrying about the kind of sex life you think you *should* be having and what you think others are having; stay out of the Orgasm Olympics. And toward this end, try to eliminate the terms *undersexed* and *oversexed* from your vocabulary: couples who fling accusations at one another are the least successful in resolving differences.

Next, establish the sexual goals you would like to shoot for, as well as other nongenital sensory or emotional experiences. Finally, begin by taking small steps. You might begin by trying for a sensuous kiss and hug once a week. At the same time, you can begin to work on some of the practical, emotional, or physical problems that may be blocking you and your partner from having the kind of sex life you'd like. The checklist on pages 29 through 33 will help you pinpoint specific areas you need help with.

Desire Discrepancy

Perfect sexual synchronicity—where people experience sexual passion and intensity at the same moment—exists only in romantic novels and films. More often than not, one partner will desire sex and the other person isn't in the mood or one person becomes aroused but the other doesn't. Usually couples who don't take it personally and blame themselves or their mates or see it as a threat adjust just fine, even when the difference in sexual "appetites" is fairly large.

With sex as with food, more is not necessarily better. The best goal is for both partners to work on adjusting their desire levels so as to achieve a satisfactory compromise.

Putting Sex in Perspective

Life is not a "blue plate special" in which we are going to get all our favorite goodies. If one of the goodies is sex—well, the surgeon general has not yet determined that having little or no sex in a relationship is dangerous to your health.

Let's assume you have to give up one of the following: Music? Exercise? Enjoying nature? Sensory pleasures such as eating? Laughing? Having sexual intercourse? Which would you choose?

Probably none of them, if you had your druthers. But in the worst-case scenario, if it turned out you would never have the quality and/or quantity of sex with your current partner that you would like, how bleak would your life be? As bleak as living without laughter? Or music? Or without your partner?

Having a super sex life most of the time is like climbing Mount Everest or maybe being a monk: very hard! And probably relatively few will achieve it. If they do manage on a few occasions to have ecstatic sex, much of the time it may be in the good or so-so range, and at others even boring or bad. Even so-so sex, however, in the context of a loving, tender relationship, is nothing to sneeze at.

And if people do not allow themselves to become overwrought over sex that is lacking in quantity or quality, and enjoy the other aspects of their relationship, they can still live happily ever after!

You don't believe that?

In their survey of 300 happily married spouses who have been married for fifteen years or more, Jeanette and Robert Lauer made these discoveries:

- Fewer than 10 percent thought that good sexual relations kept their marriage together.
- Many noted they didn't have sex as *frequently* as they'd like, but when they did, they said things like "It is a beautiful act of giving and sharing as deeply emotional as it is physical."

- Others had a much-less-than-ideal sex life but were not particularly disturbed about it and had adjusted to it. One woman married for twenty-five years rated her marriage as extremely happy even though she and her husband had not had any sexual relations for the past ten years. Married once before, she described her former relationship as "almost totally sex and little else."
- Others said they would rather be married to their spouse with a less-than-ideal sex life than be married to someone else and have a better sex life. One woman said that even though she had a much stronger sex drive than her husband, this difference was not nearly as important as the friendship, respect, and understanding they shared.

There are three factors that determine a couple's chances of improving their sex life: a positive attitude toward each other, not "obsessing" about a so-so (or nonexistent) sex life, and some willingness to experiment and be flexible.

This applies as well to *other* aspects of your relationship. If, for example, you have some fundamental disagreements on handling kids and money, the keys to being only frustrated and disappointed (as opposed to angry and depressed) are (1) having the attitude that "Well, I don't like this state of affairs, and I wish it were different, but tough—I *can* stand living in a less-than-perfect world with this less-than-perfect mate"; (2) accepting the fact that although this is how things are for now, they may change; (3) being flexible. These, in turn, will help increase your chances of working toward a better rapprochement.

As for sex—when we talk about having sex together, we're not just talking about the mechanical pushing of each other's buttons. As long as his penis and other sensory nerve endings are hooked up to his brain, both his brain and yours better not be too bogged down in anger, boredom, anxiety, or depression. Because then his fire isn't likely to get lit, and neither is yours. Or, if by some miracle it does, the sex may not be particularly good. And in all likelihood the *non*sexual aspects of the relationship—such as emotional intimacy, good communication, and effective problem solving—will also sour.

DIAGNOSING THE TROUBLE SPOTS: WHAT'S SWITCHING OFF DESIRE

By checking yourself and your partner out in each of the following six areas, you can "diagnose" your special trouble spots.

Keep in mind as you look over this list that *most people have experienced some of these problems* and that you are not "pathological" if you have responded "yes" to several of the items.

I. Is There a "Problem about the Problem"?

	Yes	No
1) Do you feel anxious, guilty, or self-denigrating about the fact that your partner wants to have sex less than you? (If so, which feelings?)	☐	☐
2) Does *he* feel self-denigrating, depressed, anxious, guilty, or angry about it? (If so, which feelings?)	☐	☐

3) Have *you,* as a result of feeling emotionally upset about the problem, engaged in any of the following *behaviors:*

	Yes	No
a) Withdrawn affection and/or efforts to connect with him?	☐	☐
b) Become angry and resentful and possibly attacked him for his shortcomings?	☐	☐
c) Had sex with people outside your marriage?	☐	☐
d) Allowed your hurt or anger to erode other aspects of your relationship? (If yes, how?)	☐	☐
e) Allowed your hurt or anger to reduce your overall enjoyment of your life? (If yes, how?)	☐	☐

4) Has *he,* because of being upset about the sex problem, engaged in any of the following behaviors:

	Yes	No
a) Become anxious about his sexual functioning?	☐	☐

b) Withdrawn affection and/or efforts to connect with you? □ □

c) Become angry and pushed you away in other ways? □ □

d) Possibly had sex outside the relationship? □ □

e) Allowed his concern about the problem to erode other areas of your relationship (e.g., spending time together, resolving problems, etc.)? □ □

f) Allowed his concern about the problem to reduce his overall enjoyment of life (e.g., become more isolated or inactive)? □ □

II. Has He Ever Exhibited Any of the Following Problems with Sexual Functioning?

Note: These may be attributable to physical causes, to psychological causes, or to both.

1) Had difficulty in achieving or maintaining an erection? □ □

2) Tended to ejaculate more quickly than he or you would like (e.g., in a matter of seconds)? □ □

3) Tended to ejaculate only after considerable time? □ □

4) Had difficulty getting himself turned on (or allowing you to help him get turned on)? □ □

5) Failed to provide you with the kind of *stimulation* you have said you need to reach orgasm? □ □

6) Failed to provide you with the sort of *emotional context* you have indicated you need for the sexual experience to be satisfactory to you (e.g., more affection, hugging, etc.)? □ □

III. Are There Any Biological Factors that May Be Contributing to His Lack of Desire and/or Activity?

1) Medical conditions such as diabetes, arteriosclerosis, neurological problems, hypertension, back problems, chronic illness? □ □
2) Decreases in energy level or physical abilities due to aging? □ □
3) Decreases due to injury? (Specify.) □ □
4) Medications such as heart drugs, tranquilizers, antidepressants, antihypertensives? □ □
5) Alcohol or recreational drugs? □ □
6) Hormonal imbalances (e.g., thyroid, testosterone)? □ □

Note: Proper diagnosis and treatment of the preceding conditions must be made through the help of a good physician.

IV. Is He Especially Uptight about His or Your Body Parts, Secretions, Oral Sex, or Sex in General?

Yes *No*

1) Does he come from a strongly religious background that may be contributing to a long-standing pattern of sexual squeamishness or rigidity? □ □
2) Is he prudish about sex (including talking about genitals or engaging in masturbation, oral-genital sex, etc.)? (Specify.) □ □
3) Does he have incorrect information on the "normality" of certain sex practices (e.g., oral-genital sex, fantasizing, etc.)? (Specify.) □ □
4) Is he relatively inhibited, inexperienced, or rigid and afraid to let himself be sexually spontaneous? If so, which? □ □

5) Does he have difficulty in focusing on erotic thoughts (e.g., he gets distracted when being sexually stimulated)? ☐ ☐

6) Does he fail to get turned on by fantasies or visual stimuli? ☐ ☐

7) Does he believe that sex is something "dirty" that you don't do with the person you love, but only with whores? ☐ ☐

8) Has he been a victim of physical, sexual, or psychological abuse? (Specify.) ☐ ☐

9) Is there any indication of a homosexual preference? ☐ ☐

10) Are there other sexual problems? (Specify.) ☐ ☐

V. Are There Problems in the Nonsexual Aspects of Your Relationship?

1) The quality of communication? ☐ ☐
2) The amount of emotional intimacy? ☐ ☐
3) The amount of time spent together? ☐ ☐
4) The way problems get resolved (or don't get resolved)? ☐ ☐
5) Your or your partner's hostility? ☐ ☐
6) Your or your partner's withdrawal (verbal or emotional)? ☐ ☐
7) Other relationship problems? (Specify.) ☐ ☐

VI. Does He Seem to Have Significant Emotional Problems (i.e., Problems Functioning in Life in General)?

1) Is he angry, depressed, or anxious a lot of the time? (Specify.) ☐ ☐
2) Is he bored a lot (with his job, his home, his life)? ☐ ☐

3) Is he experiencing anxiety over a "crisis" (illness, financial problems, unemployment)? ☐ ☐
4) Is he "stressed out" (fatigued, anxious, etc.) a lot? ☐ ☐
5) Does he have any other emotional or behavioral problems? (Specify.) ☐ ☐

If he seems to be experiencing severe depression, as indicated by suicidal thoughts, lack of enjoyment of most life activities, or sleep disturbance (especially early morning wakening), an evaluation by a psychopharmacologist is strongly recommended, as there may be a correctable chemical imbalance. Material on what you can do as his helpmate, along with information on utilizing professional resources, is contained in Chapter 7.

HOW OTHER PHASES IN THE SEXUAL RESPONSE CYCLE CAN LEAD TO A PATTERN OF LOW SEXUAL DESIRE

The sexual response cycle is divided into six different phases. Problems occurring during any of these phases could, if they persist, lead to a gradual loss of interest in sex. If a person has, or thinks he's *going* to have, problems in any of these areas, he may not even get to the first steps—the desire and initiation. His becoming extremely upset *over* the potential problem will head him off at the pass. Especially if he equates his worth as a man with his sexual performance, entry into the sexual arena becomes fraught with extreme peril.

The diagram on page 34 illustrates the kinds of problems that can occur in different phases of the sexual response cycle. Note that both *physical and emotional states* can interfere with, or even completely block, the transmission of sexual messages in each of the six phases.

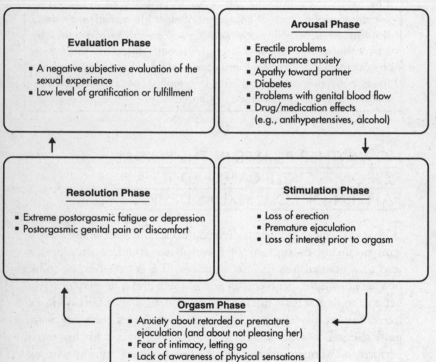

Desire (Interest) Phase

- Anxiety, depression
- Apathy/habituation
- Disgust (at self or partner)
- Anger or ambivalence about the relationship
- Turned on only by novel stimuli
- Guilt
- Belief that desire has to occur "spontaneously"
- Pressure from partner perceived as a threat

Arousal Phase

- Erectile problems
- Performance anxiety
- Apathy toward partner
- Diabetes
- Problems with genital blood flow
- Drug/medication effects
  (e.g., antihypertensives, alcohol)

Evaluation Phase

- A negative subjective evaluation of the sexual experience
- Low level of gratification or fulfillment

Resolution Phase

- Extreme postorgasmic fatigue or depression
- Postorgasmic genital pain or discomfort

Stimulation Phase

- Loss of erection
- Premature ejaculation
- Loss of interest prior to orgasm

Orgasm Phase

- Anxiety about retarded or premature ejaculation (and about not pleasing her)
- Fear of intimacy, letting go
- Lack of awareness of physical sensations
- Insufficient stimulation
- Performance anxiety
- Anger or ambivalence about partner
- Drug or medication side effects
- Other physical impairments

Problems that can occur in different phases of the Sexual Response Cycle.

This chart is based on Bernie Zilbergeld and Carol Ellison's expansion of Helen Singer Kaplan's triphasic model.

A POSITIVE PROGNOSIS

So where's the evidence that people who have been on the planet for several decades can, in fact, have good sex lives? We may not hear a lot about them—probably because of our youth-oriented ads and media—but they're all around us. Many men and women still feel warm and "fuzzy" when they look at or think about each other, and many, after five, twenty-five, or even forty-five years of marriage (including having kids), still find sex together terrific. Even more terrific, according to many of them, than it was in their less mature days.

One survey of men and women between the ages of sixty and ninety-three found that 54 percent were sexually active, with no significant decrease under age seventy-five. After age seventy-five, 25 percent were still active, with the decline due chiefly to illness in one or both partners.

In their survey of more than eight hundred adults between the ages of sixty and ninety-one, psychologists Bernard Starr and Marcella Weiner found that 41 percent of women claimed that sex is better than ever, while 27 percent of the men made this claim. The lower percentage in men was due possibly to frequent impotence. A woman of sixty-two responded to the question "What do you consider a good sexual experience?" with ". . . joking, laughing, talking, 'opening up,' good music, a shower together, bodily caressing, kissing, foreplay, a mutual orgasm." Another's advice for an ideal sexual encounter was "Take plenty of time, and when you can't stand it another minute, make it!" Another older woman said to sociologist John Cuber, "We're over sixty and have as much fun in bed—or on the floor or on the grass—as we did before we married forty years ago. Maybe one of the things that makes it all so precious, besides the great memories, is that growing awareness that we won't both be around forever, that the future gets shorter all the time."

There is, in other words, no boundary period in which sexual desire shuts off like a faucet. Like love, sexuality can last—albeit in changing forms—as long as life does.

Good sex requires:
- good working parts (genital nerves and vascular system working OK);
- the presence of adequate sensual/sexual stimulation;
- the absence of distracting thoughts and feelings (related to disturbance in the individuals or in the relationship).

Joyful sex:
- can be sustained over a long period of time with one partner— even (with some planning) with two careers and kids;
- can occur even if one partner participates more actively than the other;
- doesn't have to take place at each and every encounter;
- doesn't have to involve intercourse;
- is more likely to happen if you give up all preconceptions about a "right" or "normal" kind of response pattern or sexual scenario.

If men stop worrying about the almighty erection, and if men and women could manage better to bridge the gap between them (both very big *ifs*), couples in their middle and later years—with a more mellow perspective on their lives and more leisure—can have perhaps the best sex of their lives. The more a couple can stop seeing intercourse as the main goal, the more sex can be sensual, last longer, and produce better orgasms and/or emotional closeness for both members of the couple.

As psychologist Carol Tavris sums it up:

> Men and women aren't exactly the same, of course, but most of the differences are a result of individual histories and attitudes, not of biological programming based on gender. . . . If the sexes stopped hurling biological inevitabilities at each other, they could stop counting orgasms and sex

acts, and might actually revel in the sweet similarities of rhythm and response.

EIGHT POINTS TO REMEMBER

1. Once you get over the idea that you should be having sex at some imagined frequency or the way people seem to in movies and magazines, you will probably lose a lot of your anxiety about sex and expand your range of physical pleasure.

    Acquiring the grace to accept that you're not always going to have your sexual "ideal" is the best preparation for you to work on overcoming the discrepancies between what you'd like and what you currently have—in both the *sexual* and *nonsexual* aspects of your relationship.

3. There will be fluctuations in the intimacy of your relationship, both sexual and nonsexual; times when you're so involved with work or family that you have little time for each other. Or there may be periods of anger or even hatred when you wonder how you could possibly stay in a relationship with such a thoroughly odious person. In enduring relationships, if you don't panic, time is on your side.

4. No matter how alive or varied a long-term sexual relationship is, it's probably not going to deliver the same ecstasy as frequently as it did during your early days together. The idea of a relationship as a perpetual courtship is commercial, romantic, and unfulfillable. Sexual pleasure, even when it's no longer particularly novel or euphoric, can become a deep source of satisfaction, affection, and mature intimacy.

5. Negotiating sexual *frequency* involves the same issues as negotiating different preferences in other areas, such as decisions about money, discipline of kids, or where to go for vacations: *the absence of hurt, anger, or extreme anxiety makes every deal go down better.*

6. Life involves compromise. Try to achieve a satisfactory middle

ground by *requesting, not demanding*. If he firmly rejects a compromise between the once a year he'd like to have sex and the three times a week *you'd* like to have it, there's a good chance he may have some sort of problem with getting his battery charged and/or getting the show on the road, and some outside assistance may be necessary.

7. Active sexual desire is *not* a prerequisite for sexual excitement or arousal. What *is* a prerequisite is having the *motivation and willingness to make the time to have sex*. With the right stimulation and a proper mind-set, the desire and arousal will *then* get going. We have a much better ability to use our minds to consciously improve our sex drive than most people realize.

8. Probably the largest factor in men's sexual falloff is low frustration tolerance. He might be telling himself that things that are now *more* difficult are *too* difficult. Since he's not as easily aroused as he used to be—perhaps because of age, habituation to his spouse, or her request that he do more to satisfy her sexually— he now has to try harder. So even though he still thinks about sex, when it comes to actually *doing* it, he doesn't. Additional psychological factors may be his highly unrealistic performance standards and the resulting anxiety and insecurity over not functioning as successfully as he used to.

You can help pinpoint what may be switching off his *desire* by answering the "diagnostic questions" on pages 29 through 33 of this chapter. Then, by following some of the suggestions in each chapter, chances are excellent that you'll be able first to reduce your distress over the situation, and then to implement some positive and constructive changes.

CHAPTER 2

THE MARTIAN-VENUSIAN PROBLEM: CAN MEN AND WOMEN CONNECT *OUT* OF BED— LET ALONE IN IT?

"If marriages are made in heaven,
some had few friends there."
—Scottish proverb

Bob and Sue have been quietly reading in the living room for an hour. At bedtime, Sue comments sarcastically, "Gee, we sure had a great, intimate evening together—as usual!" Bob is stunned but, rather than risk rocking the boat any further, quietly gets ready for bed and turns over and goes to sleep, while Sue tosses for another hour, feeling angry and depressed.

Sue's Internal Dialogue

"He doesn't share things with me anymore. He's bored with me and with our marrige. He knows how upset I've been that we don't seem to talk as much as we used to, and he just doesn't care. And we especially need to resolve what to do about our vacation plans. This relationship seems hopeless."

Bob's Internal Dialogue

"My God, I thought it was so great that Sue and I had an evening together just relaxing and having some quiet time to do our own thing. And for once, she didn't bug me about our vacation plans. I can't believe that she had to ruin it by bringing up that same old 'we never communicate' business. What does she want from me?"

DO MEN AND WOMEN SPEAK TWO DIFFERENT LANGUAGES?

Bob sees Sue's "demands" on him as somehow infringing on his independence and individuality; Sue sees Bob's need for solitude as his not wanting to be married to her. He fears engulfment; she fears abandonment. Both feel angry and hurt, and the prospect is that the following evening Bob may feel anxious about wanting to take some time to "cool out" after work, while Sue grows increasingly depressed about the deterioration of their relationship. The next day, if Sue comments that she thinks his socks clash with the rest of his outfit, and Bob says "Get off my case," they continue their dance of hurt and anger. And the relationship between two people who really love each other chills, along with their sex life. As a result, each attempt or failure to attempt physical contact becomes charged with anxiety, one of the best-known suppressors of the male sex hormone testosterone.

If a man experiences the same kind of anxiety when asked to talk about feelings as he would if he were being sent to the guillotine, how do you suppose he feels when asked to "perform" sexually, when he's not sure he can even get an erection—let alone help please you physically and emotionally? He feels pressured and frightened. Visions of his past sexual and emotional failures spin through his head. He knows he should reach out, but he withdraws, from the intimacy and its attendant terrors of loss of face and of self.

Perhaps this insight can give you a sense of the sheer terror that lurks in the heart of your man and provide a different picture of this "rotten person" who doesn't give a damn about you.

What Is Really Going On Here?

How can males and females so frequently interpret the same events so differently and so misjudge the other? How can they expect to have a good sexual communication if—at least as it sometimes appears—they come from separate planets? Perhaps one of the reasons the physical connection at times assumes such overriding importance is that it seems to offer the last chance before they break totally out of each other's gravitational field.

It is helpful to view Bob and Sue's conflict as a paradigm of what the majority of battles between the spouses have at their core. Whether the *subject* of the conflict be sex or doing the housework, the underlying *theme* centers around *how much closeness or distance there is going to be in the relationship*. Usually it is the woman who wants more closeness, although it is not uncommon—particularly if a woman starts becoming more independent—for the male to be the one pushing for more togetherness.

One can take the attitude that men are just hopeless dolts or male chauvinists, who are suffering from unresolved Oedipal or testosterone problems, and who should be severely blamed and condemned for acting the way they do. If we want to have any hope of bridging the gap, however, it is far more helpful to view males as having been steeped (like us), from birth onward, in a sort of "brainwashing."

UNDERSTANDING MALE SOCIALIZATION

Uh-oh," you say. "Don't tell me I'm about to get yet another lecture on how we women have just got to be more understanding and not ask so much of these poor oppressed creatures. Why aren't *they* putting on black teddies and reading *Men Who Don't Love Enough*? Why is it always women who have to do the changing and understanding? We're sick to death of it!"

Well, ultimately, *women* benefit from learning to better understand the set of attitudes, feelings, and behaviors men are taught they "should" have—a programming that exerts a powerful grip on all but the rarest men. By learning to view his difficulties with closeness as a natural consequence of the way most men are raised, we can learn to stop taking things so personally and become less horrified and unhappy.

As we do this, it's crucial for us not to give up our strong preferences, wishes, and hopes that our mates connect with us in better ways, physically and emotionally. The goal is rather to help us give up our absolutistic demands or *shoulds*. We cannot realistically expect that someone who may be emotionally constipated *not* be emotionally constipated, or that a man who seems to be allergic to talking to us or touching us *must* immediately change. By giving up our *demands*—and facing the grim reality of *where in fact he is for now*—we maximize our chances of being a more successful agent of change.

BEING A
MAN

"I tell you, Mrs. Stanton, after all, it is very precious to the soul of man, that he shall reign supreme in intellect, and it will take centuries, if not ages, to dispossess him of the fancy that he is born to do so."
—Susan B. Anthony

The dictates of masculinity require that men not engage in any kind of behavior that might be seen as "feminine." Psychologists Deborah David and Robert Brannon have called this prescription "no sissy stuff"—meaning men should not disclose weakness, doubt, or such feelings as empathy, compassion, fear, or hurt.

A related mandate of masculinity is the "sturdy oak"—meaning that a man must be action-oriented, in control of the situation, independent, and oh-so-careful not to reveal his anxieties or vulnerabilities to anyone or imply that he doesn't have the skills to handle every situation.

In *The Liberated Man,* Warren Farrell offers "The Ten Commandments of Masculinity" as (hypothetically) handed down to the Moses of masculinity, John Wayne:

1. Thou shalt not cry or expose other feelings of emotion, fear, weakness, sympathy, empathy or involvement before thy neighbor.
2. Thou shalt not be vulnerable, but honor and respect the "logical," "practical" or "intellectual"—as thou defines them.
3. Thou shalt not listen, except to find fault.
4. Thou shalt condescend to women in the smallest and biggest of ways.

5. Thou shalt control thy wife's body, and all its relations, occasionally permitting it on top.
6. Thou shalt have no other egos before thee.
7. Thou shalt have no other breadwinners before thee.
8. Thou shalt not be responsible for housework—before anybody.
9. Thou shalt honor and obey the straight and narrow pathway to success: job specialization.
10. Thou shalt have an answer to all problems at all times.

Above all, thou shalt not let anyone pass your car on the highway or read self-help books or commit other forms of introspection.

ARE THERE BIOLOGICAL DIFFERENCES BETWEEN MEN AND WOMEN?

Sex differences have turned up in research across many cultures with considerable consistency:

- Girls seem more likely to conform to adult wishes and demands, while boys tend to try to exert dominance over others or get their own way.
- Boys seem to maintain greater distance between each other, girls less distance.
- Girls tend to exhibit more responsible behavior, including nurturing or trying to help others.
- Men display more aggression than women in most cultures.

Many experts believe these differences to be rooted in biology, specifically in the male sex hormone testosterone. Others theorize that male domination is the result of a selective process in which certain tribes kept winning key battles over less militaristic and peaceful societies. Still others argue that male domination derives from the nature of the family, where women have to stay home and nurture the young while men need to go and hunt food and defend the family.

Recently, brain researchers have speculated that one reason women may have more ability to access and communicate feelings is a structural difference in their brains; the nerve cable connecting the left and right halves of the brain (the *corpus callosum*) seems to be thicker in women, perhaps allowing more right brain–left brain communication.

There is certainly little doubt, however, that it is still the way we *socialize* our young that perpetuates the process well beyond the imperatives of biology and survival. A system in which women are expected to do most of the nurturing, while men and boys are actually discouraged from doing so, seems unnecessary to the survival of the species: to the contrary, it appears to be a major factor in the increasing amount of male violence in the world and might ultimately (as Shere Hite suggests) lead to a situation where total *destruction* is possible.

The High Cost of Being Male

The price that men pay for following their male programming is exceedingly high, as psychologist Herb Goldberg has described in *The Hazards of Being Male*. Boys are seen in guidance clinics three times as often as girls and outnumber girls in mental institutions by 150 percent. Males have three to four times the rate of alcoholism and six times the rate of narcotics use as women. They are four times more likely to commit acts of violence, and the male suicide rate throughout adolescence and young adulthood is three times as high as that for females. Moreover, males tend not to give in to pain, and are the least amenable of the species to properly attend to their physical or emotional needs or to consider going for psychological help.

Probably as a result of their programming, men wind up with

many problems in their intimate relationships, including (1) poor skills in identifying and processing feelings; (2) considerable feelings of frustration, powerlessness, and rage; (3) difficulties in being able to play or to enjoy non-goal-oriented activities; and (4) problems in connecting with their children. If bothered by unpleasant feelings, they are more likely to take a stiff drink than to risk self-disclosure or find other ways of coping with stress.

On the other hand, if they *do* decide to express emotions, they risk disapproval by men and often by women as well. And the *ultimate* fear—that of being thought a homosexual—keeps many men from risking emotional closeness with a man. Were they able to take that risk, they might experience some warmth, connection, and help with problems.

Nowhere is the high cost of being a male more dramatically apparent than in the areas of illness and mortality rates. The biggest stress triggers for men have been identified as potential failure to perform properly in the areas of work and sex—the two areas most central to a man's sense of self-worth. Tending to blame *external causes*, rather than confront their own emotions, men generally suppress what they feel, which can cause them to experience more rage and stress-related disorders, such as ulcers and hypertension, and live an average of seven years less than women. One expert, I. Waldron, estimates that as much as three-quarters of the difference in life expectancy between men and women can be accounted for by sex-role-related behaviors that contribute to the greater mortality of men.

MARRIAGE: THE TRADITIONAL SCRIPT

Marriage has had such bad press—with so many husbands, poets, and others having bemoaned it for so long—that it's remarkable that so many people still manage to make it to the altar. Although it is men who have long been depicted as the victims, sociologist Jessie Bernard pointed out in the 1960s what recent research has clearly corroborated: that marriage has more negative psychological effects by far on *women:* it erodes their self-esteem and is a major factor leading to depression.

If we examine how the marital "script" gets written and played out, we begin to wonder why the divorce rate is only 50 percent!

Choosing a Mate

It is perhaps one of the greatest tragedies in our society that our main training in choosing a life partner comes from ad men and women. Said writer Carol Botwin:

> Advertising teaches people to look for surface attributes. If he has the right car, uses the right toothpaste, smokes the right cigarettes, he will be virile and irresistible. If she has blue eyes, looks good in a bikini, wears provocative clothing, she's sexy and desirable. Advertising ignores what goes into the making of a truly desirable member of the opposite sex—the ability to empathize, cooperate, and respect another person.

From ads for Obsession to home-improvement ads, TV, even in the nineties, actively depicts half-naked women as "prey." When a man is finally caught in "the tender trap" of marriage, he is often depicted as a nincompoop manipulated by a domineering wife, who is typically fat or old.

The Romantic Legacy

To make matters worse, we are taught that the best time to select our mate is when we feel romantically in love.

Based on the French word *roman,* which means "novel," what many people experience as being "in love" is frequently sexual passion, the tension of conquest, or the uncertainty about whether or not your beloved is even going to stick around. People often feel that if they're not "madly" in love something vital is lacking, when actually, as psychologist Judith Sills puts it,

> It is odd that people seek out a period of temporary insanity as the ideal mind-set for making a crucial life decision. It would be sensible to say "I can't decide whether to marry you or not. I'm too much in love to think clearly."

We often mate on the basis not only of looks but also of *propinquity.* Many people, for example, hook up with the first person who comes along after their last relationship ended. Often we have little inkling as to how the other person thinks, feels, and behaves in a variety of real-life situations. We probably do more "research" when we choose a car or a refrigerator than when we choose a mate.

Balancing Power

Despite all our awareness and sophistication, relationships between men and women in the United States are not all that different from relationships between the sexes all over the world.

Sociologists Robert Blood and D. M. Wolfe have characterized power in marriage as "the ability to make unilateral decisions that affect both partners." If we accept this definition, then it seems clear why nearly all researchers have found that husbands generally wield more power than their wives. It is *economic and political* factors that play a major role: men's work still tends to bring in more income as well as to have greater prestige, even when it may not be more intrinsically valuable or interesting than most work available to women. Both partners tend to feed the relationship's problems.

Thirty-nine-year-old Anne relies on her forty-year-old husband Chuck's income to provide her and the kids with many conveniences, yet she has been feeling the lack of closeness attributable to his high-pressure job. She has tried to encourage him to be more expressive of his feelings and to set limits on the length of his workday. When he opens up and talks about getting out of the Wall Street rat race, however, she gets very upset. Chuck, now sunk into a heavy mortgage, doesn't feel he really has a choice. Nor does he want to give up having dinner on the table when he comes home so Anne can go back to work. He worries that if Anne starts having more power—including initiating sex—the pressure on him will only increase the heavy load he's already being asked to carry.

At the same time, while Anne originally looked to Chuck to take care of her and protect her, she now feels repelled by his controlling personality and wants more of a soul mate. As she changes, she believes a different type of mate might suit her more.

Difficulties caused by having to adjust to a partner's evolving expectations are especially complicated in the area of sexuality. As the partners grow and change, so do their needs and desires.

THE SEXUAL SCRIPT

The 1950s Version

The central character in this script is The Magnificent Penis, mighty, forceful, swordlike, thrusting, and powerful, traditionally prized for its size and extolled in literature by such writers as Joyce and Hemingway. It is stroked thousands of times by the average adolescent, each time rewarding him with the most ecstatic pleasure. Egged on by a culture that bombards him at every corner with images of sexy women, he yearns to take it out for a spin.

However, actually "scoring" turns out to be very hard work. He must initiate a date, pick her up, pay all expenses, and deliver her home again. And in between, he has to try to convince her—despite her fears of pregnancy, venereal disease, and becoming stamped as a "slut"—to have intercourse with him. Having sweated his way this far, he must still confront the ultimate terror: that he may not be able to get and sustain an erection, thus threatening him with total loss of his masculinity. He must also set the pace, introduce variations, decide when "foreplay" is to end, and the real business of penetration begins, and keep the whole process going by murmuring "I love you" at crucial times.

The women being courted must display the right combination of virtue and sensuality. She must first feign disinterest, then resist until he "wears her down." Until recently the woman (lucky creature) then had only to lie there—showing little or no response other than perhaps to pretend orgasm if she didn't happen to be having one. More often than not this was the case, as neither knew about her sex organ, the clitoris, let alone had any idea how best to stimulate it.

The 1970s and 1980s Version

With Kinsey, Albert Ellis, Masters and Johnson, and other authorities discovering the clitoris—rather than the vaginal walls—to be the center of female orgasm, women became a lot more enthusiastic about participating in sex.

From the male viewpoint, sex was now in many ways even more work than ever. Since it turns out that for most women "foreplay" is actually the main act, not merely two minutes but perhaps up to twenty minutes or more of clitoral stimulation might be in order. To make matters even scarier, he might be approached for sex at a time when *she's* turned on, but he is not particularly aroused.

Like Lilith, Adam's first partner, women are now saying, "Why must I lie beneath you? I also was made from dust, and I'm therefore your equal." Most women today also have a lot more experience than did women in the 1940s and '50s, leaving men worried about whether their performance matched that of her previous partners.

MEN'S FEAR OF WOMEN

Why has the male of the species tended to mate with someone shorter, younger, less intelligent, less successful, and poorer than he? And why might he freak out if she starts earning more money, showing more skill than he, wanting more and better sex, or implying in any way that he is less than perfect?

Some might say men seem afraid of women. Since the beginning of time men have created various depictions of women suggesting the terror they incite, ranging from harpies or sirens to witches who drain them of their vital fluids in unseen nocturnal visitations. It has been speculated that this is because women represent—because of their ability to reproduce—mysterious, uncontrolled nature, the ultimate extension of which is sexual insatiability. (Freud seemed less frightened by women, viewing them not as gorgons but as defective creatures whose existence was driven by envy and insecurity because they lacked a penis!) Although no witches have been burned in the U.S. for quite some time, it is still quite common for those who deviate from the "proper" image of a woman—the Bella Abzugs and Betty Friedans—to be mocked and for a feminist to be viewed by even highly educated males as a "man hater" or as "someone who thinks women should dominate men."

Men also fear women because, in the process of doing what women like to do best—*connect emotionally*—men see them as doing what men like *least:* compromising men's autonomy and independence. Yet at war with this is men's primitive desire to be emotionally supported and *taken care of.* I am reminded of a Jules Feiffer cartoon that appeared some years ago in the *Village Voice* that showed a woman saying:

> Men may treat women with contempt
> Men may treat women with condescension
> Men may act as though they hate women
> Men don't hate women

Men need women
Men hate needing.

Yet if a woman takes a step into greater autonomy—gets involved in a job or other interests and spends less time in husband and child care—the usual distancing pattern may reverse itself, with the male being the one who suddenly wants more closeness. He may demonstrate this either by retreating (e.g., becoming obese or withholding sex) or by becoming domineering, rageful, and possessive. Afraid that he is going to be rejected, he fears the person he perceives as having the power to *control him.* It takes a very secure and mature man to work through the stresses imposed by changing relationships between the sexes.

Most men, alas, are not all that secure. Or mature. The colloquialisms for women's assertiveness reflect this profound insecurity. The woman who asks her man to do something or in any way implies he may have some flaws risks being labeled:

DOMINATING, CASTRATING, CRAZY, A NAG, SHREW, BITCH, OR BALLBREAKER.

"The moment they begin to be your equals, they will be your superiors," the Roman statesman Cato said in a speech on the consequences of giving in to women.

The man who allows himself to be influenced by such a woman (especially in front of other men) risks being labeled:

A WIMP, HENPECKED, PUSSYWHIPPED, EMASCULATED.

It's that very sticky problem again: the worst thing for a man is to be identified with or dominated by a woman. Dozens of other "nasty names" that throw terror into men's and boy's hearts—

FAG, QUEER, MAMA'S BOY, SISSY—

also derogate him by associating him in some way with women. A man's telling an adversary "Screw you" similarly suggests a humiliating, feminine submission no "real" man would want to endure.

The conundrum that this creates is summarized by writer Barbara Grizzuti Harrison:

Men are taught, from earliest childhood, to despise in themselves what they are taught to admire in women. The worst thing a boy can be told is that he is "like a woman," which is to say, passive, emotional, dependent, soft. *Then* he is told that he must protect women precisely because they have those qualities he has rooted out of himself. No wonder this gives rise to resentment, anger and bewilderment. How can a man value in a woman what he loathes in himself?

HOW DO WE CONNECT WITH MEN SEXUALLY IF WE CAN'T CONNECT EMOTIONALLY?

Frictions between men and women on issues like communication, disciplining the kids, spending money, or how much sex to have are not the things that cause marriages to go sour; rather, *it is the way couples handle these disagreements.* Research on happy married couples shows that "intimacy motivation"—the readiness for close, warm, and communicative interactions and the ability to talk things over—is the best predictor of close, satisfying relationships for men and women. Men and women, unfortunately, have *very* different ideas about the importance, and even the definition, of intimacy and communication.

For most women emotional closeness means *verbal* closeness: a willingness to talk about feelings and negotiate problems. Socialized to connect and to be responsible for keeping their marriages in good health, women can feel utter despair when they fail to connect with their mate. Therapists report that in distressed marriages, the most common complaint of women is that their husbands are too withdrawn and do not share or open up enough. Shere Hite's landmark study, *Women and Love* echoed this. A whopping 98 percent of the forty-five hundred respondents indicated they would like their men to talk more about their personal thoughts, feelings, plans, and questions and to ask the women about theirs. When asked what their partner did that made them the angriest, the women surveyed most frequently (77 percent), replied, "He doesn't listen."

Men's most common complaint, not surprisingly, is that their wives are *too* emotional and expressive—to the point where they feel nagged. What was their most fervent wish in a relationship? To avoid conflict!

One reason that men may feel less of a pull to talk about their relationships is that, unlike women, their worth is not tied to the success of their relationship. Yale psychologist Robert Sternberg described the dramatic differences in the way men and women evaluate their relationships. The men rate almost everything as being better than do the wives, with a rosier view of lovemaking, finances, ties with parents, listening to each other, and tolerance of flaws. Thus the oft-heard line: "Everything's fine as far as I'm concerned. I don't know what you're talking about!"

Things usually start off well enough. According to Ted Huston, a psychologist at the University of Texas at Austin, during courtship, men are much more willing than they are later to spend time talking to women in ways that build their sense of intimacy. As time goes on, they tend to spend less time talking with their wives in these ways and more time on work or with buddies.

How does this happen? The biological capacity for emotional expression is available in both sexes at birth, notes psychologist Virginia O'Leary. By adolescence, however, boys have inhibited most emotions, while girls have inhibited those inappropriate for women, especially anger. Thus the dynamic of the woman-emoting/man-withdrawing creates a vicious cycle that tends to drive ever widening wedges between them.

Other studies suggest an actual *physiological* cause for husbands' tendency to withdraw from conflict. Researchers Clifford Notarius and Johnson found that husbands showed much higher levels of arousal (as measured by skin conductance) than wives while their spouse is complaining. This finding suggests that men do have an emotional reaction, whether or not they actually verbalize it. Psychologists Robert Levinson and John Gottman suggest that the anticipation of conflict or intimacy is arousing for men and that this physiological arousal may have more negative psychological and physical effects on men than on women.

Can Men Become More Emotionally Connected?

Maturity means being responsive to others and to yourself; to be able to put yourself inside another person's skin and glimpse how he or she might be feeling. To a large extent because of the way they are socialized, many men seem to have a *very* hard time with the theory and practice of empathy, sharing, emotional generosity, and supportiveness. The gap widens still further when women, to gain more insight into themselves and their relationships, read dozens of self-help books or go into therapy and become still more introspective and communicative. Also, while women seem to be trying to catch up in some of the more traditional "masculine" areas such as assertiveness and professional success, it seems men are lagging behind in trying to get caught up on some of the traditionally "feminine" skills of learning to love and become emotionally supportive.

I optimistically believe that, as we all evolve, despite having been brought up in two essentially different psychological universes, men and women can, by drawing on the best from each other's "subculture," expand their human potential through a process of resocialization. I believe that both men and women can relate to each other as equals, be vulnerable; that men can say "I'm afraid" and women can say "I want."

Let's go back to how males *acquired* their original blueprint for behavior. A boy becomes "male," as Nancy Chodorow has pointed out, by a process called *separation and individuation,* of which an essential ingredient is removing himself as soon as possible from mother's influence. Having removed himself from his mother's apron strings, he is largely on his own. Most of his prescriptive guidelines are negative: don't be a sissy, don't cry, don't run to your mother when hurt.

His father and other males provide few clues to how to relate intimately. Over the years the archetypal father described by dozens of my clients and friends is a good provider who works twelve hours a day but ignores what's going on at home, is emotionally remote except for occasional bursts of anger, and lives on Maalox. He is a model of emotional armor, likely to reward his sons for performance and independence but not for intimacy, vulnerability, or sharing thoughts and feelings.

As for developing intimate peer friendships: homophobia further inhibits a male's ability to have intimate relationships with other males, limiting male connections to friends to "hang out with" or compete with in sports. He may also narrow the range of potential cultural or aesthetic interests out of fear of being thought feminine.

Men and Women: Friends and Equals

If we improve how the sexes relate to each other, it will boost both the sexual and the nonsexual aspects of male-female relationships. A big step toward improved communication would be for both to become unlocked from rigid sex roles.

What's the payoff for men becoming more like women and women more like men? Plenty. Though the Archie Bunkers of the world yearn for the days when "girls were girls and men were men," those days seem to be coming to an end. The dichotomy of women as loving, mothering, and nondemanding and men as dominant, doers in charge of the world and stars in the relationship just won't fly anymore.

Women's assertiveness has been held responsible for the disintegration of marriage, the family, and sex. To the contrary, it is stagnation, inequality, and lack of mutual respect that have interfered with our ability to continue to love and care about and interest each other. Sex educator Sol Gordon illuminates the kind of behavior appropriate to either gender:

> What best distinguishes liberated adults of both sexes from their unliberated neighbors is their freedom to behave, and to behave *well,* to be interesting and interested, to be alternatively warm and businesslike, dependent/caring. . . . Liberated men and women have dignity. They do not feel inferior to others; they will not let themselves be made to feel inferior. At the same time, they are delighted to praise the real achievements of other people.

To repeat: the qualities of mutual respect, loving, caring, and the ability for both sexes to move freely between active and passive roles cannot help but create a more joyous sexuality for men and for women. The journey may be difficult—but it promises to be exciting.

REWRITING THE SEXUAL SCRIPT FOR THE '90S

The typical problems in male sexual expression—conquest orientation, overconcern with technical performance, emotional unresponsiveness, problems with sensuousness and playfulness, and terror of not being "a normal male"—are the same ones that affect him in the nonsexual areas of his relationships. Thus a man who avoids joining his mate in bed is probably bringing his avoidance with him. Many of the same power issues that crop up in other nonsexual areas of his life are involved: when he feels he's being pressured, he withholds.

The issue frequently gets further complicated by male-female differences in *communication styles,* much as it does when dealing with different preferences about such things as spending time together, sharing feelings, or making decisions about money or kids.

Sylvia, a fifty-two-year-old part-time real estate broker whose kids are now grown, has a reasonably good relationship with George, her fifty-three-year-old accountant husband. Although their sex life consisted of sex two or three times a week through their forties, George's diminished drive and smaller erections have caused him to just about cease initiating sex. When she makes overtures, he generally mutters "I've got a headache" or "I've had a rough day at the office" and rolls over to his side of the bed.

When Sylvia initiates certain positions, or when she expresses the desire for oral sex, he demurs with the excuse that she is acting like a "football coach," at which point she flees to the bathroom in tears. When she finally worked up her courage to speak to him about their sex life, he simply replied, "I don't want to talk about it," and began leaving an hour earlier in the morning. When she told him that she had decided to deal with her sexual frustration by masturbating, he accused her of trying to make him "feel guilty" and then added, "Anyway, you just don't turn me on."

From Sylvia's standpoint, George's response is uncaring, avoidant, even hostile. Viewed from the standpoint of male socialization, however, George's response can be seen as quite normal and natural. Feeling diminished because of his smaller erections and not in the "driver's seat" in some nonsexual areas as Sylvia becomes more active at work, he reasserts control in the only way he sees left to him: not having sex and being critical.

In response to this "activating event" (she expresses a desire to have some changes in their sex life), the woman and the man may have two different internal dialogues:

His Thoughts

1. I *should* be able to initiate and perform sexually (as I used to), but I can't. That's *awful!*
2. She *mustn't* try to push me. She's always trying to push me to

talk about feelings, mow the lawn, and on and on and on. She's a ballbreaker.

3. I *can't stand* all this pressure, on top of everything else. I feel like a failure.

4. She's a demanding person (and she *shouldn't* be). And anyway, who'd want to screw her? She's not looking all that great anymore.

5. She attacks my sexual prowess and tries to put me down and make me feel guilty (and she *shouldn't*).

Her Thoughts

1. Even if he isn't in his sexual prime, he *should* at least be willing to try to have some sexual contact.

2. He's a man—he *should* know other ways to turn me on, and he *should* want to please me sexually.

3. I can't stand this unfairness! I've made so many compromises and done so much to make this relationship work—I *should* at least be able to have sex. Some people say men are good for two things—lifting and screwing—and he can't even do those anymore!

4. He's a selfish bastard—*I can't stand him.*

Sexual *Shoulds*

Besides everything else going on between them, both Sylvia and George make assumptions about sex that work against them. For example, he assumes that not being able to "perform" the way he used to is an indictment against him. On her side, Sylvia assumes because he is a man that George should know what would please her.

Some other commonly held sexual *shoulds* in our culture include the following:

1. Men should be on top and in charge of sex, from initiation to afterplay.
2. Men are responsible for the success of the sexual encounter.
3. Men are supposed to know about sex, so they shouldn't have to ask how to best stimulate their partners nor request specific kinds of stimulation for themselves.
4. Women should wait for men to initiate sex, just as they wait to be asked out or to go to the altar. The only choice open to women is veto power over access and even then, men frequently give themselves the right to interpret *no* as *yes*.
5. The sexually assertive woman is loose, emasculating, or a nymphomaniac. (I personally like *Kinsey Report* co-author Wardell Pomeroy's definition of a nymphomaniac as "a woman who has more sexual behavior than the person who calls her that name."
6. Women need to look a certain way and can become sexually attractive by bleaching, spraying, polishing, scenting, deodorizing, squeezing, padding, waxing, starving, or even surgery.
7. It's OK for women to look sexy but not to be sexually active.
8. It's OK to be sexually responsive to your man, but not to be interested in sex to satisfy your own needs.

Can We Learn to Work It Out?

Let's return to the big question: if men and women seem to connect so poorly with each other in terms of emotional contact and negotiating differences, is there really much hope for male-female relationships?

An important step you can take to improve your chances of connecting with your mate is to begin to think of men's communication styles, as sociolinguist Deborah Tannen suggests, not as defective or noncaring but rather as different—*very* different!

Research demonstrating significant differences in the ways male and females react in relationships is mounting. Prominent among those researchers and theoreticians who have discussed how differently boys and girls perceive affiliation are Eleanor Maccoby, Carol Gilligan, Nancy Chodorow, and Jean Baker Miller. These insights have been applied to adult couples' interactions by Deborah Tannen, John Gottman and his collaborators, Daniel Goldstine, and others, who have dramatically illustrated some striking differences in the way male and female partners process and deal with the same situation. While ostensibly speaking the same language and holding many of the same goals (feeling loved and respected, balancing intimacy and autonomy), too often men and women wind up mistranslating each other, creating further misunderstandings that limit their potential for care and cooperation.

Drawing from the work of the above theoreticians and researchers, I have constructed a chart which summarizes some of the key differences in the way many men and women *view* intimate relationships and *communicate* about problems. These "processing" differences occur both in the *sexual* and the *non-sexual* aspects of the relationship.

As you read through the chart, think about how it applies to the following couple's situation and how, even with good intentions on both their parts, major communication breakdowns can occur.

She: Feels the need to talk, make love. The more he withdraws, the more she insists, pushes, demands, cries, keeps them up for hours talking about it. And she keeps asking "How do you feel?" and "Why?" Unable to stand the distance, she tries to force her way through his emotional wall.

He: Has had less interest in sex than he used to, plus experienced some problems with erections the last time they had sex. He wants to be in control of when they have sex so that it will be more likely he can "perform" successfully. He sees the marriage as OK but feels he's not capable of the kind of intimacy she seems to want.

Views About Relationships/Communication

	HERS	HIS
Intimacy in general	I need for us to talk and be close, so I can feel validated and supported. I can't bear it if we aren't close!	I need to keep her from encroaching on my "space." I need to maintain my independence!
Timing	By putting the discussion off, he's proving he just doesn't care. If we don't work through this problem, it'll keep cropping up again and causing trouble. We must fix it now!	By waiting and then bringing it up at a later time—when I'm in control of the timing, it feels more like I'm doing it of my own free will. When she tries to resolve everything right away, she's coercive and asking for trouble.
Dealing with conflict	We *must* resolve the disagreement so I can feel close to him again. I can't *stand* the distance.	We *must* not have a blowup. That's trouble—I can't *stand* it! When we're fighting, I feel suffocated and just want to be out of here.
Men's style of listening	If he's really listening to me, he would be *actively* showing interest and support.	Even though I'm silent, I'm really hearing her out. I don't know what to say or do about this problem right now; maybe later I'll think of something.

	HERS	HIS
Women's expressing anger	I know that it's "un-feminine" to express my anger, but I have the right to make my thoughts and feelings known and to ask for change. (However, I'm afraid he'll write me off as a nagging shrew—and maybe he's right.)	When she gets angry, she's pushy, demanding, complaining neurotic, behaving like a prima donna, narcissistic, a vain bitch, self-indulgent, hysterical, screaming, irrational, petty, overly emotional, aggressive, too sensitive.
Men's expressing emotions	*He's* emotionally constricted, defective, a clam.	*I'm* cool, restrained, and rational. (She's hysterical and neurotic.)
"Giving in"	If I compromise, it's a way of my *giving,* of enriching our relationship.	If I give in, I'm *submitting,* being a wimp, letting myself be pushed around.
Problem solving	He must come up with some solution, and if he doesn't, it means he doesn't care enough to take the time to work on our relationship. (Ergo, he must not love me very much and we'll never make it together and that will be awful.)	I *should* know how to solve this problem now, and I just can't. And she must not try to force me to. I feel pinned against the wall in these situations—it's awful! I can't stand it!

Having gone through this chart, return once again to the dilemma of the couple described just before the chart: where she feels the need to talk and have sex, while he has been withdrawing from both.

Do you see more clearly how, although they have the same goal of maintaining their loving relationship, by sticking doggedly to their gender role—related way of pursuing their goal, they will actually wind up driving each other further *apart?* Can you project how her pushing for closeness might easily encourage him to withdraw still further? Now try to envision how they might, if they both eased up somewhat on their stances and handled their negotiations a little more like their mates would like them to, they would achieve a much better rapprochement.

Surviving (and Enjoying!) Role Change

Being hemmed in by gender roles is constraining to men, to women, and to their relationships. Unfortunately there is no good fairy who will wave her magic wand and change men and women so that they experience brotherhood and sisterhood combined, of course, with a great sex life. Shifting *out* of traditional "masculine" and "feminine" roles is a complex process that takes a lot of time.

How can you help motivate your man to move along the continuum from sturdy oak to sensitive flower, and to adjust to the fact that you are not going to be just like dear old mom? By showing him *what's in it for him.*

He's probably most aware of the *losses* involved in giving up some of the traditional masculine role. He has to admit he may not always know what's best for you or himself. He has to go through the excruciatingly painful process of getting in touch with and expressing his feelings; he has to learn to negotiate until some viable solution between you has been reached.

These "disadvantages" of role change are overwhelmingly offset by many important *advantages:*

1. Improved ability to manage stress and reduction of stress-related physical *disorders* (hypertension, ulcers, etc.) and thus, potentially, a longer life

2. Less complaining and clinging by spouse

3. Greater two-way respect, communication, emotional support

4. Better capability for problem solving

5. Increased ability to have fun together, make life a joint adventure, share memories, plans, and dreams

6. Improved capacity for friendships and intimate relationships with others (such as parents and kids)

7. The freedom not to have to be the Chief Protector and Breadwinner

8. The freedom not to have to have an ever-ready penis but instead enjoy stroking and being stroked, mutual massages, "petting," and dozens of other delights; the opportunity to sit back and enjoy having a responsive, imaginative sexual partner

9. The freedom from alternating between feeling inferior and superior, between being one up or one down

10. Increased ability to say "I love you," or "I'm sorry," or "I hurt" or to say "I'm scared" and ask for help

11. Being freed from the need to control the universe

12. The capacity to nurture yourself and other humans—which may ultimately be the best antidote to war and violence

HOW TO TELL AN EDUCABLE MALE FROM AN INEDUCABLE ONE

On one end of the spectrum are those males who feel that women are there to serve men, including some who believe that if a woman resists or criticizes them it is their right to assault her, physically or emotionally. Obviously you should beware of such men!

On the other end of the spectrum are those males struggling to get unlocked from their rigid roles. They still may be struggling within their relationships, but at least with this group there's a sense that you're in it together.

Most men are probably somewhere in between. Many of them feel like little boys struggling to act like responsible husbands and fathers while half the time they are scared to death and want to flee, but to their credit, most don't. Some of them are loving and are working on learning to love even better. Others can't seem to love (you'd better believe them when they tell you this) and may, unfortunately, never learn to do so.

To get a clearer idea of your partner's strengths versus his weaknesses, complete the following exercise, using the checklist. Or make

Qualities	Jim	Dave	Bob	My Best Friend	Me
Sense of humor					
Emotionally balanced (not significantly anxious/hostile/depressed)					
Intelligent					
Compatible values					
Kind					
Sensitive/Empathic					
Responsible, trustworthy					
Supportive					
Loyal					

Qualities	Jim	Dave	Bob	My Best Friend	Me
Capable of being happy when alone					
Warm and affectionate					
Practical (good problem solver)					
Good sex					
Shares household tasks					
Good companionship					
Compatible interests					
Compatibile life-style preferences					
Not a substance abuser					
Likes and appreciates me					
Financially secure					
Believes men and women have equal worth and rights					
Patient (accepts fallibility in others and the world)					
Makes the most of own physical appearance					
Flexible, open-minded					

your own list of features, preferably ranked from most important to least important. Evaluate your past mate(s), yourself, as well as your best friend. Then enter for each person *yes, no,* or *?* on each of the listed traits. I guarantee you'll learn a lot—about your patterns in relationships, about the things that are "must haves" in your sex-love relationship as well as those that you can "live without."

CHUGGING TOWARD EQUALITY

> "I can see no reason to doubt that sexism
> will eventually die out, provided of
> course, that our culture does not die out
> first. If it does, it will not be the fault of
> our genes but of our will and intelligence."
> —Marvin Harris, anthropologist

If we can't be dominant, men ask, what can we be? How about equal? How best can women help facilitate this process? Not by *driving* our men to change, or by keeping them up nights pressing them to "open up" or "relate." These approaches are most likely to produce behavior opposite from what we want—i.e., further avoidance and withdrawal.

Now, let me warn you that you'll need lots of frustration tolerance for this process. Here are some guidelines:

1. *Approach the task of trying to communicate with your partner about any touchy topic as if you were trying to communicate with someone from a different culture.* Or think of yourself as an educator giving a course in emotional education.
2. *Validate and acknowledge his viewpoint even though you may not agree with it.* Don't automatically assume that *your* reality *is* reality. For example: "I know that talking about this subject is

uncomfortable for you, and you'd just as soon not have to deal with it, especially with all the pressures you've got at work. But this is something I'm feeling very concerned about, and I think we need to spend half an hour this evening and brainstorm some options."

3. *Avoid blaming or globally condemning him when he acts in an emotionally constricted, withdrawn, or other difficult way.* Try to view his behavior not as awful and intolerable, but as *customs of the culture* (like many Japanese people's habit of not voicing negative opinions even when asked). Your mate may be acting badly—but you need not take it as a reflection of your worth. By learning to overcome hurt and blame, you are promoting your own well-being.

4. *Remember to apply the "cross-cultural" approach to yourself as well:* For example, don't condemn yourself if you inadvertently slip into some of your female subculture behavior and cry, cling, beg, grovel, or scream with frustration when you feel you're not being heard.

5. *Remember that* most *men have had relatively little "empathy training"*: namely, learning to meet some of the other person's wants, whether it's convenient or not.

6. *Try to have the courage and patience to accept that some issues may not get resolved for months,* and others perhaps not for years. Don't assume that if he's changing at a barely perceptible rate, he's not changing at all. People change in *tiny* steps, not miles at a time. Compliment him on these small changes (instead of saying, "So how come it took you four months to decide to make love to me?").

7. *Don't assume rationality on the part of your mate* (even though he does). As author William Novak puts it, "Men, although frequently in an adult body, have little boys hiding inside saying, 'me, me, me,' not knowing who he is or what he wants." If it sticks in your craw to think of him as a child, you might try to think of him as an adult who is somewhat developmentally disabled. For many men, a seemingly simple task like trying

to talk about feelings is like a blind man trying to describe an elephant.

8. *Try not to fall into the trap of seeing him as not being "manly"* or successful enough if he expresses weakness, loses his job and has to take a reduced salary, or doesn't make brilliant flashy conversation at dinner parties. Women, alas—while disdaining machismo—often tend to reject many sensitive men or men in lower-paid professions on the grounds that they aren't successful enough. In fact, as I've observed, so-called "sissies" often make the best mates, while hard-driving, cigar-smoking executives may make the worst.

9. *Learn how to gracefully "lump it."* Men have a lead on us in this area, having been expected to "keep a stiff upper lip." Although they may go too far in stepping back from things they don't like, perhaps we can both strive for a better balance in learning to have reasonable expectations and when, at least temporarily, to back off.

10. *Keep trying to act lovingly,* for your own enjoyment as well as his, even sometimes when you may not be feeling all that loving. You'd be surprised at how some expression of tenderness can help warm things up.

Equality in the Bedroom

Can sex survive the fall of male domination? It can not only survive but flourish, studies suggest. Societies characterized by high female power within marriage exhibit behaviors and attitudes that Western thought sees as "healthy." "For relatively insecure people," psychologist Abraham Maslow wrote in 1942, "sex is a power weapon, related in myriad ways to dominance feelings." Secure people do not, he found, seek to dominate or be dominated. And for every man who may feel threatened by his wife's new sexual assertiveness, there is probably another who is energized by it.

Shere Hite poses the provocative question "When we think of sex, do we speak of the man penetrating the women, or of her enveloping him?" To the insecure male, female assertiveness in both sexual and nonsexual areas may be experienced as though she were going to suck out his essence, swallow him, eat him alive, or castrate him. Withholding sex may be the insecure man's way of trying to put himself back in a power position. Men's early warning system, says Deborah Tannen, "is geared to detect signs that they are being told what to do—even in so apparently affiliative an activity as making love. . . . If a man experiences life as a fight for freedom, he is naturally inclined to resist attempts to control him and determine his behavior."

I remain stubbornly optimistic that there are ways for men and women to balance power—to have our cake and eat it too—by creating a balance between the freedom to extend ourselves into the outer world and the retention of a strong commitment to our spouses.

ASSESSING THE STRENGTHS AND WEAKNESSES OF YOUR RELATIONSHIP

Take some time to write out the answers to the following questions, and try to encourage your mate to do so as well. Then exchange what you've written and read them apart from each other. They can then provide the framework for a constructive goal-setting session, in conjunction with some of the other approaches for managing anger and improving communication skills outlined in this book.

1. What are the things I like most about my spouse? What are my reasons for wanting to continue to live with him/her? _____

   _____

2. If I could have a magic wand and change three things about my *spouse,* what would they be? (Try to think of a recent, specific example.)

   _____

   _____

3. If I could change something about *myself,* what would that be?

_____

_____

4. In what ways do my usual ways of reacting to problems make me more unhappy?

_____

_____

5. What are two things I could do—specifically—to improve myself and our relationship?

_____

_____

It's hard as hell to be a man, and it's hard as hell to be a woman. And it's murder to try to create good male-female relationships. Katharine Hepburn had one possible solution. "Sometimes I wonder if men and women really suit each other," she once said. "Perhaps they should live next door and just visit now and then."

Maybe this is one of many possible options for helping us build better relationships with each other and our children, so that our planet will flourish.

In the meantime—while you are evaluating and working on trying to create a better relationship:

1. *Work at accepting your particular man*—with *all his quirks and flaws.* Try your best, for at least the next three months, not to explode when he starts acting like a jerk.
2. *Stay vitally absorbed in your own life*—not letting the majority of it revolve around his preferences to the exclusion of yours.
3. *Keep laughing with your friends, enjoying music or soft breezes blowing on your skin,* and all those myriad other things that can give you sensual and emotional pleasure.
4. *Try not to let too much ride on his always desiring you with great passion.* Even a little bit of desire can go a long way!

CHAPTER 3

WHINING IS NOT
AN APHRODISIAC

". . . women hate forever a man who self-
ishly takes his pleasure at the price of
their suffering; but they feel eternal
resentment against men who have seemed
to disdain them."
—Simone de Beauvoir,
The Second Sex

Most of the women I've talked to whose mates have less sex with them than they'd prefer say they feel pretty hurt, angry, and ashamed about it.

Barbara, an attractive, forty-four-year-old mother of two adolescents, recounted tearfully, "I've paid my dues. I struggled through two bad relationships before finding this really solid guy. I've raised my kids while giving my career a back seat to make the marriage work, and have basically done most of the compromising. I've fought through so many battles. The least I can expect is a decent sex life. But now I've got to turn myself inside out on this one, too. When does it end? I married Jim because he's a really decent person. In my previous relationship I knew I was with someone who was really limited in a lot of ways and wouldn't make a good mate and parent.

It was almost totally sexual—and little else. With Jim I've got a lot of really good things, but no sex!"

Jim's avoidance had begun to erode Barbara's self-esteem and to spill over into other aspects of her life. Her frequent sarcasm with Jim about his "heavy sex drive" and other grievances resulted in many draining quarrels. As she began to spiral downward, she found herself snapping more at her kids, withdrawing from friends, and overeating.

While agreeing that her getting upset evoked few, if any, positive changes in Jim's sexual behavior, Barbara bristled at my suggestion that maybe a first step toward solving the problem would be to work on not letting herself get so upset about it. "How can I *not* feel hurt and humiliated?" she said indignantly. "He makes me feel like I'm totally unattractive as a woman."

There's no question it's frustrating and painful when you're not having as much sex or physical intimacy as you'd like. Lying entwined with someone's body, having your senses come alive, enjoying the thrill of orgasm and all the other pleasurable feelings that can accompany sex are among life's nicest experiences. And good sex can certainly go a long way toward balancing some of the frustrations of domestic life and help you feel special to your mate in a way that no one else in his life is. If you're feeling frustrated or unfulfilled in other areas of your life as well, the lack of sex may feel even worse.

TWO PROBLEMS: HIS AND YOURS

When your desire exceeds that of your partner, you actually have two sets of problems: "his" and "hers." In turn, each set of problems can be broken down into a "practical" part and an "emotional" part.

His practical problem is that he wants to have sex significantly less than you do and isn't doing much about stepping up his sexual activity. Though less likely to verbalize it, he's almost invariably got some emotional problem about the sexual problem and usually some kind of general emotional problem as well. Common ones are depression over lack of work success, stress overload, feelings of inadequacy about his ability to perform sexually or to keep up with his partner, low frustration tolerance over having to work more to get aroused than when the relationship was new, anxiety about intimacy, anger at his wife, fear of her anger, and resentment at her requests.

"That makes me so mad," said Barbara when I pointed out that maybe Jim's sexual avoidance was a result of emotional problems. "We've *all* got problems. So how come his are so sacred? When *he's* got problems, I'm there for him to try to help him solve them or at least boost his spirits. But how about *my* stresses? I work at least as many hours as he does and have the same kids around the house that he claims make him unable to feel a sense of privacy; yet I'm game for having more intimacy. But not *him*. And when I want to talk about the problem, am crying hysterically and feeling hurt, he won't even discuss it. It's not fair!"

Unfair? Yes. Awful? No!

Yes, it *is* highly unfair. However, while most women tend to feel pain and a loss of closeness when they *can't* talk about and try to resolve problems, many men may find it equally painful to *talk* about them. So, to avoid the pain, the anger, or the blowup that might come from talking the problem through, they clam up and cause their mate's frustration to build up until she once again explodes. Or they may not even be in *touch* with their feelings in the first place.

Once again, the bulk of the burden of trying to work on the problem remains with the emotional administrators—women.

Women also have both a practical and an emotional problem. The *practical* problem can include trying to figure out how to influence him to have more sex with you, or getting him to talk about the problem with you or a therapist. Another practical problem you may have is deciding whether or not to stay in the marriage or to have an affair.

Unfortunately, most women also have some *emotional* problem—hurt, anger, or depression—about their practical problem, the sexual drought.

Barbara asserts that for quite some time she had been patient and rational. Finally, though, she "just couldn't take it anymore" and became depressed and angry. "Why *shouldn't* I feel upset? No matter what I do, he just doesn't respond to my needs. You'd think that even if he's not all that interested in sex, just seeing how upset I am might make him do something about it. How can I not be furious at him? And frankly, I'm pretty frustrated with *you*. Aren't you denying me the right to be assertive about my own needs and to express anger when there's no response? Isn't that what men have always done to women?"

The fact is, I explained to Barbara, that she did have a perfect right to feel hurt and angry. *Everyone* has a right to her or his feelings—including anger. But if our goal is to maximize happiness and minimize pain, we're probably going to be better off if we can somehow reduce the painfulness of our negative feelings. As a bonus, we're probably also more likely to get better results when we do.

When I asked Barbara how her husband had responded to her depression and anger, she thought for a minute, then admitted, in a quiet voice, "He hates it. The last time he saw me starting to get upset, he actually slid under the sheet and pulled it over his head! He says sometimes when I cry or blame him, he feels totally inadequate and unappreciated; and then of course *I* wind up feeling guilty. I hate that!"

Most of the women to whom I've spoken—especially after a long period of sexual drought—do get fed up with trying to be patient and understanding and instead become demanding, accusing, or emotionally withdrawn. But if your man is having problems in getting himself to have sex with you in the first place, he's more likely than ever to withdraw when he feels himself attacked or rejected. Few men (or women) like to cuddle up to a snarling bear.

Not only is your mate less likely to make any physical approaches when he is assaulted by your distress, but he may also—especially if he has low self-acceptance—be less willing either to talk about or to work on the problem. Because of his own shame and fear of more failure, it is more likely he will simply clam up and bury his head in the sand or a book (rather than your bosom). Unfortunate—but that's reality, sad and disappointing though it may be.

Yes, there's no question that it is unfair that Barbara and millions of others who have turned themselves inside out for their relationships are still stuck with a raw deal. "Why," they ask, "should *I* change if he doesn't?" It would, without doubt, be preferable if Jim and millions of other men worked on their problems with their mates.

But in situations like this, where your mate won't deal with the problem, you have two basic choices. One choice is to get upset—angry, depressed, hurt—and ultimately decrease your overall enjoyment of life—not to mention exacerbate his allergy to sex. But then you'll have double trouble: sexual deprivation, plus emotional pain.

You also have a second choice: to stubbornly refuse to get *overly* upset by his sexual retreat. Disappointed, yes; moderately frustrated and annoyed, yes—but not so hurt or enraged that you drain energies that might be better spent in making yourself as happy as you can under the circumstances. And when you moderate your reaction, you're doing it not so much to help him as to help *yourself*. In the process you also stand a far greater chance of helping him come to terms with his emotional problems and become sexually activated.

Let's examine these two basic choices of being miserable versus disappointed in reacting to sexual deprivation to better understand the dynamics involved.

It's *Your* Self-Worth that Suffers When You Lose *Your* Cool over *His* Low Sex Drive

Vicky, an energetic thirty-two-year-old art director in an ad agency, ended her first marriage because her corporate lawyer husband was a "critical, emotionally withdrawn workaholic." She has now been married for two years to Gene, a tall, congenial, athletic man who owns his own computer consulting firm. From the outside they appear to be the perfect couple: attractive, affluent, compatible, and with a wide range of friends and cultural interests. When they came to see me, Vicky reported that at first sex with Gene had been hot and heavy; after the first year and a half of marriage, however, it had decreased from three or four times a week to once a month or less.

Gene and Vicky like and respect each other, enjoy each other's company, and generally consider each other their "best friend." Gene gets his best physical charge from running or playing softball. Vicky's idea of physical activity is having robust sex.

Night after night, Gene watches the 11 o'clock news, ignoring Vicky's nuzzling sexily up against him. At the stroke of 11:30, after a good night kiss, he drops off to sleep. Vicky tosses sleeplessly for another hour, arriving at the following distorted assumptions about Gene's behavior:

1. "He obviously doesn't find me sexy."
2. "He must not love me."
3. "I'm getting old-looking. I've gained weight. I'm no longer attractive. His behavior proves it."
4. "If he doesn't find me sexually attractive, I am sexually undesirable and my marriage is a failure."

"It's not so easy," Vicky protested, "not to feel hurt and inadequate." And she's right. It *is* hard. A welter of cultural messages reinforce the idea that we're worth less if a man doesn't desire us.

When we get rejected, those cultural messages are released in the form of negative thoughts.

These thoughts exert their insidious effect on us, often on a sub-conscious level, throughout our life cycle, from early adolescence through our later years. In our early dating days, after a great evening, the guy says, "I'll call you." After spending several agonizing evenings waiting in vain for the phone to ring, we conclude:

"I must have done something wrong."

"I was probably too quiet, and he thought I was boring."

"I probably talked too much about myself."

"He's used to going out with model types. Why would he be interested in me?"

On the other hand, when you do find a great guy, you spend idyllic Sundays in bed, talking, making love, and reading the Sunday paper. Now, only a few months later, just as you're waking up, he dashes off to jog, never to return to bed, no matter how many entreaties to "come snuggle" or dewy looks that you throw in his direction. You conclude:

"He's bored, uninterested in me."

"I'm unattractive."

"He doesn't love me anymore. I can't stand it."

"Maybe he's seeing another woman."

"What if he leaves me?"

How does she so easily slide from *his* withdrawal to *her* inadequacy? From having a sexually avoidant male to feeling inadequate about her looks and self? Her vulnerability is especially fed by her early sex role socialization messages. The echoes of a hundred male voices and a thousand cover girls have convinced her that: "I must be glamorous, thin, and youthful to be sexually attractive." This drumbeat has kept her and most of us from loving our bodies and accepting ourselves.

Your Anger and Resentment Don't Solve the Problem—His or Yours

"OK," said Vicky, "I see the point you're making about how his avoiding me sexually doesn't make *me* a sexual failure or less of a woman. After all, even with my extra weight I still get lots of guys coming on to me in the office. But damn it! What really gets me is that I'm full of sexual energy. I've been so patient in trying to turn him on. And I've tried to talk to him about how upsetting this is for me, and I've worked my head off to understand what's going on with him. But nothing works! Then, when I finally blow up because it seems like the only way I can get through to him, he gets on my case about how all I do is nag and scream and nothing he does is ever appreciated.

"Now he's stopped talking to me about it altogether. And he refuses to see a therapist—not even for one consultation. I love him and made the decision I'd accept the way he is. But what I *won't* accept is that there might be help—and he won't go for it. That makes me *furious!*"

Some women focus on the unfairness of their partner's not doing what seems so easy and natural for "most" men to do:

"He married me because he found me so sexy. Now he finds my sexuality too much to handle!"

"I used to feel inadequate when I wasn't having orgasms. Then I learned how, and it felt great. Now I've got this husband who's really good in lots of ways, but he's not turned on to me sexually. So I'm back to feeling like a sexual zero again."

"Other men find me sexy, but I'm staying faithful to him. And he won't even touch me. How unfair!"

Still other beliefs are a result of misconceptions about marriage: namely, that it should fill just about all our needs and not have any significant flaws.

"Most normal couples have sex several times a week."

"People who really love each other will try to please the other person or at least be more sensitive when their mate is really un-happy."

"When we were dating and saw each other mainly on weekends, we used to screw more in a weekend than we have in the past year!"

"You can't possibly have a good relationship without sex."

Most of these internalized beliefs are likely to breed frustration or anger. The gist of them is this:

1. The world *should* be fair and just.
2. My mate *must* try to satisfy me.
3. He is a *rotten person* for acting this way toward me.
4. I *can't stand* being so sexually deprived.

Pouring Fuel on Your Anger: The Hydraulic Theory of Anger

A widely held belief that tends to feed the anger of many of my clients is what Erich Fromm refers to as the "hydraulic" theory of anger, also known as "it's-good-to-ventilate-your-anger."

According to the hydraulic theory, all humans cannot help feeling hostile to those who balk them; and, unless they express or let out their hostile feelings, these will inevitably grow to enormous proportions. In turn, people's feelings of anger will seep or burst out of the tank of rage built up in the depth of their psyches. This buildup of anger will then ruin their existing intimate relationships.

A great deal of recent psychological research has revealed the limitations of this theory of anger. Interestingly, we are learning that the more people heatedly ventilate their feelings of anger, the *more* irate they feel and the *more* hostile and punitively they act. Anger begets anger, and can have highly damaging effects on the process of conflict resolution and on the marriage itself.

"So," Vicky exclaimed exasperatedly, *"now* you seem to be saying that I should just sit on my feelings. Repress my anger and get an ulcer—just like my mother did because she was afraid to let my father know she was angry."

Vicky's response is common. Most people believe that we have two options: to ventilate our anger, or to sit on it and get physical symptoms such as a heart attack or colitis.

"In fact," I explained to Vicky, "you do have a *third* choice, and that is to feel and express appropriate, non-self-defeating feelings. You're probably *not* going to feel happy about not having sex as often as you want. Heck—you'd have to be crazy! Nor do I think it's a good idea for you to try to bury your resentments—they'll only resurface in even more toxic form. But you do have a choice to experience less toxic feelings. You can feel moderately disappointed, annoyed, or frustrated—rather than experiencing self-crippling rage and self-defeating hostility."

The bonus is that by feeling and acting less distressed, you are more likely to get more of what you want. Not unlike the adage, "You catch more flies with honey than with vinegar." By working on and understanding your own psyche, and challenging the irrational beliefs that fuel your hurt and anger, you will have a much better shot at understanding and influencing *his* psyche. After all, you're both human, and you share something in common—your precious relationship.

In other words, you can have little or no sex and experience only some sadness or disappointment. Or you can have little or no sex and lots of emotional distress, which can infiltrate other areas of your life.

"Easier said than done!" said Vicky. "No doubt about that," I agreed. And we proceeded to discuss some very specific tools—covered in the remainder of this chapter and the next—to help her reduce her agitation about her situation.

DETACHING INSULT FROM INJURY— OR, IS IT REALLY POSSIBLE NOT TO FEEL UPSET?

We're not talking about suppressing, repressing, or denying feelings. We're talking about *reducing the degree of distress*.

It can be very painful, at worst, and a real drag, at best, to see your images and expectations of marriage shriveling up before your eyes. First you dispense with the happily-ever-after scenario, accepting the fact that relationships involve a lot of struggle and compromise. But, at least you think, the light at the end of the tunnel includes having someone to be intimate with. You then accept the fact that maybe there's not going to be as much *emotional* intimacy as you'd like but, heck, there's still sex and *physical* intimacy. Then, oops, no sex, and you're left wondering, What's it all worth? Why me?

After you've worked your way through a few (or a few dozen) wrong numbers to find someone with a solid character and a sane personality, you quite reasonably may feel disheartened. "There's so much I've already had to put up with. Don't I ever get any reward for it all?" opined one of my clients.

Then this therapist (me!) comes along and seems to be echoing all the things society has for so long been telling women: watch your anger. Here we've worked hard at getting in touch with our anger and gone to assertiveness training groups, only to find that we now need to learn to rev it down again. Have women really come this far only to revert to sweetness and submission, despite their once again being on the losing end? We're damned if we don't assert ourselves and damned if we do. If we're going to be one down, why can't there at least be someone on top of us at night?

While it may be very natural, and very human, for the partner who wants sex more frequently to get angry and depressed, the bottom line is, *will it get you what you want?* (Namely, some nice body touching!) There's no question that it's hard not to feel very upset over your sexual famine. It may seem almost impossible to feel only frustrated and disappointed, but you need to do some hard work to keep yourself from experiencing an endless wellspring of hurt feelings.

And this work begins with your understanding that *he is not causing your distress*. True, he *is* withholding; and, unfortunately, you have limited control over that. Where you *do* have power, however, is in not letting his poor behavior give you a pain in your gut.

Start by asking yourself these questions:

- Do I want to suffer or to enjoy my life as fully as I can?
- Do I want to keep having my feelings of self-worth depend on how *others* are treating me at any given moment?
- Is my objective to make my partner feel like a wimp? Or do I want my message to reach him—body and mind? If so, I'm not going to reach him very effectively through anger and blaming.
- How much sense does it make to keep "whining" that the world shouldn't be so unfair? It makes so much more sense to make myself as happy as possible, despite life's hassles and unfairness.

Think about reducing your anger in terms of refusing to add insult to injury. Yes, he's acting "badly" by not connecting more with you sexually. But you can avoid compounding the situation by not going into a depression or rage. Don't make the mistake of letting your world spin around his penis. In other words, when it seems that having sex with him is like drawing blood from a stone, back off, Betty.

A more helpful way to feel better about a lousy situation is to put extra energy into making your world as positive and happy as possible—despite your sexual deprivation.

INJECTING PASSION INTO YOUR LIFE IN GENERAL

By injecting passion into other aspects of your life, you will reduce your neediness for more sexual passion than your mate may be able to provide.

1. *Do special things to please yourself.* Go to a play, giggle with your women friends, take a walk in the woods, buy yourself flowers, or get a massage.
2. *Focus on the positive aspects of your relationship.* Remember that things like loyalty, companionship, coparenting, and, yes, even financial partnership, are also very important elements in the fabric of your relationship and your life.
3. *Flex and stretch your muscles in some other ways*—from your toes to your pelvic muscles—by hiking, biking, doing aerobic dancing, or frolicking with your dog.
4. *Mellow out* with a relaxation tape or a warm bubble bath and snuggle up with a stuffed bear and a good book.
5. *Develop your sense of humor* and try using it with him—it can be a real sanity saver. And while he's in a lighter mood, ask him if he'll give you a nonsexual massage—no strings.
6. *Remember that no one dies from lack of sex.* And if someone else isn't going to affirm your sexuality, it doesn't mean you're not sexual or that you're worth less.
7. *Above all, make your emotional relationship with yourself the pivotal one.* Stay stimulated and absorbed in one or more passions or projects. Take some time just to be alone and meditate or listen to music.

And that screwball you love—what about him? Well, attached to his crotch is a complicated brain and psyche. He is acting the way *he* wants, as opposed to the way *you* want, not necessarily because he's malicious or uncompassionate or a wimp, but probably because he's simply wrapped up in his own concerns and feelings. Barraging him with bitter complaints, insults, or sulking isn't very likely to get you what you want.

You may succeed better in helping him get his sexual juices flowing again if you start by helping him become less emotionally distressed and withdrawn in general. I emphasize *may help* because there are, alas, no guarantees that a person will choose to deal with his problems and activate himself. But when you show him you're moving calmly on despite your less-than-optimal marital and sexual circumstances, you're at least providing him with a better model of handling frustration.

It's hard stuff—keeping sex in perspective and not feeling pretty upset when you're not "getting it." If you're ready to give it a shot, turn to the next chapter and prepare for some challenging work.

Keep your eye on the ball, being as happy as you can within the limits of Martian/Venusian mating. Stop whining about what isn't happening between you while deciding whether the advantages of your relationship outweigh its disadvantages and what risks you're willing to take to increase the amount of partnered sex in your life.

KEEPING SEX IN PERSPECTIVE

Sex Is:

- tension-releasing,
- a sensory treat with zero calories,
- a way to get exercise,
- a means of enhancing intimacy,
- a nice nightcap,
- an eye-opener/great way to greet the dawn,
- a way to express loving and tender feelings.

Sex Isn't:

- a proof of your femininity,
- a measure of your self-worth,
- something to make up for your lack of fulfillment in other areas,
- a way to resolve marital conflict or boredom,
- another black mark against your mate (when it isn't happening),
- just intercourse; it's also touching, stroking, sharing warm feelings.

CHAPTER 4

THE KEY TO EMOTIONAL SELF-MANAGEMENT: TUNING IN TO YOUR IRRATIONAL SELF-TALK

Most people think in terms of other people causing their feelings: "*He* makes me so mad!" "*He* makes me feel really unattractive."

Sometimes others do treat us badly or reject us. It's pretty much the human condition, and it's quite normal and appropriate to feel frustrated, disappointed, or somewhat sad when they do so. But when we buy into the notion that we must feel deeply upset when they do, we are adding to the hurt. We make *ourselves* vulnerable to loss of self-esteem and rage.

How do we get over this emotional knee-jerk habit of feeling put down when we get rejected or badly treated? "It's so ingrained," dozens of my women clients have said.

The Greek philosopher Epictetus said more than two thousand years ago: "It is not things in themselves that disturb us, but the views that we take of them." Many years ago a creative and inno-vative psychologist, Albert Ellis, began to use a similar principle in his therapeutic work, which became known as rational-emotive therapy. Since that time, research has demonstrated its effective-ness, and rational-emotive therapy and cognitive behavior therapy have increasingly been applied as self-help systems for being your own emotional troubleshooter.

By following some of the guidelines outlined in this chapter—many of which are derived from rational-emotive therapy—you can help yourself deal more successfully with all kinds of relationship issues.

1. You can learn to handle your own hurt and anger.
2. You can learn to accept yourself—even if your partner seems to be avoiding you like the plague.
3. You will be able to talk about the problem without getting emotionally overwrought.
4. You will be able to brainstorm solutions more clearheadedly.

WE FEEL THE WAY WE THINK: THE ABC THEORY OF EMOTIONAL DISTURBANCE

At point *A* there is an *activating event:* Your husband has not had sex with you for over six months. He has refused several overtures on your part during that time and will not discuss the problem except to say vaguely, "I'm just not into it."

At point *C* you experience an *emotional consequence:* you feel hurt, depressed, and angry.

I am fond of taking polls. And one of my favorite polls is to ask women in the workshops that I conduct how they would react to a given situation, and thus determine cause and effect. In this case—if *A* caused *C*—every woman would feel the same way when the husband they loved and wished to have sex with rejected them.

Nearly always, around 80 percent of these women do, in fact, feel hurt and angry. However, almost invariably a distinct minority feels only sad, disappointed, or frustrated—but not deeply humiliated or enraged.

"So how can these women feel this way?" protested my client Vicky. "Maybe they're some kind of saints—but that's not *me*."

With some further explanation my two clients Barbara and Vicky grasped that even though they had not been able to react in a non-disturbed way in the past, it was something they could learn to do. And did.

It really clicked for Barbara when what she considered the "last straw" occurred.

"We never seem to get around to making love for months. His weeknight excuse is 'I'm too tired.' On Sunday morning it's that 'The kids are around—I can't relax.'

"So I figure we'll go to a romantic place. I get my folks to stay with the kids. I spend weeks making plans to go to this wonderful place in Barbados.

"And what happens? Nothing! Days go by, and no matter how many sexy bathing suits or slinky dresses I put on, he just doesn't respond. He played tennis with me and was sweet and nice. Most of the rest of the time he was off jogging or windsurfing. But no sex!

"The last night, we finally get around to having it. Probably because he knows he'd better! And in three minutes it's all over! I've never felt so depressed and hopeless and furious as I do now!"

Barbara's anger spilled into tears as she told me this story.

"I really hate that Jim ruined this trip by acting his usual asexual self," she said with a sigh.

"And if you thought only *that*, Barbara," I responded, "you wouldn't be so miserable.

"But I think you also have some additional beliefs in your head—as you frequently do when Jim is being withholding. Here's where point *B* comes in: your *beliefs* about the activating event.

1. "How can he keep treating me this way?" (Translation: *He shouldn't be nonsexual.*)

2. "He's awful for ignoring me sexually and being such a lousy lover when we *do* have sex." (Translation: *He's rotten and selfish.*)

3. "I can't *stand* being ignored this way—especially when other guys would give their eye teeth to have such a sexually responsive woman!"

4. "I feel like an unattractive, insignificant human being." (Translation: *I am worth less.*)

"Yes," responded Barbara, "that's exactly how I feel!"

"Let's challenge each of these beliefs," I suggested. "That is, let's see if you can look at the situation in a different way—and, in the process, feel less upset. First, let's look at your thoughts 'How can he keep treating me this way' and 'he *shouldn't* be so inconsiderate in ignoring my needs.' "

After a long, pensive silence, Barbara said quietly, "I guess I finally see what you've been getting at. When I've been thinking, 'He shouldn't be acting the way that he is,' it's like saying it shouldn't be raining—when it is."

"And your belief that it's awful and intolerable—is that a *fact* or a *belief?*"

"I guess they're my own beliefs—catastrophizing, as you've been trying to get me to see. The fact is, maybe cancer or having my child die is awful. And while I think the situation stinks and is unfair, I can stand it. And I guess I'd better learn to stand it better, because so far there's no end in sight. So I may as well get used to it!"

"Do you see," I asked Barbara and Vicky, "that it's perfectly reasonable to believe that it's a pain in the neck not to have sex and that your marriage would certainly be closer and more enjoyable if you did? And that if you thought only this way, you would feel *only* frustrated and disappointed? But that when you add the beliefs that he absolutely must not act this way, and that it's awful and unbearable, *you create your own misery?*"

When Vicky came in to see me for our next session, she showed that she really understood the power of rational self-talk. She reported that she had had the calmest discussion ever with Gene and that, although he didn't say much, he'd actually listened and understood.

"I told him, 'I wish you weren't being this way—avoiding me sexually or even any discussion of sex. I feel sad and frustrated. I wish we could work together to find a solution. I think it's really sad for both of us that we're missing this delicious thing.' And guess what? This morning he actually gave me the longest hug he has for a long time and told me he loved me!"

By not overstating the problem, Vicky was better able to reach Gene.

The following chart is designed to show you how your own as

Women's Self-Messages	Women's Behavioral and Emotional Consequences	Men's Self-Messages	Men's Behavioral and Emotional Consequences
1) Poor me. I'm finally in my sexual prime and have someone to sleep with nightly. And he won't touch me! He *shouldn't* act like that!	Depression, anger Self-pity Whining	1) How can I get aroused by this person I've been with so long? I *must* have a newer and more exciting partner!	Boredom Flirting with other women Avoiding wife

Women's Self-Messages	Women's Behavioral and Emotional Consequences	Men's Self-Messages	Men's Behavioral and Emotional Consequences
2) I don't feel like a *real* woman without someone sexually interested in me. I *need* his interest in me.	Self-downing Overeating, drinking	2) Every time she makes a crack about our sex life, I feel *emasculated*.	Self-downing, anger Drinking, overeating
3) If my marriage is so lacking in passion, *I'm a failure*.	Self-downing, depression Overeating, drinking	3) I feel like a total *failure* on my job, because I haven't been made a partner.	Self-downing, depression Overeating, drinking
4) Why bother? I'm sick of trying. Nothing I do will help. It's *hopeless*.	Depression, high frustration Withdrawal	4) Why bother? I'm sick of trying. Nothing I do in this marriage seems to help. It's *hopeless*.	Depression, high frustration Withdrawal

well as your partner's self-defeating self-messages encourage physical and emotional distancing.

A good deal of the time, the disrespect you think is coming from your mate is actually coming from *you*. As you become more self-accepting, you'll find you're feeling a lot less hurt by your mate's behavior, more realistic in accepting his limits, and more effective in communicating with him.

THE ROLE OF SELF-TALK IN PERPETUATING ANGER

Once again, it is negative, irrational self-messages that cause debilitating and unproductive levels of anger.

The following chart illustrates the typical kinds of *should*ing and other destructive self-messages that lead to anger and high levels of frustration. Note how similar men's and women's evaluations of their mates' behavior are—and how they both lead to hostility, withdrawal, and various kinds of passive-aggressive behavior.

Women's Self-Messages	Women's Behavioral and Emotional Consequences	Men's Self-Messages	Men's Behavioral and Emotional Consequences
1) I'm a good, nurturing wife. My mate *should* satisfy me sexually. I *deserve* some affection!	Anger Avoidance	1) I bring in the money and tolerate her weight. I *shouldn't* also have to have sex with her if I haven't initiated it. I *deserve* some peace.	Anger Avoidance

Women's Self-Messages	Women's Behavioral and Emotional Consequences	Men's Self-Messages	Men's Behavioral and Emotional Consequences
2) My mate *should* be willing to talk about the problems (or go for counseling). *I can't stand the stress of not talking* and working things out.	Anger Yelling, pushing for long conversations	2) I have enough tensions and criticisms at work. I *shouldn't* have to face this crap when I get home. *I can't stand these talks.*	Anger Withdrawal Verbal attacking
3) When I want sex, he *should* at least be willing to have it some of the time, just to please me. This *proves* he just doesn't care about me.	Anger, depression Sulking, withholding Verbal attacking	3) If I'm just not turned on (or turned on to her), she *should* understand, even if we don't discuss it. This *proves* she just doesn't care about me.	Anger, depression Sulking, withholding Verbal attacking

Women's Self-Messages	Women's Behavioral and Emotional Consequences	Men's Self-Messages	Men's Behavioral and Emotional Consequences
4) He *should* give me regular sex; he's my husband. Doesn't he love me?	Anger, hurt Withdrawal	4) She *shouldn't* see me just as a sex object. Doesn't she love me for myself?	Anger, hurt Withdrawal

The last set of beliefs is an amusing turn of events. How different things were just a decade or two ago.

OVERCOMING SELF-DEPRECATION AND ANGER

Many women repeatedly blow up at their mates only to feel guilty, angry, or ashamed of themselves later for losing control.

"I can't believe that, once again, there I was groveling, with tears and mascara running down my face, for a little human contact from my husband—this man who claims to love me. How could I have made such a fool of myself?"

My advice to my clients is always to *accept yourself*—including your overreactions. That doesn't mean you're not going to try to act better next time: but you're *human. And humans make mistakes.*

The following steps can help you greatly reduce your *dysfunctional* anger: that is, the kind that eats at you and gets you poor results.

1. *Assume responsibility for your feelings.* There is no question that your mate's negligent, rejecting, or even hostile behavior contributes to your own negative feelings. But *you* determine your level of disturbance about his neglect.

2. Acknowledge that you'll be better off feeling *4* on a scale of anger or depression rather than right up at the top at *10*. And you're likely to handle the situation better if you feel appropriately frustrated rather than *in*appropriately angry.

3. However, it's important to stop putting yourself down when you do have a full-scale blowup. If you condemn yourself, as Vicky originally did, for "losing it," you actually make yourself feel *more* inadequate. You can view your emotional distress as bad, but *you* are not a bad person for having it.

4. Continue to work against being overly vulnerable to hurt or anger. If your husband's actions make you feel there is something wrong with you, then you might have a tendency to deny your hurt feelings and turn your anger toward him. Even if your mate says, as Vicky's husband once did, "How could anyone want to go to bed with a nagging shrew like you?" you do not have to see yourself as one or to respond with anger at your spouse.

   Getting rid of self-deprecating feelings will not eliminate all your feelings of depression and hostility. But it will certainly go a long way toward dissolving some of them.

5. Keep working on your emotional muscle tone by disputing your irrational beliefs, over and over again, until you internalize a more rational belief system—emotionally as well as intellectually. (Look at the two charts in this chapter at least once a week so you can check out which irrational beliefs you may be holding.)

   In challenging your irrational beliefs, ask yourself questions such as these:
   - "Where is it written that I absolutely *must* have sex with my spouse twice a week rather than twice a year? *(It would be nice, but . . . it's just not happening right now.)*"

- "Why *must* my spouse act the way I want? Why *must* I get every important thing I want in my marriage? *(It would be great, but few people do. Marriage involves compromise and trade-offs.)*"
- "Where is it written that my husband *must* not avoid sex, or even be downright neurotic? *(The fact is, he is flawed and fallible—like all humans. And the less crazy I make myself, the better the model I provide for him to overcome his frustration and stress.)*"

The last rational thought cannot be emphasized strongly enough, for if you are ever going to influence your mate's erotic urges, it is more likely to occur if you minimize your own distress.

By confronting your own unrealistic assumptions about how your mate *should* be, you stand a better chance of helping him counter the *shoulds, oughts,* and *musts* that create *his* disturbance.

Some of your mate's *musts* may include the following: "My wife must be thin for me to have sex with her . . . I can't stand it if she isn't!" Or "I have to really feel loving and excited in order to have sex" (as opposed to getting into it because my partner is eager to and *then* getting aroused).

Men and women may be more alike than different. They put themselves down for different things, or jump to different conclusions and overgeneralizations, but their irrational demands on themselves are similar.

When you learn to help counter your own *shoulds,* anxieties, and tendencies to put yourself or your partner down, you are acquiring some tools you can pass along to him. This has to improve the quality of the interactions between you.

The smart woman decides to face disappointments as challenges. It's not that she doesn't have concerns and insecurities or feel down when something bad happens. She just decides not to marry herself to her misery. She has developed self-acceptance and the ability to keep hassles from escalating into horrors. If she experiences a setback, she tries not to blame others or herself, but to understand it and move forward.

The A-B-C theory of disturbance just described offers a simple yet profound method for eliminating or reducing anger and depression in your relationships. It helps you recognize that you create your own anger and depression about your mate's poor behavior: through *should*ing, *catastrophizing* or *condemning yourself or him* for the problem.

It shows you how to replace these *shoulds* with more realistic wishes and preferences.

The bottom line is, you really can't *make* him be different: less depressed, withholding, or stressed out. You can only work on your side of the problem. This book is focused on *you* and how *you can take care of yourself* and not make yourself miserable about something that may or may not get "fixed."

"Isn't this once again putting all the burden on women?" many women argue. It sounds that way. And to some extent it's true. But we can't change others: only ourselves. And if our goal is to maximize pleasure and minimize pain, and to be as successful as we can in achieving some of our life goals, we had better learn to come to terms with others' disappointing or unkind behavior.

It's not easy. At first it may seem that rational thinking does not work. No matter how much you understand things intellectually, you still *feel* depressed and angry. But if you truly practice accepting—not liking—grim reality, you will find you will feel significantly less disturbed. An excellent way for you to internalize a newer, more rational belief system would be to actually shout aloud—twice a day—your new rational countermessages at the end of this exercise until they become a part of you.

You do have *choices*. Freed up from your disturbance about your mate, you can stop overfocusing on trying to light his fire and start concentrating on getting involved in other absorbing activities.

You can let him know you're there for him, but if he seems to be unduly stressed, depressed, angry, or anxious, calmly encourage him to change his attitude by your good example and to seek out some psychological "coaching." Stop trying to charge him up sexually, and instead try to show him how he can help himself feel

---

Exercise

A: **Event** about which I am upset:
My husband rarely initiates sex and rebuffs me when I do.

B: **My irrational beliefs** about this event (the thoughts that are creating my distress):
1) *He shouldn't be neglecting me.*
2) *He's really selfish in always expecting me to respond to him, but thinking it's fine if he rejects me.*
3) *It's awful!*
4) *I can't stand it (or him).*

C: **My emotions** and **behaviors** (disturbed or dysfunctional ones):
> **Emotions:** Depression, anxiety, anger
> **Behaviors:** Yelling or sulking; storing up tension in my neck; spending hours obsessing about the situation

D: **Rational countermessages** (more realistic preferences and evaluations) I can give myself to reduce my distress:
1) *I wish he weren't neglecting me, but tough—he is!*
2) *I'd prefer he didn't have this double standard.*
3) *It's a pain in the neck, but not awful or catastrophic.*
4) *I don't like his behavior, but I can stand it. He's not **totally** rotten—he just has some rotten traits and habits.*
5) *Just because he's treating me poorly doesn't mean that he doesn't care about me or that the entire relationship is hopeless.*
6) *I'm going to calmly keep trying to do things to make my life happier.*

---

more comfortable in his own skin and function more effectively and enjoyably in his life in general.

Let's face it. Male-female relationships are not easy. But if you choose to continue yours, be prepared to put considerable energy into keeping yourself relatively undisturbed, while calmly encouraging your mate to do likewise. Over the years I have become increasingly impressed with people's tremendous abilities to use their rational capacities to live more happily and effectively—with themselves and with others.

Full steam ahead!

CHAPTER 5

HE SEEMS TO HAVE A SEX DRIVE— BUT HE ISN'T USING IT WITH ME

"She understood, from absences of enthusiasm . . . that he no longer found her appealing or even adequate to his needs. . . . She was exactly the same person he had fallen in love with. . . . Catherine could not understand what she had done wrong or in what way she had failed, but she knew she had failed, and was miserable."

> —Phyllis Rose (written about Catherine Hogarth— Mrs. Charles Dickens)

At the age of forty-six, aside from occasional one-night stands at sales conventions and one brief, not very serious affair, Robert seemed to have shut down sexually in his marriage. Married for sixteen years to an attractive and successful art director, Robert had his last sexual contact with his wife, Martha, six months before they came to see me.

In the earlier days—when he was in his twenties—they had sex five or six times a week. Now, although somewhat abated, his sex drive had far from disappeared. He masturbated at least three or four times a week, got regularly turned on by young miniskirted women on the street or at work, and frequently watched X-rated movies on cable TV on out-of-town business trips.

Robert rated his marriage to Martha as largely satisfactory, enjoying her companionship in the many activities and interests they shared and having relatively few conflicts other than his complaint that "she keeps getting on my case to spend more time with her on weekends, when it's the only chance I have to get caught up on my own stuff."

He attributes his longtime lack of sexual attraction to her to a variety of things, including fatigue, kids trekking in and out of their bedroom, and the lack of any "chemistry." Other than a friendly hug and peck on the cheek when they meet at the end of the day, there is little physical contact of any kind between them.

Martha was always less interested in sex than Robert but was nonetheless upset at the nearly total fizzling of their sex life. She would express hurt that he no longer seemed to have much interest in her and make him swear he was not involved with anyone else. She accused him of being responsible for her substantial weight gain: "Why should I go to all the trouble to lose weight if you're going to ignore me anyway?"

Laurie and Mark are a couple in their mid-twenties who are living together and are engaged to be married. When they came to see me, she complained about sex having plummeted steeply since she moved in with Mark. "I don't think I'm unreasonable," she exclaimed, "to want intercourse once or twice a week." She says, "I don't know if he's really interested in me." He says, "Of course I am—why would I be marrying you? I don't think sex is the only reason to get married."

I asked Mark, "Do you ever get the desire to have sex?" He replied, "I don't know about other guys, but for me sex is hard work. I'm exhausted at the end of the day." "So you find sex to be very demanding?" I asked him.

Mark: "You sweat when you have sex, don't you?"

Laurie: "Can you imagine what it will be like when we get married?"

I saw three other cases—all quite similar—within a four-month period:

Carla has been married for twelve years. She and her husband, Ted, had sex almost daily before they were married and in the early stages of marriage, but for the past six years Ted has not approached her sexually. Once a year or so she attempts to discuss it. The only explanation her husband gives her when she asks him about it is "I don't know." He refuses to go to couples counseling, claiming, "We've got to work it out ourselves. What's a shrink going to do?"

Fifty-four-year-old Lester says he goes for months without being interested in sex. He travels a good deal, is overweight and often tired. He is angry at his boss and complains that his wife "nags" him about being overattached to his daughter from his former marriage and demands "too much time, talk, and attention." Occasionally he gets hold of some cocaine and has terrific orgasms, but gets bored when it takes twenty minutes to help his wife orgasm through oral or manual stimulation. As a young man, he claims to have been very sexually active and "never seemed to get enough of sex." Now he finds he has trouble sustaining erections, and this difficulty—along with his anger at his wife—has pretty much made him remove himself from the sexual scene. On the rare occasions his wife indicates she'd like to work on this problem, he says, "I'm just under too much stress and don't want to talk about it."

Sandy, a forty-five-year-old woman now six months into her second marriage to a "really terrific guy," says her husband is rarely interested in sex. He teases her about being such a "horny broad" but claims he can't keep up with her. With tears in her eyes, she said, "I don't know what's wrong with me. It seems that ever since I started being myself with a man in bed, they seem to reject me. The other night we were making love, and I was really enjoying it. I playfully rolled on top of him and started kissing him, and he said, 'I can't handle this.' So I guess I'll have to tone down my behavior. But I'm angry—when do I get to be myself? How do I satisfy my desires?"

WHAT'S GOING ON? (IS IT SOMETHING IN THE WATER SUPPLY?)

Ted thinks the reason he's turned off to Carla is that she has now become a mother. "You don't screw Mommy," is how he puts it.

Robert says his reason is "My wife just doesn't turn me on."

Mark claims he's "too darned pooped at the end of the day . . ." and adds, "Laurie's just getting too sexually aggressive for me."

All three men confide that if Michelle Pfeiffer should happen to come along and whisk them off to her hotel room, they'd be on her like a bull in heat. It seems more probable that if any of them were married to Michelle for twenty years, and she was after them to help out more with the household and kids, or if she started initiating sex or wanting more varied sex play, they'd probably be doing exactly the same avoidance dance they're now doing with their own wives. Or if their partner was relatively servile, they might be even *more* turned off: doormats can be pretty boring.

"But isn't it natural not to be all that turned on by your mate after being together for years, day in and day out?" I'm asked.

Undoubtedly being with the same partner for many years, combined with the aging process, a busy schedule, or even women's increased sexual assertiveness may *contribute* to making sex harder to get into than it may have been previously. But *more difficult* to get aroused is not the same thing as *impossible*.

If we think of such situations as being married for many years or having young kids as activating events, then the same important principle described so far is operative: *It is not these conditions in themselves—but rather the attitudes or beliefs he has about them—that cause his reactions.*

Just as it isn't your mate who causes *your* hurt and anger when he rebuffs you sexually, so do *you* not cause *his* lack of desire. Just as it is what you tell *yourself* about his rejection that hurts you, so it is *his* own negative self-talk—rather than the long years you've been together or your growing independence—that causes him to avoid sex. His feelings and behavior are dictated by what is going on in his head. And even if you hang from the chandelier in your sexiest negligee, so long as he is feeding himself antisexual beliefs, he still won't get turned on. Negative self-talk in and of itself will produce his sexual boredom, low frustration tolerance, anxiety, or anger, all of which are powerful antiaphrodisiacs.

To illustrate the crucial role of attitudes and feelings in whether or not a person gets aroused or turned off, let's look at the cases of Scoop and Droop.

Scoop and Droop are both forty-four-year-old men, whose attractive, caring forty-four-year-old wives don't look as young or as trim as they did twenty years ago. Both men have three kids, ages seven, twelve, and fifteen, and a workday that, including commuting time, is twelve hours long.

Both men find it much easier to get aroused by the *Sports Illustrated* swimsuit issue or by nubile young women on the street than by their wives, and both find that as they've gotten older it takes longer for them to get an erection. Not only does their hardness wax and wane, but they are not always able to orgasm or ejaculate. Both wives are still raring to go sexually, and have communicated to Scoop and Droop that it isn't off-putting to them if intercourse is not possible. They find clitoral stimulation—with or without intercourse—just fine and dandy.

Droop finds one excuse after another to fend off his wife, especially when he's not very sure of his erectile potential. He feels es-

pecially intimidated by her initiating sex. His wife, Joyce, who has tried to hang in and be as supportive as possible, has become increasingly discouraged not only by the infrequent sex but also by his apparent unwillingness to deal with the situation and her feelings. Feeling insecure, Droop occasionally has a fling with a call girl or work associate to reassure himself he's still sexy.

Scoop, whose wife would prefer to have sex twice a day and three times on Sunday, finds he's in no way ready for that kind of frequency. He manages, however, at least every week or two, to get himself turned on and initiate sex because he knows she'll enjoy it. At other times, when she initiates sex and he's not particularly in the mood, he sometimes starts playing around with himself or her (at times with the help of a fantasy), which then helps him get aroused and in the mood; and sometimes, when he really *is* beat, he demurs. Even though he occasionally feels a bit taken aback by his wife's assertiveness during their sexual encounters, he appreciates the positive side of her being turned on and active; it makes less work for him! Although ideally she'd like to have more sex, Scoop's wife is satisfied with the quality of the sex they do have and the fact that he's trying to meet her halfway. When he occasionally fails to get an erection or ejaculate, instead of getting upset and withdrawing, he simply gets involved in helping please his wife. Some of the time he gets turned on again in the process.

By now, two things should be quite clear to you:

1. You do not "cause" his lack of sexual interest in you.
2. It is your mate's *attitude* that is causing the main "short" in his sexual circuit.

"That's all very well," said Droop's wife, Joyce. "You and I understand that he's got this attitudinal blockage; but does *he* understand this?"

Probably not. For now, being less enlightened than you, your mate probably believes quite strongly that these external conditions are inevitably causing his reactions, and he would strenuously deny that his behavior had anything whatsoever to do with his attitudes or beliefs about these conditions. As for his feelings of anxiety, insecurity, or anger, he's probably so caught up in his avoidance or blaming of external situations that he's utterly out of touch with the impact his own feelings have on your relationship. Remember his male socialization? He's acting, if you think about it, just as he "should," even though you'd prefer he not.

So how do we get through this predicament?

Having recognized that it's his sex organ between the ears that may be temporarily inoperative, let's first examine the ten reasons—or excuses—for male sexual turnoff. Bear in mind that as we review these excuses, I am assuming the man's sexual apparatus is basically in working order.

TEN REASONS MOST FREQUENTLY GIVEN BY MEN FOR BEING SEXUALLY TURNED OFF

Applying the A-B-C model outlined in Chapter 4, let's consider each of these reasons or excuses as *A*s, or activating events. Then we'll look at the *C*s, or emotional and behavioral consequences, that your mate is likely to be having in each of these situations, along with the *B*s, or irrational beliefs that are causing these emotional reactions.

Excuse #1: "The Romance Is Gone"

Ralph has seen June's body nude at least three hundred times now. The first several times he touched her, he had explosive feelings. She was fresh and new, a challenge, and neither of them ever knew exactly what was going to happen next. But by the tenth or thirtieth or hundredth time, touch alone rarely evoked that explosive response. They've woken up together, seen each other at their worst, and been in the john together. And scores of disagreements, along with lack of personal time, have gradually taken their toll. He may be bored coming home to a wife who talks about the problems Johnny is having in school or a fight with her boss "and all that other stuff I just don't feel like hearing about." He may even resent the additional burdens and demands made on him by the kids or feel angry with his wife for having had them and taken attention away from him. Monogamy, he believes, equals monotony—and the death of passion.

Desire and sexual activity may get reduced in the context of domestic routine, but they needn't die. Sexual passion, however brief it may be, does involve a flight from normal existence. Passion doesn't swoop down on you, however; you have to take the time and effort to promote it, to get emotional and sexual feelings flowing—kids or no kids, ideal conditions or not.

Excuse #2: "It's Become So Routine"

> "What was it about marriage, anyway? Even if you loved your husband, there came that inevitable year when fucking turned as bland as Velveeta cheese: filling, fattening, but no thrill to the taste buds, no bitter-sweet edge, no danger. And you longed for an overripe Camembert, a rare goat cheese: luscious, creamy, cloven-hoofed."
>
> —Erica Jong, *Fear of Flying*

Many people believe that once you've done the same things hundreds of times with the same person, sex can no longer get you excited because there's nothing new to expect. If he hasn't seen you for three months, perhaps he might have a rekindling of interest; but even if you dressed up in a different sexy outfit every night, it's still good old Maude inside that lacy contraption.

It's true that repeated sex over a period of years may make it harder for men (and women) to get *quickly* or *simultaneously* turned on. But where is it writ that in order to have sex, your sexual switch needs to be *automatically* turned on by looking at or thinking about your partner? In his head! If we all waited until we got turned on by things, or "naturally" felt like doing them, we'd *all* be procrastinators. This is true whether the activity is sex, going out to jog, or writing a report. You don't reach your goals in life without somehow kick-starting the operation—in this case that means overcoming low frustration tolerance.

This need for instant turn-ons is often underscored by the next myth: that sex, to be enjoyable, must be spontaneous.

Excuse #3: "It Just Isn't Spontaneous—the Way It Used to Be"

Well, of course it isn't—at least most of the time—going to "just happen" the way it used to, when the relationship was new and you just "magically" fell into bed with each other and didn't have to do anything to rev yourselves up. The fact is, however, that when you were courting you didn't "just happen" to have wonderful sex. You made dates ahead of time. Frequently you had not seen each other for several days. You sometimes dressed up, had an intimate candlelit dinner, or had sex in "forbidden" spots. There was actually *more* planning, in certain ways, than there is now. Certainly more attention was lavished on the preprogram!

Along with the spontaneity myth is the myth that you have to have just the right conditions for great sex to happen: for example, candlelight, a bottle of wine, a moonlit beach, or outfits like people on the TV show "Dynasty." The fact is, you can have just as great sex, in the middle of the day wearing shorts and a T-shirt, or even hair rollers. Our greatest sex organ is between our ears. Your mate can either wait for the sexual desire circuit in his brain to pop on, or he can help switch it on, then allow good stimulation and absence of distractions to do the rest of the job.

Excuse #4: "She's No Julia Roberts"

Men are subject to all kinds of conditioning, and millions of them, conditioned by the media, believe that if their mate is no longer thin and young, they can't get turned on or enjoy sex with her.

Albert Ellis has astutely pointed out that a man sees a beautiful woman and may wrongly believe that "the very sight of her . . . arouses him sexually, when, in fact, it is his beliefs and values about what is beautiful in a woman that affects his choice."

In other words, if a man thinks, for example, that medium-sized breasts are sexy and a woman has a flat chest or pendulous double-Ds, he may not feel aroused or may even be turned off. Or he may convince himself that if she has some other anomaly—such as a face that is average or below in attractiveness, or a large nose—he can't enjoy sex with her.

The myth we have been led to believe is that men want to "do it all the time." More accurately, they are always ready to make love to the media's image of a perfect woman and even then only *on a short-term basis*. A twenty-eight-year-old man of my acquaintance confided, "My girlfriend is terrific-looking—but then I go down to the beach and see these incredible girls in their string bikinis. I've been with my girlfriend for a year and know pretty much what sex is going to be like with her: no way am I going to get the instant turn-on with her that I would with one of those other beach bunnies. My other friends feel the same way: if their girlfriend is away, and they get a chance to have a fling with someone new, they go for it!"

Let's face it: there are very few perfect-looking people. The notion that a teenaged, unevolved nymphet *is* sexy—while those over forty-five or with average looks or with a fair amount of body fat on them are *not* sexy—brings us smack up against the next of the top ten reasons.

Excuse #5: "She's Too Old"

In our culture, women's sexual attractiveness depends to a large extent on how well they stave off the signs of aging on their faces and bodies. In an effort to maintain a look that is physiologically natural only in their youth, women in our incredibly ageist society risk their health with cosmetic surgery, harmful diets, and poisons on their hair, skin, and nails. "I believe," says Delores DeHardt of California State University, "the construct we call femininity was invented to cover up men's revulsion of women's bodies—the kind of revulsion that makes people shudder when they see a 60-year-old woman and a 20-year-old man making love on the screen. Involved is denial of our physical selves, our secretions, our body fat, our skin texture. . . ."

Bombarded as we are by images of sexy young nymphets, it's hard to imagine a woman who might be photographed, as Picasso was, at the age of ninety wearing only shorts. The undressed body of an old woman would be considered repulsive, obscene.

Men still prize beauty and youth in women, probably not because they're trying to perpetuate the species as reported recently in the *New York Times* or are turned on by her fertility, but because they're still hung up on traditional sexist norms. These norms are so ubiquitous that many are not even aware they hold them. The sad result is that a tremendous amount of psychological damage has been done to wonderful, mature women because of the misogynistic and ageist ways beauty has been defined—just as blacks have been damaged by a society that sets up white as the standard of beauty.

There are many, many advantages to becoming emotionally and sexually close to a mature and evolved woman: one with experience in living and loving and confidence in herself as a person. Would that both men and women appreciated this more fully; hopefully, someday soon, we all will.

Excuse #6: "Her Goddamned Diaphragm" and Other Gripes about Birth Control

"Her diaphragm hurts my penis."

"It's a real turnoff when she gets up to put it in—I wish she'd go back on the pill."

"Wear a condom? Yechhh! That's like taking a shower with a raincoat on."

Women have always had to bear the overwhelming responsibility for birth control, not to mention unwanted pregnancy. In addition, they have to bear the burden of men's discomfort with just about whatever form of birth control they decide to use, with the possible exception of the birth control pill. (As an aside—if you think there is any chance your mate may be having sex outside the marriage, latex condoms better be your method of choice in preventing not only pregnancy but sexually transmitted diseases as well.)

Excuse #7: "I Can't Handle Her Becoming Pregnant"

It's getting around to that time that you agreed several years ago would be the year you'd start trying to have kids. He is not sure he's ready—and who is? Afraid to risk the possibility either of impregnating you or of one of those long and painful "fights" about it ("We agreed on this: if not now, when? You'll never be ready," etc.), he avoids you like the plague.

Or, if the relationship between you has been somewhat tenuous, he may start backing off when you want to have sex because of that nagging fear in the back of his mind that women often try to hold on to a relationship by getting pregnant.

Excuse #8: "That Fertility Business Has Really Gotten to Me"

Maybe efforts to get pregnant have been going on for months or even years; and sex has been required at peak times every other day, sometimes followed by frantic rides to the lab. Or there have been visits *ad nauseam* to gynecologists and urologists and fertility clinics, followed by miscarriages or other disappointments. At best, you may both be left feeling ambivalent about sex—or frankly turned off.

Excuse #9: "I'm Too Stressed Out"

"It's been a long day. If I have an hour or two to unwind, I'd just as soon spend it with a beer and the Bears game. If she's around the house, fine—as long as she doesn't bother me." To him this includes not only trying to initiate sex but also attempting to relate in just about any meaningful way.

Stress varies in intensity, depending on who is experiencing it. What one person may see as a traffic jam worthy of horn honking and swearing another may view simply as a minor irritation that's all in a day's work. Stress researchers conclude that it's these *differences in attitudes* rather than the types of stress themselves, that play the major role in causing emotional upset and even stress-related diseases.

Excuse #10: "I Just Don't Feel Comfortable with the Kids in the Next Room"

"The kids could walk in any minute."

"With Scottie sick in the next room, we're probably going to get interrupted."

"Sarah's home from college. You know she's always making cracks about 'What have you two been up to?' if she hears us making love."

No one in his or her right mind would ever claim that your sex life—let alone your love life—is anything but highly complicated when one or more kids are on the scene. Two A.M. feedings, dealing with kids' illnesses, homework, and dozens of other needs, combined with jobs, marriage, and umpteen other responsibilities, make it extremely difficult to carve an oasis of quiet time.

But although sex may get more sparse or certainly harder to plan, making use of things like locks on bedroom doors and grandparents and other sitters can be a big help. By no means does every couple with kids give up on sex. And surely you can cuddle and be physical to some extent with kids around: having parents who openly show affection provides good role models for your youngsters.

SO, HOW ABOUT ME?

I can well imagine that most women, having read these ten excuses, must be about ready to burst by now.

"*I'm* getting pudgy? How about his paunch? He looks like he's six months pregnant!"

"He finds my diaphragm inconvenient? Well, excuse me! How do you think I like having to get up and put it in, then walk around for eight hours afterward with all that glop dripping out of me?"

"Fertility-schmertility! Who's the one that had all those painful procedures, had their tubes shot up with dye, did all that temperature taking, and reminded him 'It's tonight, dear'?"

"He's tired from work? Well, I work full-time and pick up after him and the kids, and *I* can still have sex! He sits there like a lump."

Et cetera, et cetera.

The point is, we all have our beefs and our reasons (good and bad) why we might not be that interested in having sex with our partner—especially when it isn't entirely comfortable or convenient. But some of us do it anyway. Which goes to show that most of the "reasons" don't stop us—unless we somehow *tell* ourselves that they must and thus allow the resulting emotional blockages to keep us shut down sexually.

HOW DO WE SHAKE LOOSE OF THE DOMESTIC DOLDRUMS?

After three years of marriage and two major career changes, Josh and Alissa's daily sex life had fallen off to once every couple of weeks. As Josh's work pressures became more intense, and Alissa switched from being a secretary to being an account supervisor, the intensity that each of them had once put into sex seemed to have been diverted to other aspects of their life. Getting caught up on some professional reading before bedtime seemed a lot easier than the prospect of having sex.

Several months ago, after a pregnancy scare and a yeast infection, they began, at Alissa's insistence, to use condoms. Josh feels they very much get in the way and are a major reason he'd just as soon forget about sex most of the time.

For many painful months they both grew increasingly anxious about what they felt was the end of their passion, and discussions only seemed to make matters worse. When Alissa suggested they make use of sexual fantasies to help get revved up, Josh protested, with hurt and indignation, "If we need to start thinking about others to get turned on, it's really over with us." When he suggested that to prevent sex from getting squeezed out of their busy schedules they write a "sex appointment" into both of their calendars, it was Alissa's turn to become upset: "That takes away all the spontaneity!" she protested. Eventually, by helping each other stop feeling upset about having to kick-start sex, and instead just doing it, they found to their delight that with a little work, a sexy African sculpture, and a handy bottle of massage oil, things are rolling along nicely again.

SOME LESS OFTEN EXPRESSED
REASONS—WHICH HE MAY NOT
BE AWARE OF

Your Increasing Independence

With the kids in school you're now working full-time. You're becoming more independent, more turned on by things outside the home. Gone are those four-course gourmet meals on the table every night and laundry sorted and put away. Not only is he eating tuna sandwiches for dinner, but he's helping out more with the housework.

You're even going to out-of-town conventions from time to time—and who knows what you're doing there?

His distress may come out indirectly, in the form of attacks on you as a lousy mother or complaints about there not being any clean shirts. Behind his anger, however, is probably more hurt, dependency, or fear of abandonment than he'd care to acknowledge. He may actually welcome your getting on his case as an opportunity to blame you instead of facing his own fears.

Not having sex with you may be his way of saying "I know you're interested in sex, but since you aren't acting the way I want you to (as you *should*), I'm not going to 'give it to you' until you shape up and return to mothering me."

Inability to Deal with Your Pointing Out His Imperfections

> "A man ends by hating the woman who he thinks has found him out."
> —Jenny Jerome Churchill

In your frustration at his lack of affection, communication, or help around the house, you may periodically have let him know that you wish he'd act differently. Even when you've consistently delivered the message with relative calmness, he may start feeling inadequate because his flaws have been exposed so fully and so often. Or he may feel angry because you've seen through him. A tactic he might use is to deflect conversation away from the legitimate content of your complaint onto your "bitchiness" or "nagging." In this way, he tries to take the focus off his flaws while at the same time punishing you, through his emotional and sexual withdrawal.

Or he may find that an "easier" route to feeling better about himself is to go to someone else who thinks he's great and doesn't complain about his flaws. Of course she doesn't bear the brunt of them; and because she's new, he's not making himself anxious, and he functions better sexually.

Irritation at Your Personal Habits

Perhaps he's disgusted by months-old piles of unattended-to lists and magazines in the bedroom, and of course those self-help books you've placed strategically on *his* bedside table, complete with underlinings. (One of my clients recently confided that he occasionally moved these books around to make it look like he's read them.)

In my years of practice I've heard just as many men complain about their women's untidiness as I have the other way around. Men are definitely not the only slobs. Although frequently his complaint is legitimate, at other times he may simply be marshaling a roster of your character flaws to avoid having sex.

You May Have Shown a Lack of Interest in Sex in the Past

Earlier in your relationship you may not have been that interested in sex, possibly because it wasn't very satisfying to you. Or you may have shown a lack of interest in doing some of the kinds of things he's wanted you to do—such as fellatio or dressing up in sexy lingerie—so he's decided you're really not that interested, even though you may be now.

He May Feel Intimidated by Your Sexual Assertiveness

You may have begun to be more active, or have tried to get *him* to do certain kinds of things sexually—such as doing oral sex on you, or trying some new positions.

He can, theoretically, be *excited* by this and see it as creating new opportunities for sexual enhancement. If his sex drive has waned, however, he may feel threatened and experience your sexuality as placing more demands on him. Or he's anxious about not being able to give you the kind of tenderness and affection you want. So he has backed off out of fear of not being able to live up to your expectations.

And there's that *third* party, his penis. Especially if he (and you) believe that his long-lasting erections are essential to sex, he may—in the face of not being sure he can "keep it up" with you—have decided that he'd better stay out of the fray altogether.

Mid-Life Crisis

He's heard that men are headed for the sexual skids in their middle years; he's noticed that it's definitely taking him significantly longer to get aroused than it used to, and it's harder to remain erect. Once again, if he allows his fear of not being able to "perform" adequately take over, he'll avoid having sex, and the more he avoids it the less likely he will be to want to have sex and the more apprehensive he'll be when he does have it.

He's Having an Outside Affair

If he is having an affair, he almost certainly doesn't plan on telling you about it—although he may have left some trail of evidence, such as a charge bill for a lacy nightgown you never saw. Maybe you've confronted him, and he's "gaslighted" you—told you that you were crazy for thinking such an insane thing when in fact it turns out that he *was* having an affair.

Even though he may have stopped seeing the other woman, your hurt and pain have been so deep that you've closed off; and although you've gone through the motions of having sex after several months of being frozen, you feel you can never trust him again. And he, sensing this from you, has gradually distanced himself too. If this is the case, it's crucial to seek competent couples' counseling. Even if he refuses to go, you had better do so, so you'll have some support and help with your feelings of hurt or anger.

AVOIDANCE STRATEGIES AND THEIR PSYCHOLOGICAL CAUSES

Most people have characteristic ways of responding to situations, especially ones that are uncomfortable or seen as threatening. In both nonsexual and sexual situations, Berkeley psychologist Daniel Goldstine points out, they adopt certain strategies to get what they want or to protect themselves from what they fear. These choices are not always made consciously.

In response to potential sexual situations, a person's attitudes and emotions are involved at least as much as his nerve endings. If he's angry at his mate, scared he might not "get it up," bored, or frustrated that sex isn't as "easy" as it used to be—he's more likely to feel aversion than arousal. And he's more likely to avoid connecting than to attempt to connect. Once again, his reaction is determined by his beliefs and attitudes about the situation. *In other words, he feels and acts the way he thinks.*

The main four emotional culprits that are likely to lead to his avoiding sex are low frustration tolerance, anger, anxiety, and depression. Let's examine each of them and the thoughts and attitudes that produce them.

Low Frustration Tolerance

Assume that the situation, or activating event, is that your mate is not particularly turned on to you spontaneously, and to get things going he might have to push himself. He tells himself a **rational belief** ("It's hard") and an **irrational belief** ("It's *too* hard"). If he has a low tolerance for behavior that can prove frustrating or disappointing, he is less likely to extend any effort in getting himself geared up.

Instead of finding a way to turn himself on, he chooses, although not necessarily consciously, an *avoidance* behavior—such as making himself unavailable for most of the weekend by running, playing softball with his friends, and remaining glued to his Nintendo or basketball games in between. When you both get back from a lively Saturday night party and you're feeling particularly sexy, he pleads fatigue; and the next morning, just as you are rolling over to kiss him, he waves cheerily to you on his way out the door to jog. When he returns, he buries himself in the Sunday paper.

The antisexual beliefs causing his low frustration tolerance are:

1. Sex is work—I'm going to have to push myself to get into the mood and turned on, then do all kinds of other time-consuming stuff she likes. Weekends are supposed to be relaxing!
2. It's *too* hard, *too* uncomfortable (and it *shouldn't* be).
3. Why bother, when I can jerk off in the shower or while she's out?

Anger

If he is angry at you for wanting more participation in the household, or resentful at being tied down in marriage, his avoidance behaviors may range from the more passive ones of falling asleep in the living room and getting up two hours before you to blaming his lack of sexual interest on your flabby thighs. If you try to pin him down and discuss his avoidance, he may switch to anger and attack you for being a nag or tell you, "There's nothing wrong with me. I'm sexy—women come on to me all the time; you just don't turn me on."

His irrational beliefs are:

1. She *shouldn't* be treating me this way.
2. It's *awful*—I can't stand it. (Sound familiar? See Chapter 4.)
3. *She's* rotten and should be punished.

The lower his self-acceptance, the more likely it is that he will use anger and other defensive behaviors to establish distance from what he perceives to be the source of his problems: you. It's far easier than admitting to his own feelings of inadequacy. And if, after a time, he meets with counterhostility, he comes more and more to believe that he is the beleaguered innocent victim.

Anxiety

Harry, like many sixty-two-year-old men, found his erections had gradually become less hard and, especially when anxious, difficult to maintain. His wife, Alice, would have been happy just to cuddle or at times to have him stimulate her to orgasm, and had often reassured him that his not being hard all the time did not make her think any less of him. Nevertheless, Harry's embarrassment led him to avoid sex for weeks at a time. When he wasn't blaming his lack of sexual participation on rising prices, falling stocks, sick parents, having to visit his daughter, or a rough day, increasingly he was involved in time-filling projects, the latest of which was building an amplifier in the garage, from scratch.

If he's afraid that he's not going to function well sexually (get erect, stay erect, be able to satisfy you sexually and emotionally), he's probably telling himself the following:

1. I *should* be able to stay erect and satisfy her and give her umpteen orgasms.
2. I *must* not fail or be thought of badly by her.
3. It would be *awful* if I couldn't perform sexually; I *couldn't stand the discomfort* or embarassment.
4. It would make me a wimp, a failure, not a real man.

Let's say that Harry, in addition to his problem with erections, had problems with intimacy and with being asked to do things around the house. His anxiety about sexual contact with his wife would further increase if, in addition, he was telling himself the following:

1. I mustn't get too close to her—I couldn't stand the discomfort.
2. The more I give her, the more she's going to want from me (even *more* intimacy and housework).
3. That would be awful! I couldn't stand that.
4. That would make me not a "real man."

Although one of the three emotional responses discussed may be the predominant one in a given situation, they tend to feed off each other, and more than one may be going on. In the preceding case, for example, Harry is feeling a combination of anxiety and low frustration tolerance.

Depression

A fourth emotional response—depression and its related symptoms of feelings of helplessness, hopelessness, and worthlessness—may also enter the picture. In fact, after marital conflict, depression is the second leading cause of inhibited sexual desire. Because of its complicated nature, however, this will be discussed more fully in Chapters 6 and 7.

SEX IS PROBABLY NOT THE ONLY SITUATION HE AVOIDS

The way he deals with sex or intimacy is often a metaphor for the way he deals with other, nonsexual issues.

- If he has *low frustration tolerance* (LFT) about cranking himself up sexually when he's not particularly inspired, he may often procrastinate on other uncomfortable activities such as doing taxes or mowing the lawn.
- If he has *anxiety about sexual intimacy,* he's probably anxious about other aspects of intimacy, such as talking about feelngs or negotiating conflicts.
- If he's *anxious or ashamed about his performance* in the area of sex, he probably also has performance anxiety in other areas in which he ties his self-worth or manhood to his functioning—such as job income or sports success.
- If he gets *angry* and tends to withhold sexually, chances are that he also has problems managing and expressing anger in appropriate ways in other interpersonal situations, such as with kids or work associates, and probably engages in withholding behaviors with them as well.

Because of his male programming, unfortunately, he is not likely to be in touch with how he's feeling, and even less amenable to discussing it. His reluctance puts you in the delicate position of trying assertively to do something about increasing sexual communication with a man who may, at the first scent of "pressure," flee, burrow, or blow up.

YOUR RESPONSE TO HIS SEXUAL AVOIDANCE MAY ALSO REFLECT YOUR RESPONSES TO DIFFICULT NONSEXUAL SITUATIONS

If your tendency, for example, is to get hurt and angry when others, such as your kids or your friends, treat you poorly in nonsexual situations, you're likely to have the same kind of response in sexual situations. These reactions may only exacerbate his. When Harry's wife, after much patience, finally blows up at him for his latest avoidance ploy, he tends to become more anxious, angry, and withdrawn. When she responds with hurt and depression, he starts making himself feel guilty. All these reactions combined create an emotional climate in which the possibility of arousal and good sex are not very likely to occur.

IT'S NOT FAIR!

Right again: it's not fair. It seems women get dumped on, then get told they just have to "be understanding"—and clean up the mess!

Some of the double binds we are in are truly mind-boggling. For example:

- If you don't work at anything very stimulating outside the home, you're boring; if you do, you're threatening.
- He can't have sex with you if he's angry; but he can't have sex with you if there's comfort or friendship, because that's not a turn-on.
- If you want to "prepare" for sex, it's artificial, not "real" or "spontaneous." If you *don't* set aside time for it, it just . . . isn't.
- He can "make love" with a sex object; but he can't do it with a person he loves and respects (the Madonna/Prostitute Complex).

- You're willing to put yourself through the pain and discomfort of trying to connect with him; *he* would just as soon *skip* the pain and discomfort and avoid trying to connect with you. Thus your work becomes twice as hard.
- He's distracted and stressed by having the kids around—but, of course, they're his kids too, though you sometimes wouldn't know it.
- He was attracted to you because you were loving and nurturing; now he sees that as your "neediness."

It's easy and natural for you to feel disgusted, discouraged, and angry at his apparent unwillingness—physically or emotionally—to meet you even an eighth of the way. While you are racking your brain and exhausting yourself trying to light his spark, he's biding his time for the magical automatic "high" that may never come and seems not to be willing to try to light some matches of his own. Or rub two sticks together, if necessary.

Once again, you're faced with two seemingly grim choices: *upsetting* yourself and creating more distance, or trying to keep yourself sane while maximizing your chances of getting him to connect better.

HOW TO KEEP *YOURSELF* FROM DEVELOPING A HEADACHE OVER YOUR MATE

Here are some pointers to help you maintain some emotional equilibrium and a clear head while pursuing the difficult task of trying to connect with him.

1. Examine Your *Shoulds*

Check to see if you hold any of the following *shoulds*; if so, question them as you've learned to do in the previous two chapters.

- It's awful and intolerable that men find it so difficult to relate; and that the more they withdraw, the harder we've got to work—and then get called "nags" for our efforts.
- A man should have an erection at just about every sexual encounter, and if he doesn't he's defective.
- "Real" sex *must* include intercourse. *Note:* Sex doesn't have to include intercourse. A whopping 70 percent of women do not orgasm from intercourse alone.
- In a good marriage people should never have to masturbate.
- A man should really be in charge in the sexual arena and should know how to turn me on without my having to show or tell him, possibly many times, what I need.

(If you need help in disputing some of these beliefs, turn to pages 243–247 in Chapter 9.)

2. Accept Yourself

Let's start with your feelings about your body, since women are ever-so-vulnerable in that area. It is very important—for both of you—that you not allow his lack of sexual interest in you to make you doubt your sex appeal and decrease your feelings of physical attractiveness.

Is it just men who lay this trip on us that we have to look like *Playboy* centerfolds to be attractive? Yes and no. No one can make you feel physically inadequate or unattractive without your consent. Whether or not *he* can accept you as a sexy person—with your real or imagined physical flaws—*you* can accept you.

Women, it turns out, often have even more rigorous standards for themselves than men do and possess a real ability to distort things like the amount of "fat" they have. In a recent article in the *Journal of Abnormal Psychology* women indicated that their ideal body weight was even lower than the weight they thought men liked most. When men were asked about what kind of woman's body they found most attractive, it was *heavier* than what women thought to be ideal—and also heavier than what women *thought men liked*. He and you are not turned off because your breasts are small or your behind shakes like jelly—the turnoff comes from his or your *attitudes* about them.

As an exercise in physical self-acceptance, look in the mirror each morning and pick out three things about your appearance you *do* like. Perhaps you have a wonderful smile, nice breasts. Acknowledge your good points. Even say out loud to your image, "You're OK!" You had better learn to accept yourself with an imperfect body before you can expect him to.

3. Resist Feeling Hurt or Resentful if He Dodges a Sexual Opportunity

Let's say you and your mate have made a date to spend Saturday evening alone. You were really looking forward to spending some intimate time together. During the week, though, when he drops hints like "Maybe this weekend isn't such a good time, since I've got such a backlog of work to get caught up on," you finally blow up and tell him to forget it when he suggests a special country weekend the following weekend as a "rain check." Resentment by you, combined with anxiety or guilt in him, can provide a powerful antidote to pleasure and will probably reinforce his tendency to want to be spared the whole business.

Or maybe you were in bed beginning to make love after a nice anniversary celebration when all of a sudden he says, "Darn! I have to get up early tomorrow morning," sets the alarm, and turns over to go to sleep. Instead of feeling he is negating your entire relationship, try again on Sunday afternoon, when he's less distracted. Avoid convincing yourself things are hopeless and diving into a depression and withdrawal, for this will only continue to fuel *his* continued withdrawal and create a stalemate between you.

Once again I must remind you: male-female relationships take considerable persistence, fortitude, and high frustration tolerance. Sorry—but that's the way it is.

4. Give Him "Hot Tips" and Praise

No one taught him in sex education class that the clitoris existed— let alone how to stimulate it. And even if they had, only *your* brain is hooked up to your nerve endings, and only *you* can give him correct feedback on how the stimulation you're getting feels.

I'll have a lot more to say on this subject in Chapters 8 and 9. Let it suffice for now that you've nothing to lose by clueing him in on how best to stimulate you. Moreover, by bringing to his attention that his having an erection is not necessary to please you, you may help relieve him of a lot of his anxiety about performance. Try to avoid harsh negative feedback, such as letting him know what a truly lousy kisser he is. Men are vulnerable just as we are. Don't underestimate how inadequate he may feel about his sexual skills. And be sure to give him exuberant praise when he pleases you, letting him know what felt good so he can do it again next time.

5. Remember that Role Changes Are Hard for Just about Everyone

Although on one level he may feel pleased that you're coming into your own sexually, or proud of your new career, it may not be happening at the most convenient time in his life. He may, for example, have to take on more home responsibilities just at the point when he was getting ready to slow down in his job. Sometimes it feels safer to him to try to undermine or retreat from the marriage than to go through the pain of thrashing out the conflicts in uncharted territory.

6. If He's Had an Affair, Keep Working at Lancing the Boil

A smart woman will not leave her husband if she sees that his affair had less to do with the state of their union than the temporary state of his ego. If the affair is now over and the pain has dropped to a bearable level, and if you ultimately feel that the advantages of your relationship outweigh the disadvantages, try to put it behind you. When you know that while you've put in all the sweat and tears another woman has been reaping the rewards, this is very, very hard to do. But it's possible.

Try to remember that however sneaky, cowardly, or destructive his behavior may have been, it probably came out of weakness and neediness. To him the "other woman" may have felt like a safe haven, a person who would listen to him and not challenge him or criticize him. For a time he might have been able to salve a weak ego by feeling young and virile again with a twenty-six-year-old. You might decide to leave him, but I've talked to dozens of women who have lived to regret divorcing a man who turned out to be a basically "good" person, his adulterous lapse notwithstanding. I've also seen relationships where couples were able to get past the hurt, pain, and anger into a vastly improved relationship. Ironically, often the improvement might not have happened without the jolt caused by an affair that came perilously close to dissolving the relationship.

7. Go for Some Hugs and Affection

Sex can be a lovely part of your sensuous life. So can hugging and other expressions of affection. When not just sex but his hugs and kisses as well have long since dried up, many women, 75 percent of them according to one survey, have thought seriously about getting out of their marriage.

If he's not "by nature" a hugger or a physically expressive person, gently train him to become one. Tell him you know it feels weird to him, but hugging is something you'd like to do with him from now on, when he leaves or comes home or falls off to sleep. You may be surprised that once he gets the hang of it, it starts feeling pretty good—to both of you. Then you still have some nice possibilities for snuggling and warmth, whether or not sex gets off the ground.

8. Don't Be Afraid of Fantasizing about Others

Even former president Jimmy Carter admitted to committing adultery "in his heart" in his famous *Playboy* interview. Your fantasizing about a sexy guy who works at the health club or his picturing Julia Roberts can definitely enhance sex—*unless* you worry about it. Better that he should have adultery in his heart or head than in reality. Fantasy could, of course, involve the two of you doing exotic things with each other—but this may not always be as big a turn-on as your private sexual fantasies.

IS REKINDLING DESIRE REALLY POSSIBLE?

Perhaps most couples will never really recapture that first "rush," when they thought sex was going to send them to the other side of the moon.

Because most couples never make it to the sex therapist, there are not many data available on success rates in overcoming sexual boredom. One source estimates that the success rate—in therapy at least—has almost tripled in recent years. Couples who tend to stand the best chance of being helped are those whose rage doesn't run too deep, who haven't let the sexual moratorium go on for too many years, and who still basically care for each other.

Even, however, if it's been years since you've had sex, and you've almost forgotten what it's like to feel desire and warmth for each other, you can get the fires burning again. The two important conditions are being free of emotional blocks and being willing to organize a scenario where good stimulation and the absence of physical and mental distractions can occur.

Spending some quiet, friendly uninterrupted time together and making a deal that you're going to try to do three "special" things for each other every week are a good start toward helping you feel that you're part of the same team.

On your weekly date, make sure there are no chores, no conversations to settle something, no other agenda than just to be together and feel close. After a time you can add some heavy petting, preferably with clothes on. Design a special plan for Saturday night, for example, that includes sending the kids out on sleepovers; or have a quickie when they're out at a Sunday matinee.

Even though many couples find sexual satisfaction decreasing after the advent of children, you can beat the statistics, *if* you work at it. Rekindling desire *is* possible. Witness the case of Grace and Paul.

Grace and Paul

Grace, a forty-six-year-old fashion buyer, has been married to her fifty-one-year-old dentist husband for thirteen years; it is a second marriage for both of them. They have a nine-year-old daughter, Jodi, and Brad, her seventeen-year-old son from her first marriage, lives with them.

When they lived together for the first year, "sex was great," said Grace. "I was usually the more assertive one, because I think I'm basically higher-sexed than Paul, but we had sex at least twice a week and sometimes even several days in a row." Paul, who worked six ten-hour days a week, would always have sex in the evenings before bedtime. "He hates it in the morning or on weekends," Grace said. "It doesn't fit in with his schedule, and he's always nervous about Jodi walking in."

Three years ago, at a time when sex had trickled down to about once every three months, Grace came to his office unexpectedly and caught him in a clinch with his receptionist, a thin, tall, twenty-eight-year-old blonde who wore tight clothes. Confronting Paul, Grace made it clear that if he continued to see his assistant, she would leave the marriage. Paul responded by protesting his love for Grace, stating that he had been unable to resist the woman's flattering seduction and was relieved it was over because he had been feeling tremendous guilt.

He then went away to a dental convention, during which time the "girlfriend" came to see Grace and proceeded to give her a blow-by-blow description of all the sexy things she had done with Paul, adding to Grace's hurt as the gymnastics sounded like "far more than we have ever done." But what upset Grace the most was that during the time of the affair Paul had continued to rebuff her sexual advances, claiming that he was too busy and had too many financial problems. He was also quite disturbed at the constant bickering going on between Grace and her son and resentful of the time she spent with their daughter.

Once, when Grace had asked him if he was involved with someone else, he had accused her of being "paranoid." Grace put on fifty pounds. She had lots of sexual fantasies involving other men and told Paul about them but didn't act on them, although from time to time she tried to reassure herself of her attractiveness by going out for drinks with men.

Following his return from the dental convention, he resumed sex with her, being more the initiator than ever, as well as warmer and more affectionate. It was hard to get over the pain, she said, but she felt it was worth it because she knew they had a basically good relationship and friendship.

When I spoke to her last, Grace was going to suggest to Paul that they start doing "some new things sexually," something that until recently she'd felt brought too many associations with the "affair" for her to feel comfortable with. Now that she and Paul are having sex regularly, "I lost weight fast," she said with a sparkle in her eye. From time to time, usually when Paul is experiencing financial strain, "sex goes down the tubes, and it's hard to get it going again. But we do!"

Paul and Grace were unusual in that they managed to work things out on their own: normally, marital therapy and possible individual therapy may be necessary to work on other issues and unravel what led up to the affair.

Several factors seemed to be responsible for Grace's being able to resolve this painful situation successfully. First and foremost was her being able to think it through in a clearheaded fashion. Although initially devastated and ready to walk out of the marriage then and there, she was able to realize that (1) Paul's choosing to go to bed with another woman did not reduce her value as a woman or as a human being; (2) although she strongly disliked his behavior, he was not a rotten, terrible human being; and (3) although she didn't at all like what had happened, she could stand it.

With her emotional distress reduced, she was then able to calculate more clearly that the pros of the relationship outweighed the cons, as long as Paul did not repeat this behavior. At least part of her ability to get through this painful episode she attributes to the support of her women friends, friends in the best sense of my friend Betti Franceschi's definition: "A friend is someone with values similar to yours, who helps you think clearly when your mind isn't working rationally."

Paul, in turn, was helped by several conversations he had with a male friend who had been through a similar crisis and had grown from it. In large part because of Grace's emotional resilience, which made her better able to communicate effectively with him, Paul also began to see clearly that here was a woman of depth and substance—qualities he was now able to appreciate as ultimately a lot "sexier" than a young pretty face attached to blonde hair and long legs.

Chapters 6, 7, 8, and 9 will provide you with further specifics on how to handle the emotional and practical aspects of dealing with a man who's not connecting the way you'd like him to.

CHAPTER 6

THE BODY POSITIVE: ENCOURAGING GOOD HEALTH MANAGEMENT AND A GRACEFUL APPROACH TO AGING

Once there was a planet inhabited by an extraordinary set of humans with highly evolved brains and amazingly complicated bodies. With good care, these remarkable creatures might survive seventy-five or more years. Yet many of them did not do a very good job of taking care of themselves, thus dying prematurely or living in a rather deteriorated condition.

Some did not get adequate fuel, and their pipes clogged up. Or they tried to ignore a rattle until something finally fell off or broke down. Others poured toxic substances into their lungs, stomachs, or veins, damaging many body parts, including their brain cells.

These creatures also had vehicles to transport themselves in: two thousand-pound hunks of steel called *autos*. On these they lavished the best of care:

- Good "nutrition"—fed them fuels with just the right "octane" that were almost never allowed to run out
- "Medical" care—headed for the car-doctor when their vehicle was sick, injured, or just sluggish
- Good preventative maintenance—took their autos in for regular checkups and adjustments (even though if worse came to worst and it conked out, it could be replaced)

What are these strange creatures called? The majority of them are called *men*.

While their cars thrived, these creatures' own bodies and organs frequently suffered myriad unpleasant and inconvenient consequences, including the following:

- Aches and pains that restrict comfort and mobility
- Preventable illnesses
- Reduced energy levels
- Interference with participation in many activities, including sex

Norman unwinds from his day on Wall Street by watching a movie or reading detective stories until 12:00 or 1:00 A.M., leaving him with an average of five hours of sleep a night. A half-dozen cups of coffee each day help keep him awake, but he frequently suffers from headaches and colds. In addition, with less energy for exercise, his weight has shot up and he feels "tired and old." Dinner with his wife, Sheila, and their two kids is tense as Norman has become increasingly cranky, and they are more relieved than disappointed when he plops onto the couch in his study. Quality time with Sheila is down, as was Norman on the last three occasions she tried to initiate sex. His last general physical exam was four years ago.

Al's ulcer can be kept pretty well under control if he follows his recommended diet. But despite his wife's efforts to prepare suitable meals, he eats forbidden foods frequently enough during the day to keep his stomach crying for a truce. When he manages to take a lunch break, he dashes from the frenetic treadmill of his office to forty-five minutes on the treadmill at the health club.

Ed is diabetic but is sloppy about following the diet necessary to maintain good blood sugar levels. Scott has been given a series of exercises to do, which helps alleviate his chronic back pain, but he doesn't do them for days or even weeks at a time. Nate's weight, cholesterol level, and family history put him at high risk for cardio-vascular disease: his father and all his uncles died in their fifties or early sixties. But unless his wife removes all unhealthy food from the house and continually reminds him about his nutrition, he persists in eating his way into the grave.

What's the last thing any of these men is interested in doing? Having sex. And although they may not yet be ready for a nursing home, they have about the same energy and sex appeal of men much older than they are.

As we've seen, men have a difficult time taking care of their psyches. But what keeps a grown-up from getting enough sleep, eating properly, fastening his seat belt, or going to the doctor for a checkup or treatment? Why can't our mate take care of his one-and-only-body?

The answer goes back to the programming that teaches men to be "sturdy oaks." Trained to deny any form of weakness, men typically disregard signs and symptoms of ill health, making 25 percent fewer visits to doctors than females, and still fewer visits to counselors for the emotional problems that are often exacerbating their health problems. Nor are they likely to seek help or information from self-help books or friends. Because of their higher likelihood of ignoring symptoms, they wind up being hospitalized 15 percent longer than females for the same disease or condition.

While anxiety about appearing weak interferes with good health care, the addition of low frustration tolerance can further complicate things. The attitude that "it's too hard to follow that god-damned diet when I eat out so much" will cause him to stray from potentially life-preserving health regimens. In addition, when people worry too much about their condition, the net result is that they do not fully appreciate those aspects of life still left for them to enjoy, nor do they look for new sources of satisfaction to replace those no longer available to them.

Shame may exacerbate the problem. He might feel embarrassed about paying attention to physical or emotional needs, feeling he is "weak" or "feminine" and "I should be able to tough this out myself." Whether the area is marital or family problems, work problems or health difficulties, millions of men fail to turn to readily available help to alleviate the problem. And if they don't know where to begin, they resist asking for help from appropriate sources.

Seeing a mate allow his health to deteriorate while he withdraws increasingly from life can be both a physical and an emotional turnoff. A wife may lose respect for a partner not because of his condition but rather because of his refusal to do something to improve his quality of life.

THE RELATIONSHIP BETWEEN GOOD PHYSICAL HEALTH AND GOOD SEXUAL FUNCTIONING

"I figured there were two organs we had to be concerned about," Elaine protested. "His sex organ and his brain. Now you're telling me his body has got to be healthy? How many more hurdles to overcome? By the time he's in shape to have sex, he'll be dead!"

It probably comes as no surprise that the brain and the penis are parts of the body. And if you don't treat your body well, your brain and genitals are hardly likely to function their best. And sex isn't likely to be so hot—if it takes place at all.

Do you remember how much sexual desire you felt the last time you had a cold or a pulled muscle? Almost any medical condition that involves discomfort can affect sexual desire. It should come as no surprise, then, that more serious untreated health problems, recreational drugs, and poor overall care of the body are anathema to good sexual functioning. Moreover, they are likely to have more direct effects on male sexual response than in the female, since strain and illness can lower testosterone levels, which are responsible for the male sexual drive.

These conditions not only are likely to decrease desire, but also may affect other aspects of the sexual response cycle, including erectile capacity, ejaculation, and sensation during orgasm. And of course, knowing in advance that there may be problems with functioning or lower levels of gratification flowing from the sexual experience is likely to make him simply want to avoid the whole process altogether!

Very frequently, by checking things out with one or more competent professionals, you will find that something can be done to improve sexual functioning. But if your man avoids seeking help and instead crawls off into his corner and totally avoids sex, you are both probably going to be stuck with his sex problems, as well as his upset feelings about it.

What effects can physical health problems have on sexual functioning? There may be *direct* effects, as in the case of vascular, drug, or hormonal problems, which can affect arousal, erections, or ejaculation. Or there may be *indirect* effects, such as when poor general health habits or handling of stress results in physical fatigue, a low energy level, or the development of diseases, thus causing a general reduction of one's effectiveness or enjoyment of life.

Because of the complicated interplay between mind and body, some "kinks" in sexual functioning such as mild changes in arousal or erectile ability due to fatigue or aging may, if unchecked, spiral into an ongoing cycle of further sexual malfunctioning or avoidance. Sex therapist Helen Singer Kaplan draws the example of a man who may have trouble getting an erection 10 percent of the time. If he fails to seek information or medical evaluation, stress arising from his failure to get an erection pumps adrenaline through his body, causes the blood to be drained from his penis, and stops an incipient erection. As a result he may become fully impotent and avoid sex.

The payoff of encouraging him to take better care of his health can be high—for both of you. Many physical conditions, if properly diagnosed and treated, may result not only in the restoration of sexual interest and functioning, but in better functioning and interest in life in general.

If there turns out to be no physical problem, a visit to a physician still can result in reassurances of normalcy and other information that may help reduce his anxiety and alleviate the sexual dysfunction.

MEDICAL CONDITIONS

Medical conditions can play a major role in making people back off from sex. Often it is not the medical condition itself that precludes sex, but rather that the person is procrastinating about taking care of it or is making himself anxious about the condition. Once again, the extent to which a person gets diverted from sex or other activities is heavily influenced by his attitudes and feelings *about* his physical problem.

We've all seen people with severe conditions, such as multiple sclerosis or paraplegia, who enjoy life more than others who might be in perfect health but bog themselves down with anger, low frustration tolerance, anxiety, or self-pity.

As is the case with nonmedical stressors, the key to preventing medical problems from conquering you is to conquer your low frustration tolerance *about* them and to engage in good health management. In so doing, you stand a better chance of staying on top of the physical condition and of living with it as comfortably as possible.

How Emotional Self-Management Can Help Us Cope with Major Medical Conditions

So much is being written today about the role of attitude and emotions in disease processes that the public has been given the impression that if you have a strong enough "will" you can prevent or cure certain conditions. This impression is especially unfortunate when people with diseases such as cancer or ulcerative colitis wind up actually blaming themselves for having caused them.

This oversimplification of the influence of the mind on the body notwithstanding, emotions and attitudes do play a part in helping you head off certain problems or better manage or even recover from others. Similarly, attitudes and feelings about changes in sexual functioning related to medical conditions can play a major role in either overcoming or exacerbating sex difficulties. Given equal degrees of impairment, for example, the diabetic male with high frustration tolerance and self-acceptance is likely to have a far better sex life than one who becomes depressed over his disease or feels inadequate and thus avoids sex altogether.

What follows is a look at major areas of potential medical problems, with special emphasis on the sexual dysfunctions that may accompany each. Because the problems that show up most commonly are those concerning sexual arousal and erectile ability, the incidence of these problems, along with the relative role of psychological and physical factors, will be our special focus.

Hypertension

While hypertension in its "pure" form is not thought to interfere with sexual functioning, the stress of other illnesses that often affect hypertensives may. Frequently it is actually the medications used to treat hypertension that tend to cause a falloff in arousal and difficulties with erections. Partly out of fear of creating self-fulfilling prophecies, physicians often fail to alert patients to these potential side effects, and thus in many cases increase the chances of anxiety and avoidance when sufferers discover that their penis isn't operating up to snuff. By discussing the problem with his physician, he may be able to switch to a similarly acting drug with fewer sexual side effects.

Your mate's emotional and psychological state can play a role in hypertension and its effect on his sexual functioning. Both repressing anger and ventilating hostility in an inappropriate way have been implicated in the development of hypertension, which in turn can lead to stroke or heart attacks. And anxiety about hypertension can turn a man who only occasionally has problems with erections into one who is almost never able to get erect and who consequently may avoid sex altogether.

Heart Attacks

Frequently the sexual difficulties following a heart attack originate in the mind rather than the body. They may stem from his fears of another heart attack, from depression, or, in some cases, from his *partner's* queasiness about resuming normal sexual functioning. These fears are largely unfounded, as the maximum stress at the moment of orgasm is no greater, according to Masters and Johnson, than that of walking up two flights of steps; and the incidence of arrhythmia accompanying sexual activity is no greater than it is in moving one's bowels.

Some men who have had heart attacks are so anxious about a possible recurrence that they become reluctant to engage not only in sex but in many formerly enjoyed nonsexual activities as well. This diminished range of activities tends to make them less juiced up about life, which in turn perpetuates their loss of interest in sex.

Yet other men who have had heart attacks or surgery do not abandon sex. If they now find the missionary position of intercourse too taxing, for example, they are often delighted to find that by experimenting with new sexual positions and activities they actually wind up *increasing* their sexual pleasure.

Vascular Problems in the Penis

Many experts believe that this is the most common physiological cause of impotence in men in their later years. According to Dr. Adrian W. Zorgniotti, professor of urology at New York University, "The arteries in the penis grow old faster than the rest of the body."

Other experts, such as Dr. Robert Kolodny of the Masters and Johnson Institute, believe that reduced blood pressure in the penis may not be as important as has been thought in causing impotence. They cite as supportive evidence a French study of impotent men with vascular disease with whom sex therapy alone had a high success rate. When a *variety* of contributing factors is present—including impaired circulation, psychological factors, and neurological problems—improvement in any one area may help the man function sexually again.

By using a special cuff to measure penile blood pressure, in conjunction with Doppler ultrasound, physicians can actually check out whether erectile problems may be vascular. Nocturnal penile tumescence (NPT) monitoring in a sleep lab may also help determine whether an erectile problem is organic or psychogenic.

An interesting phenomenon which several researchers speculate may temporarily occur in some men is a "pelvic steal syndrome," a condition in which pelvic thrusting causes the large gluteus muscles to shunt blood away from the penis. As a result, certain men's erections may disappear during "missionary position" intercourse; yet with the woman on top there may be no problem!

Diabetes and Other Metabolic or Hormonal Problems

It is estimated that at least half of all diabetic men have trouble getting or maintaining erections. Diabetes is generally considered the most common physical cause, accounting for one-quarter of the men over fifty who are impotent.

While in the past it was widely assumed that most diabetics with

erectile problems had a choice between a life without coitus or penile implants, many physicians suggest that impotence is psychogenic for nearly a third of the diabetics it afflicts. Many may actually have only minimal impairment; that is, they may be able to
get partial erections. If they become stressed or anxious about their
sexual functioning, however, it is this stress, rather than the erectile
impairment itself, that may lead to more chronic impotence.

If your partner has nocturnal erections or is able to masturbate
to orgasm, chances are he can function adequately in intercourse at
least some of the time, since only approximately 67 percent of normal erectile capacity is needed for penetration. Dr. Joseph D. Wax-
berg, a Stamford, Connecticut, psychiatrist and sex therapist who
takes an optimistic approach with impotent diabetic patients, suggests that taking advantage of sleep erections may be a powerful
way of getting many men with this problem over their anxiety.
"The wives," he says, "know to reach over in the night when hubby
has one and gently caress him. He wakes up, see what he has, and
they have intercourse."

Often it is not vascular or neurological impairment but poor
management of his diabetes that interferes with his sex drive and
functioning. If poor management occurs regularly enough over a
period of time, the likelihood of serious problems such as vision
loss may be increased, leading to restrictions on his life-style. This
can be emotionally debilitating and result in further neglect of his
physical and emotional health. Consequently not only sex but other
important relationship components as well, such as the expression
of affection and good communication, are likely to fall by the wayside.

Low Testosterone Levels

Many physicians who treat men with problems of low sexual desire
or erectile difficulties believe that before such conditions are blamed
on psychological or other causes a measurement of serum testoster-

one, and probably of serum luteinizing hormone, should be obtained. (This can be done through his primary care physician.)

Low hormone conditions, often due to pituitary tumors, may be involved. In such cases treatment with testosterone will often improve sexual desire and coital capacity. In other instances, where severe psychological stress may be responsible, psychotherapy may help restore sexual functioning.

Prostate Problems

Benign enlargement of the prostate—common in middle-aged men—may interfere with urination as well as sexual pleasure, as can urological infections such as urethritis, venereal disease, or lesions in various parts of the urogenital tract. In many men's eyes problems in the genitourinary domain are associated with potential "loss of masculinity" and are especially likely to receive the "ostrich" treatment. As a result, many conditions that might be easily treated through a visit to a physician go unresolved. And sexual accompaniments of prostate difficulties, such as slowness in getting erections, become the cause of increasing amounts of anxiety and sexual avoidance. Ironically, many medical experts agree that having a regular sex life may be one of the best safeguards against prostatitis and may help to extend healthy sexual expression into old age.

Women are also increasingly faced with genitourinary problems as they grow older, but are more likely to have their anxiety and fears dispelled because they are accustomed to routine gynecological exams. They also have a greater willingness to consult doctors, friends, or other informational sources to understand what's happening and to learn of possible treatments—much as they seek out help with emotional and relationship problems. With men, on the other hand, both benign and malignant conditions may go untreated and result in prolonged periods of anxiety and physical discomfort, or even potentially preventable death. (Prostatic cancer is the third leading cause of cancer deaths in the U.S.)

Gastrointestinal Problems

Sex is not likely to be particularly high on his agenda if your man's guts are hurting or jammed up. As is the case with other body problems, poor emotional self-management may result in poor physical self-management. Certain conditions may be triggered by his failure to manage his diet properly, while others may go undiagnosed and, like any other problem, will grow worse from neglect.

Even when there may not be any disease present, poor nutrition can result in conditions such as constipation or diarrhea. Neither is conducive to emotional well-being or sexual desire.

Difficulties in handling feelings—in particular the inability to express dependency needs or anger—have frequently been associated with the development of a range of problems from spastic colon to perforated ulcers.

In the presence of other gastrointestinal problems, mild problems with impotence may escalate as a result of medication or the aging process if psychological problems, such as anxiety about body image, are not dealt with. Body image problems can occur when any one of us loses or has an impaired organ or body part. When it is related in our minds to intimacy, the problem can be quite painful to deal with but should not be ignored.

Alcohol and Substance Abuse

Dave has a few beers a week but discounts any suggestion that he may have a drinking problem, because he practically never drinks "hard liquor" and can "hold his booze."

Len smokes a joint a few times a week to unwind or occasionally uses some cocaine as a "pick-me-up." "But for heaven's sake," he says scornfully to his woman friend, "I'm hardly a dope fiend. What a prude you are!"

As any expert on alcoholism will tell you, it is not the *amount* of alcohol one consumes, or how drunk one gets, that is the determinant of addiction. Rather it is the *reason one drinks* and *the way one reacts* to alcohol that are the hallmarks of a substance abuse problem.

Although men frequently indulge in alcohol or recreational drugs to help them function better sexually, much of the time this consumption actually results in significant sexual impairment. Often, as a result of having had occasional problems sexually when drinking, men become worried. They then drink again the next time to build their courage to have sex, thus launching a cycle of continued erectile failure.

According to Masters and Johnson, 30 to 40 percent of alcoholic males show decreased libido and 40 percent have erectile problems. Others estimate that up to 80 percent of men who drink heavily over a long period suffer from erectile problems or loss of sexual desire. Testosterone tends to be decreased in those men who use so-called hard drugs, such as heroin and other addictive substances. One-third to one-half of those men tend to have problems with erections, and approximately 66 percent have low sexual interest. Marijuana smokers' testosterone decreases as they use more, with 20 percent of those who use the drug habitually having problems with erections and 30 percent with decreased libido.

Because nicotine constricts blood vessels, smoking can also prevent erections. One study showed that in twenty men with erectile problems who were long-term smokers of more than a pack a day, after six weeks without tobacco more than a third could get erections again.

Other factors connected with heavy drinking or hard drugs also decrease the chances of a good sexual connection. Mood swings (especially anger and depression), general fatigue, and neglect of family and other life responsibilities will all contribute to creating a personality out of sync with himself and the world. This does not make him very happy or a harmonious sexual partner.

Other Medical Problems

Conditions such as asthma, emphysema, migraines, allergies, or seizures may, although they have a definite organic basis, be exacerbated by stress or poor health management. Smoking in the face of respiratory problems, drinking coffee at night when one has problems with insomnia, not using prescribed inhalers for managing asthma, and skipping meals are all anathema to good physical, emotional, and sexual health. Ironically, while he makes sure his car chassis and engine are in good working order, he clanks or drags his way through life thinking it sissifying or weak to take care of his own body.

Other physical conditions which can cause sexual dysfunction include spinal cord injury, multiple sclerosis, or other neurological disorders; and infections or injuries of the penis, testes, urethra, or prostate gland.

"AGING" PROBLEMS

Aging does involve physical changes, many of them disagreeable. The discomfort of small physical ailments, chronic pain, worry over weight or loss of hair, however, can magnify when people distort how serious these changes are.

For many men arthritis, prostate problems, or major surgery serve as a preview of old age and incapacitation—which means, among other things, being out of control. While some men and women fall into despair and view the remainder of their life as one long downhill slope, others have a more upbeat attitude and learn to accept the frustration of physical change. They focus on drawing as much pleasure as possible from life, building on what they've learned from their mistakes, and harnessing their strong points. They see their later years as a time of liberation, with more rather than fewer options, owing to greater wisdom and a sense of perspective. In the area of sex, these people can spend their time focusing on all the things they *can* give their partners—such as love, affection, and marvelous clitoral and body stimulation—instead of what they *can't* do, such as have intercourse for an hour.

Coping with declining physical functions can be especially difficult for the many men married to women eight, fifteen, or even twenty-five years younger than themselves. Attitude, once again, is all-important.

Lou, sixty-one, married Nancy ten years ago after his divorce, when he was a Porsche-driving, tanned tennis player. She, at thirty-four, was thrilled finally to find a successful and mature man after all the sophomoric "boys" she had dated. But while they used to have sex almost daily, Lou's sex drive has declined substantially, partly as a result of the medications he needs to control his blood pressure, and they now have sex two or three times a month. Increasingly insecure about his sexual prowess, he watches Nancy like a hawk and feels a sinking, anxious feeling when he sees other, younger men chatting with her at parties. His moroseness, jealousy, and the infrequency of his attempts to physically caress her, which result from his fear that caresses might lead to his having "to perform," have turned her off far more than any decline in his libido.

Like Lou, fifty-nine-year-old Herb gets apprehensive from time to time thinking that his forty-three-year-old companion of three years, Cheryl, might be wishing she were involved with someone closer to her own age. Since Herb, unlike Lou, does not focus his energies on jealousy and anxiety, nor does he flirt with other women to prove he's still attractive, Cheryl isn't tempted to compare him with other men. Instead, while accepting that down the pike it's possible for any person to be "left," he focuses on living as healthy and positive a life as possible and on being a good, loving, caring, affectionate mate to Cheryl. Appreciating this, Cheryl has felt only mildly frustrated at the decreased number of times they have sex leading to orgasm for both of them, but feels pleased that he's still willing to do things to satisfy her although he may not always orgasm.

Both men and women may lose sexual desire over the years, with the frequency of intercourse declining for both sexes. Generally, however, this is a result of lower expectations concerning sex, boring sexual routines, or mid-life stresses. Sexual decline is not an inevitable result of the lessening capacities of the body. Many husbands complain that their wives lose interest in sex after menopause, and some wives complain that in middle age their husbands become impotent or uninterested; *these changes are usually socially caused,* not hormonally programmed. "Presuming some continuity [of sexual expression]," said Dr. William Masters in an interview, "the only thing the male or female needs for effective sexual functioning is a reasonably good state of general health and an interested partner." To which Virginia Johnson amended, ". . . and an interesting partner."

CAN TOO MUCH "HEALTH" BE BAD FOR YOU?

While evidence seems increasingly to support the importance of good diet and exercise in promoting good health, as with any activity, excessive preoccupation can be problematic. A person may, for example, become absorbed in health management to the exclusion of nearly all other interests and activities. Even worse, extremist practices (e.g., extreme macrobiotic diets or overly rigorous exercise regimens) can actually have *negative* effects on health, including serious bodily injury or death.

As a result of our nation's preoccupation with physical fitness, a relatively new phenomenon called *overtraining* has occurred. Any of you who are "exercise widows" and whose husband is apt to be streaking out the door to jog just when you're getting ready to snuggle know the syndrome. Or there's the boyfriend too exhausted for sex because on their romantic Caribbean vacation he was off Windsurfing or scuba diving for nine hours a day.

According to a recent report in *American Health,* overtraining can lower a sexually healthy male's testosterone level 17 percent and sperm count 29 percent—not to mention inhibit his libido. "Sports anemia," a phenomenon consisting of weakness, irritability, and fatigue, is common among overtrained men. Fortunately, when exercise is brought down to a more moderate level, almost all of these problems correct themselves.

GETTING HIM TO SEE A DOCTOR

Felicia fumed when I suggested that somehow her forty-one-year-old husband, Roger, needed to be hooked up with a good physician who could help him address his excessive weight, work stress, and smoking. These, in combination with his family history and recent hyperventilation problems, made him a prime candidate for major heart and respiratory problems.

"Now you're telling me that, in addition to having my breasts and cervix checked out, and researching the pros and cons of estrogen replacement, I've got to research *his* ailments and then try to get him to go to the doctor and to follow his advice? Gimme a break!"

"Short-term pain for long-term gain," I replied. I agreed with her that he was acting childish, insisting on abusing his body and then wondering why his sex drive had fizzled. But until he's willing to do it himself, you're going to have to keep plugging away at the idea that "sturdy oaks" need care if they are to remain sturdy. Otherwise you may wind up as a widow—or a nurse to an invalid.

How to Handle His Resistance

You will probably notice that some of the excuses he comes up with for neglecting his health strongly resemble those he uses on other occasions to avoid such difficult or uncomfortable activities as having sex or figuring out his taxes:

"I'm just too busy/tired now. I'll go to the doctor or start exercising when I have the time" (meaning next year).

"Doctors are mainly quacks. They can't really do anything—except sock you with high bills."

"You're just being neurotic about this—as usual."

As for his perhaps most common excuse for avoidance and procrastination—"I'm just too busy"—try asking him, "What would you do if your car was having this kind of problem?"

Or you might say, "We have a problem. You don't seem to be feeling up to snuff physically the way you used to. What should we do about it?"

Handling his resistance to taking care of himself or at least allowing you to help him manage his health is like everything else we've discussed in this book—a pain in the neck, but there you have it—life isn't fair. In general, of course, while there are no easy answers, it's best to try to follow the same principles we've been discussing—don't attack, don't blame, and try to maintain your objectivity so that seeing a doctor doesn't become the main issue rather than his good health. One client, Sue, tells me she finally got through to her husband when she had just about given up trying to get him to go for an annual checkup. During a quiet dinner one night, when the kids for once were elsewhere and they were alone, she asked him how he would feel if she were ill and how he would like to go on without her. By turning the tables on him, Sue was able to make her husband see that she wanted him to care for himself because she loved him and did not want a life without him. And it worked—he went for a checkup and was given a good bill of health. Now Sue is hoping that maybe next year he won't be so afraid.

How to Find a Doctor Who Can Help

How do you find a doctor who can advise your husband if he is exhibiting problems with his sexual drive?

1. Ask friends or colleagues for recommendations of physicians who have treated them conscientiously. Basically you are looking for a physician who specializes in internal medicine, and it would be good to find one who emphasizes preventive health measures.
2. Check with your county medical society or with the head of internal medicine at your local hospital. One affiliated with a medical school is preferable.
3. Since many internists know too little about treating sexual problems, your best bet if your mate has a sexual dysfunction may be to consult the human sexuality program at a nearby university medical center, ask the local medical society to recommend a medical sex therapist, or write to the following:

• American Board of Sexology
  Registry of Diplomates in Sexology
  P.O. Box 1166
  Winter Park, FL 32789
  (202) 462-2122

• American Association of Sex Education Counselors
  and Therapists (AASECT)
  435 North Michigan Avenue
  Chicago, IL 60611-4067
  *(To receive a list of sex therapists
  in your state, send a self-
  addressed stamped envelope.)*

Consulting a physician comfortable with and knowledgeable in sexual issues can be of tremendous help in relaying corrective information and relieving your husband's anxiety. It will help ease his mind to know that it takes longer to get erections as one gets older, or that certain medications may reduce erectile capacity. And a good communicative doctor can get across to your husband that there are a lot of things a man can do that are enjoyable that don't require an erect penis. As we've seen, it's anxiety about performance that leads men to jump ship and avoid sex.

After the Appointment Is Made

If possible, go with your mate to the appointment so that you have an opportunity to get important questions answered. If your mate balks at this, consider calling or dropping a note to the physician in advance to alert him to certain questions he or she might ask so that important information does not get missed. Some possibilities are "How is your sex life?" and "How many ounces of alcohol a week do you consume?" and "What is your standard day of eating like?" Or suggest that the doctor probe for depression.

Establishing a relationship with a good primary care physician can also provide your partner with someone to whom he may be better able to confide emotional problems than you. Such a doctor may also, where appropriate, be able to convince him to see someone for psychotherapy, biofeedback, or sex therapy.

In assessing sexual functioning (especially in the case of arousal, erectile, or ejaculatory problems), the physician should cover the following issues:

1. When did you first notice changes in arousal or erection?
2. At what stage in sex do your erections tend to subside?
3. Does the pattern vary depending on the situation? How?
4. Do you have erections at night? During masturbation?
5. How long does it generally take you to ejaculate after penetration?
6. What are your common masturbation or partner sex fantasies?
7. Do you experience any guilt, fears, anxieties, or depression about sex?
8. How do you feel about your mate? What turns you on or off about her, sexually or nonsexually?

9. Specifically what is your alcohol or drug consumption (prescription and recreational)?

Perhaps one of the best things that can come out of your mate's getting hooked up with a sensitive and competent primary care physician is the attitude that taking responsibility for your body is not being a sissy, but rather being a life-affirming, responsible adult. And by realizing that it's not so terrible to have *physical* imperfections, he may be more likely to accept the fact that *sexual* or *psychological* imperfections are not so shameful either, and that there may be some help for them as well.

Be Patient!

At the risk of sounding a bit repetitious, there is no substitute for calm perseverance, high frustration tolerance, and good self-acceptance in trying to help your partner to take better care of his health.

Some Final Words to the Wise

1. You can lead a horse to water, but you can't make him drink. If your mate continues to abuse his body or neglect his health, despite your best efforts, you, sadly, may not be able to stop him.
2. Don't demand that he change. Suggest that you would prefer he take better care of himself.
3. Remind him that it has repeatedly been shown that fit people tend to be more productive, better organized, get more done, and have more fun doing it.
4. If, after all forms of nonblaming encouragement on your part, he stubbornly refuses to get unhooked from alcohol or drugs, seriously consider getting unhooked from *him*. Living with a committed substance abuser is bad news.

5. It is likely that, being male, he will have a shorter life span than you. Therefore, if you neglect nurturing other intimate friendships, interests, or sensory experiences while putting all your eggs in his basket, your life will be less rich—as well as more difficult if you become "unmarried."

6. Continue to take good care of your own physical and emotional health and to be a life-enjoying, responsible hedonist, hopefully inspiring him and others close to you to do so as well.

Remember, however, that avoiding disease is only part of the picture in taking care of the body. It's time to look at how to reach the highest possible level of physical self-acceptance and enjoyment.

ACHIEVING ORGANISMIC BRIGHTNESS

Fueling your body and taking care of parts that aren't functioning properly can be viewed as getting things to "sea level." The next step, if you want to shoot for an optimal state of physical well-being, is a less easily definable process that I call "organismic brightness," or feeling good in your skin. Included in this are:

1. feeling OK about your*self* and being relatively comfortable with your body;
2. generally maintaining an overall state of relaxation; and
3. having well-developed senses (touch, smell, taste, sound, vision).

Developing Physical Self-Acceptance

As you probably know all too well, it's very hard, in a culture that teaches us to define self-worth by how closely we resemble a movie star, to feel OK about ourselves when we have a bulging stomach, skinny arms, or, God forbid, a small penis. Some of the same exercises suggested earlier in the book to help you feel more accepting of *your* imperfect body can also help *him*. You can even do some of them together.

1. Suggest that he stand in front of a mirror, naked, and point out three features he really likes. For example, "my hairy chest, my calf muscles, my smile." Then add, "My body is a wondrous thing to be appreciated."
2. Have him talk about the parts of his body he doesn't like (such as his sagging chin or narrow shoulders) and help him accept each of them and not base his total self-image on them.
3. Carve out moments when you're occupying a quiet space together and enjoy the pleasures of touch by snuggling, holding hands, or walking arm in arm. It is a marvelous way to free touching from its automatic association with sex, and experience the pure pleasure of being alive and connected to another human being. This is especially important for males, who have been taught at an early age that it's unmanly to nestle in a lap or to touch except in sports or sex.

If he seems hung up about touching or being touched, you might explore with him the possibility of his having experienced early sexual or physical abuse. One of my clients, hurt and angry that her mate seemed to have such a hard time hugging or stroking her, was surprised to learn one night, when she asked him gently where this avoidance may have originated, that as a child he had been beaten regularly. Small wonder that he found it hard to experience his body as a source of pleasure. This realization helped free him of a lot of the guilt he had had about depriving his wife of physical contact; and by freeing himself of guilt about it he was able, over a period of weeks, to engage first in brief caresses and then, later, in more prolonged snuggling sessions.

4. Both of you might experiment sleeping with a nice cuddly stuffed animal, such as a teddy bear. It's a fantastic way to reclaim the feelings of physical comfort one had as a young child. Expect him to balk—as the husband of one of my clients did, vocifer-

ously—and then, on trying it out, to find it a great soporific as well as a way to escape temporarily from his tension-producing, be-a-man, keep-a-stiff-upper-lip world view. My client's husband, by the way, now rarely goes to sleep without the bear. Incidentally, one hospital in Florida routinely gives teddy bears to all patients before bypass surgery. Apparently cradling the "care bear" to the chest helps lessen the pain of bypass chest incisions.

Learning to Relax

> "You will find that deep place of silence right in your room, your garden, or even your bathtub."
> —Elisabeth Kubler-Ross

The tensions and physiological changes that can be triggered by stress can sap your energy and lower your resistance to all manner of unfriendly bugs. They can also produce increased heart rate, rapid breathing, migraines, insomnia, elevated blood pressure, or other serious problems.

A good deal of the stress that permeates our lives, all the way to the bedroom, comes from our work lives. If much of his life is structured around being productive at work, and play or relaxation is seen as wasteful, try to encourage him to do as many things as possible that do not add to the gross national product. Suggest those that are appropriate for him: for example, if he goes at a hectic pace at the office all day, suggest a quiet lunch in the park instead of racing to the gym to hit the treadmill.

1. *When he comes home, try to provide him with an hour or so to unwind,* during which time no phone calls will be put through to him. He can then do gardening, take a short nap, fantasize, or listen to some music.
2. *Encourage him to take "mini-relaxation breaks" at work* as well,

pointing out that any time he loses will be more than made up for by increased efficiency. A brief procedure, which can be used at any point during the day when his body and brain are racing, is to spend two or three minutes sitting in a quiet room (the john, if necessary), breathing slowly and deeply through his diaphragm while repeating to himself (or aloud) the word "C-A-L-M."

3. *Put on a relaxation tape for ten to twenty minutes.* You might even do this together, unless one of you needs to mind the kids. Preferably get one that takes you through all the muscle groups in your body, first tensing the muscles, then relaxing them. Once you've mastered the procedure, you will be able to achieve a relaxed state in less time. You can then "scan" your body to discover where you are tense and see what you can do to relax that part.

4. *Try suggesting the two of you lie motionless for ten to twenty minutes.* Visualize the flow of the cosmos and your connection with the universe, imagining that you are all flowing with the same sexual energy.

5. On a day when he hasn't been racing around crazily, *suggest he try jogging, swimming, biking, or walking* in a pastoral setting, which increases the heart rate and thus brings more oxygen into the bloodstream and releases endorphins.

6. *Give him a gift certificate for a series of massages.* Or take a massage workshop together so you can take turns helping each other mellow out after a tense or tiring day.

7. *Encourage him to have occasional deluxe masturbation sessions.* With the door locked, the phone unplugged, and, if he wishes, his favorite erotica or music, suggest he take at least half an hour to slowly allow his sexual sensations to ebb and flow, trying not to focus on the goal of orgasm, but rather on the pure joy and richness of loving and pleasuring himself. And never fear— in all probability this will help him get into a *more* sensual frame of mind in general, with some nice spillover to your joint sex life, especially if he calls you in before he orgasms!

8. *Take play breaks.* Try some of these diversions:
   - Put some playful but not too strenuous dance music on your stereo, such as *The Nutcracker Suite* or some soft rock, then lie down on the floor so that your two bodies form one straight line and your toes are touching, knees slightly bent. Begin to move your legs to the music, flowing with the rhythm and with each other, trying neither to lead nor to follow.
   - Turn down the sound on the television and make up silly scripts.
   - Read a play or poem aloud.
   - Play music together.
   - Rent a canoe or rowboat.
   - Go to some gourmet take-out place and buy a selection of different items. Then go home and feed them to each other in the dark, guessing what you're eating.
   - Put on some music and do "silly dancing" together: make up your own steps and become as loose and playful as you want. It's one of my mate's and my favorite play break activities; it's aerobic; it takes only a few minutes and can be done at any time, and it's "dis-inhibition-training" for the man who is afraid to be loose, look awkward, and just let himself go—both in and out of bed.
9. *Suggest he take a "mental health day" off from work.*
10. *Most importantly, read Chapter 7 so you can teach him the best stress reducer of them all: rational thinking.*

Increasing Sensory Awareness

One of the main vehicles sex therapists use to help people overcome anxieties about sexual performance and stop focusing on intercourse is called *sensate focus,* developed by Masters and Johnson.

These and other exercises will be described in Chapter 9. Even before embarking on this exercise, which is done nude and is at least quasi-sexual, I like to help people expand their *overall sensory appreciation*—that is, of touch, sound, sight, and smell.

These exercises can be done in many ways and in many settings, both separately, where he may be more fully able to get into his own feelings, or together, where you may have a joint aesthetic experience without the tensions of anticipated sexual performance.

1. *Lie in the grass or the sand,* feeling the sun and the air caress your skin, taking in the sounds of the birds, the kiss of the breeze, the smell of the flowers, the pungent odor of fall leaves.
2. *Play a tape.* Relaxation tapes are available in health food or music stores. They guide you, through words and music, to imagine yourself traveling through nature or even through the universe. Or use your own imagination and, closing your eyes and relaxing in a comfortable position, transport yourself to a lovely beach or the middle of the Milky Way, allowing waves of relaxation to flow over you as you imagine your body being softly caressed.
3. *Pick a quiet place and listen to some ethereal, soothing music.*
4. *Take turns planning a "time-warp trip."* Every other week one of you plans time together, arranging for the baby-sitter and appropriate props, such as music or a satin comforter. The trip can be an imaginary trip to any place, in any time, in which case the partner planning it can provide some pretty interesting props.
5. *Take a nap in a silk bathrobe*—together or separately.
6. *Eat sensuous foods,* taking turns feeding each other, with the receiver's eyes closed, savoring the tastes and textures of the food.
7. *Walk in the rain.*
8. *Lie naked on a thick rug in front of the fireplace.*
9. As a warm-up for developing your sexual senses (much more to follow in Chapter 9), *try exercising your pubococcygeal muscle,* located in your pelvic area. To find this muscle, practice stopping the flow of urine several times. Then, as sex therapist Bernie Zilbergeld suggests, start by squeezing and releasing your pelvic muscles fifteen times: just squeeze and let go. Do one set of

fifteen twice a day until you are able to squeeze only the pubococcygeal muscle. Then you can do the exercise anytime you want: while driving in a car, watching TV, or even sitting in a meeting! It's a great way—for both males and females—to sensitize yourself to your genital sensations.

CHAPTER 7

HOW TO HELP
YOUR MATE WITH HIS
EMOTIONAL AND
PRACTICAL PROBLEMS

"Today we know that human nature isn't
something that is fixed and inexorable, the
equivalent of fate or predestination, but
something that is eminently malleable,
and while it is true that the leopard cannot change its spots, we can certainly
change ours, if only we are willing to devote ourselves to the task."
—Ashley Montagu

It's not easy to live with someone who is tense and inhibited, is highly self-absorbed, seethes with anger and impatience, or is mired in a bleak outlook on life. Chances are he finds himself hard to live with as well. People with a significant amount of emotional distress tend to have low self-acceptance and get poor results in their interpersonal relationships and other endeavors. And, ultimately, they wind up not enjoying their lives very much.

"So what am I supposed to do about it? I'm not a trained mental health professional—I can't be expected to be his therapist!" I hear you protest. One woman I know wryly refers to this part of her helpmate job as being "Our Lady of the Perpetual Band-Aid."

By now, it is hoped, you've learned the basics of how to keep *yourself* from being disturbed when those around you aren't giving you what you want. Also, you've made some progress in keeping your ego intact even if you're not receiving a lot of "strokes" from your mate assuring you of your desirability.

By taking some of the rational thinking skills you've been practicing on yourself and teaching them to him, you may help your man increase his own feeling of self-worth. This growth will help him feel less stressed out and better able to handle his personal problems. Best of all, he'll be better able to connect with you, emotionally and physically.

Your goals with him are the same as for yourself. You want to help him:

1. increase self-acceptance and trust in his own abilities,
2. increase his frustration tolerance and reduce his anger when others act badly or the world fails to give him what he wants,
3. learn to reduce anxiety and stress and increase relaxation,
4. acknowledge mistakes and develop a sense of humor,
5. acquire problem-solving skills as well as the ability to better balance his life, and
6. increase his enjoyment of life—emotionally, physically, and spiritually.

As was the case with you, the main process for his accomplishing these goals involves replacing his self-defeating thinking with more rational attitudes—ones less likely to result in unproductive feelings and behaviors.

Think of yourself as a firm, kind "peer counselor" who combines the ABCs of rational thinking with patience, friendship, gentle confrontation, understanding, and a sense of humor. Continue to make clear what you'd like him to do, and help him work on identifying and dealing with any attitudes or feelings that may be getting in the way. In so doing you'll be continuing to reinforce your own rational thinking processes. Then, at the end of three months, evaluate the situation to see if it's any better, and decide where to go from there.

Hank, fifty-seven, is a middle-level manager in a large electronics manufacturing company. The closer he gets to retirement, the more time he spends sleeping or watching television sports rather than exploring retirement opportunities. He responds to his wife, Mary, in monosyllables, if at all, and barely glances up when his daughter and lively year-old grandson visit.

From the moment Ray gets into the shower and shouts that "the goddamn kids have left the shampoo cap off again" to the time he curses his way home from work along the traffic-clogged expressway, he is a tightly coiled spring. Once home, he wraps himself in an impenetrable curtain of anger until it's time to go to bed. He despises his sales job and everyone he works with, claiming they're the "biggest bunch of cretins on this planet."

Ernie comes home feeling "like a whipped dog" from his job in his father-in-law's construction business. His daily interactions with his aggressive and explosive father-in-law have gradually taken their toll, and he has been experiencing a fair amount of depression and inertia. He loves his wife, Cynthia, but is jealous of her success as a public defender. He feels particularly inadequate if she exhorts him to "stop being so darned passive with Dad and everybody else" or pushes him to think about becoming a parent in the next year or two. Increasingly distressed about the "spare tire" that seems to be forming around his waist, he still has not managed to make it to the gym. Similarly—despite his constant complaints of fatigue— he has procrastinated for two years about going for a physical checkup to investigate possible physical causes for his exhaustion.

How did each of these men get to be this way? Here are some possibilities: (1) His parents didn't toilet-train him properly. (2) He has an unresolved Oedipal fixation. (3) His father always told him what a failure he was when he got a B in a course and never praised him for his accomplishments. (4) His Catholic school background has left him with a permanent problem in dealing with authority figures.

Here is a far more likely reason: Whether or not he suffered from a traumatic childhood, he has taken with him into adulthood the same kinds of irrational beliefs we discussed in Chapters 3 and 4.

By helping him identify some of his irrational beliefs and encouraging him to replace them with more healthy evaluations of himself and the world, you may be giving him the best gift ever: good emotional health. Even if you don't succeed, at least you'll know you've given it your best and can feel good about that.

SO WHAT IS "GOOD EMOTIONAL HEALTH," AND HOW CAN I HELP *HIM* WHEN I'VE GOT MY OWN PROBLEMS?

Most professionals seem to agree on the following criteria of mental health:

1. *Self-acceptance:* the ability to stubbornly refuse to put your *self* down even when you haven't performed as well as you'd like or when others reject you
2. *Autonomy and self-efficacy:* the sense of being able to function in the world, along with some basic skills for doing so
3. *Resilience:* the ability not to get bogged down for any significant period of time in *anger, anxiety, depression or guilt*
4. The capacity to become *vitally absorbed* in one or more vocational or avocational interests
5. Having *close relationships*—which could include intimacy on an emotional, social, sexual, intellectual, or recreational plane—with one or more people.

Perhaps emotional health is only another name for maturity or being a grown-up.

Increasingly, the evidence is mounting that the most important foundation for emotional health is *having a good, rational philosophy.* Dr. George Vaillant, a psychiatrist at Dartmouth Medical School, and his wife, Caroline Vaillant, in their important longitudinal study of how men fared at age sixty-five, reported that those with "strong stoicism" at forty-seven were doing well at sixty-five. They found little evidence that several factors long assumed to be important in psychological development, such as being poor or orphaned in childhood or having parents who were divorced, had much effect on well-being at sixty-five. "In the long run," says psychologist Daniel Goleman, summarizing the Vaillant study results, "people are extraordinarily adaptable. Given enough time, people recover and change; a half-century perspective shows that time heals." The secret of emotional health seems to lie in their ability to handle life's blows without passivity, blame, or bitterness.

HOW DO I GET HIM TO ACCEPT MY EMOTIONAL HELP?

It might be a good idea to let him know that you'd love it if both of you made the next month "Rationality Month." And though he may not be ready to admit your progress, if you actually have been thinking more rationally and handling things better, you are now in an especially good position to influence him. If he has found you too "needy" or "emotional" in the past, your new "rational mode" can't help impressing him.

If you can induce him to listen to an introductory audiotape, the following tapes (available from the Institute for Rational-Emotive Therapy, 45 East 65th Street, New York, NY 10021) are excellent: Albert Ellis's *Solving Emotional Problems* and *Conquering Low Frustration Tolerance.* If he continues to insist that he's fine, and *you're* the problem, then get him a copy of Albert Ellis's *How to Live with a Neurotic* to help him to tolerate *you* better!

If he's distinctly resistant to self-help materials, you'll need to describe the process to him verbally. You might begin by explaining that for you "developing emotional muscle" has boiled down to accepting that it's not the lousy things that happened to you that caused you to get upset (mad/depressed, anxious, withdrawn, etc.) or the poor treatment you received in your childhood that causes your current distress. Rather, you became upset by allowing people and things to push your buttons. But now you've learned to catch yourself when you're starting to overreact or catch yourself indulging in "stinking thinking." These responses, you can go on to explain, almost always take the following three main forms:

1. *Should*ing or making unreasonable demands on yourself or others. This, you explain, has led you to make yourself angry at the person who has "let you down"—even if that person is yourself.
2. *Catastrophizing*—taking a hassle—past, present, or future—and making it into a horror. Give him some of the examples from Chapters 3 and 4.
3. *"I can't stand it–itis"*—telling yourself something that's difficult, unpleasant, or uncomfortable cannot possibly be endured, even though you are obviously still alive.

Next, give him an example of a situation in which you successfully turned around your thinking. Your boss's unfair criticism of you for one small error in a stupendous report you had prepared in record time might be one. Describe to him how you started making yourself angry but reminded yourself, "It's a hassle, not a horror." As a result, you were able to respond calmly and not stew over it for hours—and what a liberating feeling that was.

Ask him if he's up for trying this method out for the next four weeks, with an option to renew. If he asks what's in it for him, tell him that "life may just become a little easier with both of us less bugged about things and able to handle the stressors of our lives more effectively. Wouldn't that be worth a try?"

Here's how one woman, Rhoda, whom I worked with in therapy, used this process in dealing with her husband, Brian.

Brian and Rhoda: An Example

It was Brian's playfulness and exuberance both in and out of bed, along with his intelligence and family background of "really solid values" that attracted Rhoda to him. Thirty-six years old, Brian ran his own business and seemed to have his brief first marriage in perspective: "I was only twenty-three and just too young to know what marriage was all about."

Thirty-two and married for the first time, Rhoda—an ebullient elementary school teacher who had been through some really rough times in her twenties—was thrilled finally to see the light at the end of the tunnel: a mate she loved who came from a similar family background and who shared her life goals.

A year into their marriage, the tunnel appeared to be darkening. Between a $40,000 bill for back taxes that she thought he had paid, his frequenting the local tavern for a few beers, and a business that was faltering badly, Rhoda's once-stable financial situation became a shambles after she helped bail him out. The affection they had started out with deteriorated into much mutual sniping. He called her a "princess" because she insisted on buying a new outfit each season and attacked her because she reserved two nights a week to keep up with her friendships and her weekly volleyball team; she was on his case because of his increasing financial instability and total physical rejection of her.

When she came to see me, Rhoda was feeling "betrayed and furious" at being drained financially and emotionally, with no end in sight. The last straw was their not even having physical contact, to her one of the bonds of marriage. At first she had tried to "reason" with Brian. But now her frustration level was at such an all-time high that she felt she might explode if he "looked at her cross-eyed." Although Brian came in for one joint session, he insisted on continuing to see the psychoanalyst he swore was helping him but acknowledged they never discussed his drinking, lack of sexual arousal, or tax delinquency. Rather they were still dealing—after two-and-a-half years of twice-weekly sessions—with his childhood.

First Rhoda and I worked on helping her get over her feelings of depression and inadequacy at the seeming failure of her marriage and at Brian's sexual rejection of her. In doing so she came to realize that she could survive on her own if worse came to worst and the marriage didn't work out. We accomplished this important groundwork by means of the process described in Chapters 3 and 4 and then developed a three-month plan for her being more helpful in dealing with Brian.

Diagnosis and Treatment Plan

Although both Brian and Rhoda felt Brian's beer-drinking habits did not make him an alcoholic, he completed the self-scoring "Signs of Alcoholism" inventory from the National Council on Alcoholism during his one session with me, and it indicated a significant drinking problem. This result confirmed what I already expected from Rhoda's descriptions of some of his emotional patterns of yelling and belligerence in the evenings and depression and exhaustion much of the next day.

Since Brian would not come to couples therapy, Rhoda and I agreed that the main problem areas she needed to help him work on were:

Emotional: • Help Brian overcome depression and work boredom.

             • Help him overcome his low frustration tolerance over (a) having sex with Rhoda when he is no longer spontaneously "turned on"; and (b) having to deal with irate customers.

Practical: • Brian and Rhoda were to maintain a budget.
• For now, Brian is to hug Rhoda and give her a kiss lasting at least one minute each day, morning and evening.
• Brian would go without any alcohol for two weeks to see if abstinence created any difference in his depression level.

Overall • To see to what extent, with Rhoda's help, Brian
Relationship could become the helpmate Rhoda wanted to go
Goals: through life with.
• With both of them reducing their anxiety over their marriage, to see if they could learn to relax and have more fun and sex together.

Coaching Tips

I then gave Rhoda the following tips on how to be a good "coach" to help Brian better accept himself, tolerate the frustrations of everyday living, and rely on his own emotional self-management, rather than on alcohol. Many of these tips may be helpful with your own mate.

1. When you see him putting himself down for any of his behaviors (e.g., calling himself a "lousy husband" or a "failure" in his business), show him how to damn his *behaviors,* not *himself.* Say, for example: "Yes, you did mess up at that, because you're a fallible human being; but making mistakes doesn't make you a totally rotten, hopeless person. All it does mean is that you're going to have to work harder if you want to improve in the future."
2. When he exhibits low frustration tolerance (e.g., overreacts when things don't go his way or thinks he "can't stand" something), say "Yes, it *is* uncomfortable, inconvenient, and a pain in the ass—but not awful or intolerable."
3. Most important, through "modeling," show him how you have

changed and how you can now accept yourself, even when others are not affirming you.

4. Try not to upset yourself when your mate gets off track. Instead, praise him when he does something positive. If he kisses you, for example, say something like "I've been feeling really close to you and optimistic about how things will work out."

The final tip that I gave Rhoda and offer to you is: the best way to keep yourself from going crazy if your mate continues to do all the things you're trying to help him stop doing is *not to take it personally*. You did not create his disturbance; he's probably been talented at it his whole life. Also, accept that you may not succeed in helping him change.

HOW TO HANDLE HIS RESISTANCE

Probably your man is *not* going to react to your efforts by saying "Dear, have I thanked you lately for all the help you've been to me in getting over my anger, intimacy, and insecurity problems?" Much more likely you will get some of the following reactions:

"What are you, my shrink?"

"Stop pulling all that psychology stuff on me."

"You're reading too many of those darned self-help books. I'd love to burn them all."

"*I'm* perfectly happy. You're the one with unrealistic expectations. We have a good relationship, but you're never satisfied."

"Relationships aren't supposed to be this hard. They're supposed to be easier and more natural—not so much talking and working at them all the time."

Experiment with some of the following answers to his objections:

Him: *"I don't want to talk about this anymore."*

You: "OK, when do you want to talk about it? Can we set up a time?"

Him: *"Why are you always nagging?"*

You: "Because I'm human. I love you, and when I don't know any other way to get through to you, I start falling back on my old bad habits. It would be helpful if, next time I lose it, you say something humorous like 'Hey, Blondie, there you go again!' And I'd like to have the same right to call you on it when *you're* shutting down. What could I say or do to help signal you when that starts happening?"

Him: *"I'm perfectly rational—what's wrong with you?"*

You: "Yes, I certainly can overreact at times. Maybe it could be that we've *both* got poor ways of handling certain things; and if we both help each other, rather than attacking each other, we can both improve.

Him: *"I'm sick and tired of all your self-help books."*

You: "They may not have all the answers, but trying new things can help. Let's try what I just suggested and see how it goes." [Then stop!]

or

You: "You know, I think you're right. Sometimes I think we should just stop 'talking-about-talking-about' and just *talk*. We'd save lots of time!"

If he starts shouting:

Walk out and come right back and start over as if he hadn't been yelling at you. Or say, "You must really be feeling ragged after twelve hours of traveling."

If he says, seemingly with no other goal than shutting you up, "I really do love you" or "You're right":

Say: "Actions speak louder than words." [Then shut your mouth and don't go into overkill.]

In general, you're much better off making your interactions short and then rewarding him for his brief interest. Avoid shouting and being repetitious; he will only tune you out.

DEALING WITH SOMEONE YOU PROBABLY CAN'T HELP

Hank is unhappy with his job, his siblings, his house, and his wife, Phyllis. Hurt and frustrated by his emotional abuse and sexual neglect, Phyllis spends increasing amounts of time out of the house "just to survive." "Every year," she claims, "he's becoming more and more like his father—a stingy, uptight guy who blamed everyone in the world for his problems and who was one of the worst sourpusses I've ever met."

My first step was to help Phyllis recognize that her husband was disturbed. She was counseled to take even his most vitriolic attacks on her as accurate measures not of her worth but of his *disturbance*.

Her second task was to avoid self-pity and depression over her relationship by telling herself, "It's not great being married to Hank, and I sure don't like how he abuses me verbally. *But even though I don't like it, I can stand it* (at least for now)." In terms of responding to his behaviors, she was coached to do the following:

1. *When he tries to put you down, use the "to-me-ness" principle* advocated by my friend and colleague, Dr. Penelope Russianoff. "To you I'm a lousy, boring friend; to me I'm a caring, involved person. We see me differently."
2. *When he acts negatively, warn him once or twice.* When he complains about the theater seats, the restaurant, and just about every other aspect of the evening, tell him you will leave for the evening if he continues to act negatively. If he persists, leave.

3. *When he acts somewhat rationally, reward him in some way,* verbally or with a special treat. If he reverts to acting badly, leave for the day and do something enjoyable for yourself.

4. *Keep in mind that the goal is improvement, not perfection.*

5. *Try to keep your preference that he behave better from escalating into a* must.

6. *Maintain a sense of humor* by trying to see some of the absurdity in your mate's obnoxious behavior.

7. *When you find yourself on the verge of letting him push your buttons, take a slow, deep breath* and inhale while thinking to yourself "C-A-L-M." Then remind yourself, "Don't expect a nut to act like a non-nut."

8. *Try very hard to keep this approach up for several weeks.* Once you've managed not to be so upset over his disturbed behavior, reevaluate the situation and decide whether it makes more sense to stay or leave.

COPING WITH THE "BIG THREE": ANXIETY, ANGER, AND DEPRESSION

Whether your mate is basically emotionally healthy or deeply disturbed, he probably suffers at times—as do all humans—from some amount of anxiety, anger, or depression. The following is a brief layperson's guide to recognizing and helping him deal with each of these emotional problem areas, be they situational or chronic patterns.

ANXIETY, STRESS, AND GENERAL UPTIGHTNESS

Recognizing the Signs

1. Does he obsess about the possibility of making a mistake or failing and engage in a lot of "*what-if*-ing"? Does he procrastinate because he's afraid to fail?
2. Is he compulsive about doing things properly and according to schedule, to the extent that he rarely enjoys the activity?
3. Is he excessively devoted to work? Does he turn leisure activities into work and apply the same perfectionist standards to them?
4. Does he have difficulty tolerating various discomforts and thus avoid them? These can be anything from public speaking to taking plane trips to having emotional dialogues with you.
5. Does he suffer from free-floating anxiety, chronic tiredness, inability to sleep, poor concentration, hostility? Or various somatic complaints, such as high blood pressure, backaches, or digestive disorders?

In the Area of Sex:

1. Does he become excessively anxious if his body does not respond in the way he thinks it should?
2. Can he "perform" only under certain conditions—e.g., in bed at 11:00 at night with the lights out, or only on weekends or when the kids are out of the house?
3. Is he uptight about the way his body looks or performs? Does he decide he'd better not risk it?

This sort of overconcern not only robs people of a good deal of *life* satisfaction, but is also a major barrier to *sexual* participation and satisfaction. Barring any physical disorders, anxiety is *the* key factor in arousal disorders such as male erectile difficulties and female orgasmic dysfunction. Anxiety also plays a major role in premature ejaculation and inhibited sexual desire. By helping your mate manage his anxiety better in nonsexual situations, you can help him increase his and your overall enjoyment of life. As he becomes less fearful of letting go, failing to perform, or trying new things in nonsexual areas, things are bound to pick up in the sexual area as well.

What Are the Causes of Anxiety and Stress?

If you ask most people what's causing their stress or uptightness, they will tell you "it's my boss," "my wife," "my son's new earring," "financial pressures," etc. They will, in other words, insist that various activating events are causing their emotional reaction.

But by now you know better. We've learned that it is not these events in themselves that are causing his anxiety but rather the view he takes of these stressors, meaning *the various irrational beliefs he holds about them*.

Along with these irrational beliefs and disturbed feelings often come certain *physiological* changes, which is why anxiety is felt particularly strongly in our bodies. Perhaps you've heard about the fight or flight syndrome. In brief, our adrenal glands secrete some thirty stress hormones; as a result of overstress or anxiety, our heart rate may increase, or we may begin to breathe faster or experience muscle tension or fatigue. If there is no real emergency, our body, all revved up for disaster, will eventually begin to produce acids such as lactic acid and cortisol to reduce the increased hormones. The result is the fatigue that is often the main symptom of stress.

Helping Your Mate Identify His ABCs

Suggest that he make a list, in order of importance, of the problem situations (or activating events) that result most often in throwing him off kilter. Next, have him list the self-defeating reactions (emotional, behavioral, and physical) that he has to these problem situations. For example, does he start to feel down on himself or get the urge to overeat or drink?

Finally, help him learn to identify the irrational beliefs (or "killer Bs" as psychologist Art Lange calls them) about himself, others, or the situation that cause these reactions. Be sure to help him distinguish thoughts from feelings: e.g., "I feel you don't care about me" is actually a *thought*—one that usually leads to a *feeling* of depression, anxiety, or anger. The process may be helped by showing him how to use his bodily sensations to help him identify his feelings. For example, neck or back pain may be his body's way of reacting to anxiety. When he feels this pain, you might suggest he ask himself what is upsetting him.

These are the irrational beliefs generally associated with anxiety:

1. I cannot live with what has happened (or may happen in the future).
2. This event or just the possibility is too awful!
3. I couldn't stand the discomfort, rejection, or failure.
4. If I fail or am rejected, I am a bad or hopeless person.

After identifying what his irrational beliefs are, help *him* identify what is true about these beliefs and what is not true, rather than deciding for him. Then you might help him substitute realistic beliefs.

To minimize the chances of his resisting your efforts, try beginning with situations not related to you or your relationship. Then, when he starts accepting that *he* is responsible for his own reactions, add some situations involving you. Here is a sample troubleshooting form worked out by Brian, in conjunction with his "coach," Rhoda:

Troubleshooting Form

Activating Events:

- Large debts, slow business
- Wife pressuring me for sex

Self-Defeating Consequences:

- Emotional: Anxious, stressed
- Behavioral: Drinking, avoiding sex

Irrational Beliefs:

- I *mustn't* have all these debts and so little income; *I can't stand it*—I'll go bankrupt and look like a *jerk*.
- My wife *mustn't* pressure me; I *shouldn't* be avoiding her sexually, and since I am I feel like a *wimp*.

By encouraging him to look at the worst that could happen and to change his evaluation of these events to a less catastrophic one, Rhoda was able to help Brian come up with the following:

Rational Countermessages:

- It's unfortunate if I go bankrupt, but I won't die or lose my worth as a person. It will simply wipe the slate clean so I can start reconstructing my finances in a better way.
- My wife has a right to want to have sex. I don't like the fact that I'm not really feeling up for it, but it doesn't mean I'm a wimp. Even though I'm not aroused, I can still provide her with some pleasure and affection.

Other Techniques You Can Teach Him for Managing Anxiety and Stress

1. Do something tension-reducing, such as yoga or working out.
2. Distract himself by getting into some absorbing activity he enjoys, such as playing the piano.
3. Use "thought stopping" when he finds his mind grinding over the same thing: coach him to imagine a voice shouting "Stop!" or actually have him say it aloud every time he finds himself ruminating unproductively.
4. Set aside ten minutes a day just to worry; and tell him not to allow himself to do any worrying *outside* this time period.
5. Do a relaxation procedure, such as inhaling slowly through the nostrils, allowing the diaphragm to expand; then exhale slowly while thinking "Calm" or "Relax." Repeat ten times. Or play a relaxation tape.
6. Use some coping statements, especially if he's in the middle of a crisis and there isn't time to go through the entire process of disputing irrational beliefs. Such statements can include "It's a hassle, not a horror" or "This too shall pass."
7. Take an improvisation workshop or a Dale Carnegie public-speaking course, where there is regular practice in getting through uncomfortable situations.

Tips for You

Once you've helped him understand that he doesn't have to be a helpless pawn of external events, step back and see how he does on his own. For as history professor Peter Stearns, author of *Be a Man! Males in Modern Society,* says: ". . . If men do in fact need some special comforts, some lifelong mothering, they will have to provide it themselves, or strive to rearrange their outer world so that it requires less domestic solace."

ANGER AND LOW FRUSTRATION TOLERANCE

Anger—meaning rage—is generally not too hard to spot—particularly if you're the target of it. The symptoms of low frustration tolerance overlap in certain ways with those of anger. While these feelings are also different in certain respects, I shall address them together because they both involve having a "short fuse" and the same core irrational beliefs.

Recognizing the Signs of Anger

1. Does he seem to need to be in control constantly, to dominate, or to be right all the time?
2. Does he have a tendency to be unrelentingly critical of you or others and to devalue your opinions?
3. Does he take small annoyances, such as your slight memory lapses or clumsiness, and make federal cases out of them?
4. Does he refuse to take responsibility for his own emotions, generally blaming other people for causing them?
5. Does he try to intimidate you or others by yelling, making threats, or engaging in character assassination? Or by withdrawing money, sex, affection, or conversation?
6. Is he jealous, possessive, or competitive with others for your attention?
7. Do you frequently feel afraid, guilty, angry, or overwhelmed? Do you feel that you must walk on eggshells or twist yourself into a pretzel to please him? Do you find yourself making excuses for him to others?

In the Area of Sex:

1. Does he demand that you be available when he wants sex, but is hostile or unavailable when you are the initiator?
2. Does he like porn movies that involve violence?

3. Does he insist you don't love him or attack you for being a prude if you don't have sex the way he prefers?

Recognizing the Signs of Low Frustration Tolerance

1. Does he get impatient and give up easily when things are difficult? Does he tend to wallow in his inertia for days or weeks at a time?
2. Does he avoid things that are uncomfortable?
3. Does he yell at cars that are going too slowly?
4. Does he want to do exactly what he wants to do, just as if he had no marital and family responsibilities?

In the Area of Sex:

1. Does he give up easily if not aroused effortlessly or if he loses his erection?
2. Is he easily distracted or put off by not having sex when, where, and how he wants it?
3. Does he find it easier to masturbate or run to a hooker than have to make an effort to please you or to work at getting himself aroused? Is he aroused only by certain limited "fetishes"?

What Are the Causes of Anger and Low Frustration Tolerance?

In many ways anger and problems with tolerating frustration are natural by-products of the male role. If a major part of being male involves being strong and in control, then anything perceived as a threat to his control, power, or centrality in your life is likely to make him feel fear and anxiety. Since, however, men are not "supposed to" be vulnerable, these feelings of insecurity or fears of being deprived or abandoned are often unrecognized or covered up. They may tend to be directed *outward:* either at the perceived source of threat or at the nearest available scapegoat. He attempts to regain his feeling of control by trying to strip others of *their* self-confidence and power, thus making them dependent on or subordinate to him. In the sexual arena, this might involve covering up insecurity with anger so as not to risk failure. (For a more complete review of the kinds of irrational beliefs leading to anger and how to counteract them, review the discussions in Chapters 3 and 4.)

Tips to Help Him Manage His Anger and Low Frustration Tolerance

1. Point out that *really* being in control would mean not allowing other people to push his emotional buttons and that being truly strong means being able to admit weakness without feeling he's less of a man.
2. Point out that there are few real traumas in life and that it isn't necessary to get so discombobulated over the "small stuff." Suggest that a more appropriate response might be for him to lower his expectations about people and even to be able to laugh at some of their silly behavior.
3. When he is argumentative, try being unusually cooperative, compromising, and loving, even if you think he does not deserve your good treatment. You may then be able to see more clearly that nothing will work, and decide it isn't worth staying with him.
4. Try dealing with him the same way you would with a youngster or co-worker who is behaving badly. Be firm and set very clear limits as to what is and is not acceptable. And be prepared to leave the room or the relationship if he consistently violates those stated limits. If he uses any physical violence, leave *immediately*. No one deserves to be hit.

DEPRESSION

Recognizing the Signs of Depression

1. Does he experience feelings of worthlessness or excessive and inappropriate guilt?
2. Does his pleasure in nearly all activities seem to be markedly decreased?
3. Has he had significant weight loss or decrease in appetite?
4. Does he experience insomnia nearly every night? Or does he sleep excessively?
5. Does he ever express suicidal thoughts?
6. Does he exhibit extreme fatigue and physical slowness? Or agitation and unusual irritability?
7. Does he seem to be unusually withdrawn or engaging in more drinking or drug use than usual?

Note: Having several of these symptoms is an indicator of major depression, and the person should immediately be encouraged to go or, if necessary, be taken to a licensed mental health professional who may prescribe or refer him for antidepressant medicine.

A less severe form of depression, called *dysthymia,* has some of the same symptoms, though not in as extreme a form. Because of the tendency of most males to deny and repress feelings, signs of depression may be somewhat difficult to detect. Unfortunately, the effort he spends in trying to mask his feelings may actually cut him off even further from the empathy and interactions he needs.

What Are the Causes of Depression?

Common triggers for depression are serious loss, particularly more than one at a time; retirement or loss of a job; death of a loved one; personal disease or injury; and failure to succeed at work. A history of depression or alcoholism in his immediate family may indicate a biological tendency toward depression. Other biological causes are hypothyroidism or alcohol or sedative abuse.

Helping Him Identify His ABCs

First, have him list the activating events (or *A*s) about which he is feeling most depressed and the self-defeating consequences (*C*s).

Next, help him pin down the kinds of irrational beliefs (*B*s) about these events that are causing him to feel so down:

1. I should not have done this (or this should not have happened to me).
2. Because I/it did, I am no good and can never be happy again.
3. I deserve to suffer or be punished.

Finally, help him challenge or dispute these irrational beliefs until he arrives at a new, more rational set of self-messages. Because he may be firmly wedded to the idea that he is a worthless person, it may be helpful to employ examples related to others. For example, ask him, "If a friend of yours lost his job or made a bad mistake or failed at something, would that friend be a rotten, condemnable person?" And "If not, why not?"

This process is most helpful if you can write down these thoughts together on a troubleshooting form. An example follows:

Troubleshooting Form
Activating Events: • Loss of job • Death of father **Self-Defeating Consequences:** • **Emotional:** Depressed • **Behavioral:** Procrastinating on completing résumé; obsessing about the things he wishes he had told his father

---

Troubleshooting Form (Continued)

Irrational Beliefs:

1. I *shouldn't* have lost my job.
2. I'm a *total failure* who will never be able to succeed.
3. I *should* have behaved better with my father.
4. I'm a *rotten person* because I didn't.

By encouraging your partner to dispute the idea that failing or behaving badly makes him a hopeless, rotten person, he might arrive at something like the following:

Rational Countermessages:

1. It's *unfortunate* that I lost my job, and it probably would have been preferable if I had done certain things differently. I am, however, a *fallible human being*.
2. It's *unfortunate* that I didn't tell my father how much he did for me; but that doesn't make me a rotten person—*just imperfect, like all humans*.

Other Techniques for Combating Depression

See the following section, "Light Those Fires!" In addition, try some of these suggestions:

1. Let him know that even though these things are very, very painful, and it seems as if the pain will never end, frequently we can learn a lot from them: they become stepping-stones to doing better in the future.
2. Have him state aloud two positive things about himself every day, morning and evening, to remind him that he also has *good* traits and accomplishments.

3. To help him move toward a more optimistic view, encourage him to use the term *temporary*. For example: "I am now out of a job, *but that is temporary.*" "I am now feeling very depressed over my dad's death, *but my depression is temporary.*" Coping statements, such as "This too shall pass," can also be helpful.

4. If his depression is biological, keep reassuring him that even though his worthlessness and hopelessness feel incredibly "real," they are occurring partly because he is probably "off" chemically.

5. Remind him that sometimes acting in a more positive and enthusiastic way will often get much better results and cooperation than acting negatively or moaning about how lousy everything is.

Light Those Fires!

The best antidote to boredom and burnout is to develop some vital, absorbing interests, which will help each of you become more emotionally alive. With a relative absence of anxiety, hostility, or depression, you can be freed up to pursue what interests you. Many of these methods for getting your nonsexual "juices" flowing can and should be done separately; they will provide an opportunity for some independent activity, which you can then share with each other. Others—such as some cultural activities or a couples' massage course—can be done together.

Such energizers will provide you with an alternative to your reliance on him to stoke your fires. And it will provide him with creative alternatives to vegetating or to having outside affairs to feel young and alive.

Stimulate Your Minds

Learn something new or revive an old interest:

1. Take a writing workshop (short story, journal writing, poetry) at a university or community college or YMCA.
2. Take singing lessons.
3. Learn to play a musical instrument (or go back to the one you abandoned in high school).
4. Sign up for a photography or drama class.
5. Learn three new words a week.
6. Watch public television to improve your intellect and broaden your horizons.
7. Read a work of literature or a self-help book at least once a month.
8. Learn a new language and reward yourselves by taking a trip to a country where the language is spoken.

Do Good Deeds

Doing good deeds for others—without expecting any compensation—is one of the very best ways to enrich your life and overcome inertia, boredom, or depression. In addition, it's a fine way to meet potential new friends.

1. Join a political or social "cause," such as a wildlife preservation group or a political campaign.
2. Volunteer to raise money for public television.
3. Join a church or synagogue group.
4. Volunteer in a community agency such as Big Brothers, a hospital, or an organization for the homeless; call your local United Way or other charity organizations for more ideas.
5. Help carry an elderly person's packages.

Do Something Playful or Spiritually Uplifting

1. Do some physical activity—at a level that's right for *you*. Discuss a workable plan with your doctor.

2. Watch inspirational films.
3. Listen to music with your eyes closed. Attend a religious service. Take a meditation course or get a massage.
4. Walk barefoot in the mud. Ride a carousel horse. Sing in the shower. Let a puppy lick your fingers. Allow yourself to experience the aimless playfulness you had as a child. Be willing to look foolish and laugh at yourself.
5. Change the image you project by starting to wear jaunty hats or jazzy socks or consciously eliminating put-downs from your conversations. Often, by projecting yourself differently and drawing different reactions from people, you eventually become the new improved person you're projecting.

Encourage Some Solitude

Couples tend to have a better chance of having a good relationship if they don't feel they own each other's time and resent their mate's independent activity. Solitude can soothe the soul when you learn how to use it. Some people like to spend three or four hours alone a day; others find it difficult to handle any time alone. What's "healthy"? Spending almost all of your waking hours alone probably isn't the best choice; nor is never having any time to yourself. The key is *balance*.

Many men, despite their protestations of independence, seem to have a harder time being alone than do women. Even though your mate may be there only in body, he still wants you by his side. One reason may be that he doesn't know how to fill the solitude, and that frightens him.

Help Him Become Nondependent and Develop Outside Friendships

If you want your man to develop some survival skills, first teach him how to microwave. It's amazing how even in the nineties many men have so few basic skills. And don't allow yourself to feel guilty if he has to heat up his dinner or make a salad.

Another way of helping him develop more autonomy as well as better intimacy skills is to encourage his having intimate friendships. Although many males have men they "do things with," such as golf competitors, drinking buddies, or business friends, you rarely hear a man talking proudly about his "best friend." Maintaining his lawn is usually given far greater priority than maintaining his friendships.

You might coach him to deeper friendships by picking someone he already knows and potentially could become closer to. Encourage him to have dinner alone with his associate, during which he might open up about himself and attempt to get his friend to do so as well.

Another good way to help him bond with other males would be to encourage his participation in men's groups. Because of the publicity surrounding two books—Robert Bly's *Iron John* and Sam Keen's *Fire in the Belly*—men's groups are beginning to burgeon, much in the way that women's groups did in the 1970s. There are also at least two national quarterlies devoted specifically to the men's movement—*MAN!* and *Wingspan*.

Growing Older Gracefully

Your own attitude and emotional response to growing older not only can help make *your* middle and golden years enjoyable but also can help provide your mate with a good coping model.

SEVERE SCREWBALLS

Heather, who comes from an "uptight WASP family" headed by her rigid, stuffy father, was swept off her feet by André's burning black eyes, intense intellect, and dazzling poetry.

Don'ts	Dos
1. Overstate your own aging processes.	1. Emphasize the attractive attributes you both continue to have, be it a flair for dressing or a twinkly smile.
2. Focus on what you *should* have or *could* have done. The past is the past.	
3. Avoid trying new things because you're "too old" or it's "too late."	2. In discussing your own or your mate's past, assess the things you're not happy about (e.g., not being a better parent). Then work on what to do about these issues now rather than engage in self-recrimination.
4. Preoccupy yourself with the horrors of being widowed and thus cling to him.	
	3. Redefine your personal goals. As a joint project, make a list of your "Second Half of Life Goals," in five-year segments, up to age ninety-five.
	4. Learn to value wisdom and find ways of celebrating what you've learned about life over the years.

In dark, romantic cafés he pressed her hand, told her how much he adored her, and recited poetry to her. They talked for hours. He was "the first man I'd ever met who could really talk about feelings," she confided wistfully. It took her many months to realize that the talk and the feelings were overwhelmingly about him, rarely her.

For three months they had wonderful, passionate sex. Then, without warning, he became increasingly moody, critical, and withdrawn, attacking the very things he had loved about her three months before. Her free-lance commercial art business, once an impressive sign of success to him, became labeled as "hack work—a sellout." When she dressed up in the sexy short skirts that before had so turned him on, he now got angry and called her a whore. He made little effort to write or to earn money, claiming "*I'm* an artist. I can't just grind work out like *you* do."

She lay awake night after night, wanting him to come to bed even if only to talk, but he continued to avoid her. At times she would gently touch him, but he would literally brush her off. The more he withdrew, the more desperate she became for sexual contact "to validate who I was." She thought, if I do better, I'll make him want me again. The many friends she turned to remained loving and supportive. Eventually, though, she began to feel so ashamed about her "addiction" to him that she distanced herself from her friends.

Anger, low frustration tolerance, anxiety, and depression are present to some extent, in varying degrees, in most of us. In people like André, however, these traits are embedded in a defective "character structure" that makes them far less likely to be changed. These more serious disturbances are known as *personality disorders*. If you recognize in your mate any of the following descriptions, your chances of getting him to connect better with you, sexually or nonsexually, may be slim—especially without the aid of a competent therapist. And your attempts to alter his hurtful behavior will only succeed in making him act more unfeeling.

NARCISSISTIC PERSONALITY DISORDERS

One of my friends recently quipped, "My ex and I had one thing in common: we both loved him and hated me!"

Narcissistic people, as psychiatrist Otto Kernberg describes them, are people concerned with their own gratification. They find it nearly impossible to empathize with another person's needs or viewpoint, but have a strong sense that they deserve others' approval or admiration. They want love but are incapable of giving and are fearful of attachments lest they become dependent. They often have a strong need for new experiences. When confronted with their self-absorption, they are likely to turn things around and call you a chronic complainer. Frequently very charming, they find it easy to surround themselves with those who will dote on them and find little need to listen to others' "trivia" or worry about the kind of impression they are making. Often they are emotionally shallow, exploitative, have a sense of emptiness and meaninglessness, or experience bouts of insecurity, which they immediately try to stanch by seeking new admirers. They are especially allergic to the kind of give-and-take and stick-to-itiveness required in successful long-term relationships.

The narcissist, according to Kernberg, may have a generally impoverished sex life. He will frequently value and talk about a sex partner's body parts more than the partner herself, out of a need to deny her importance. Ultimately he is likely to become bored with his partner and seek out women, especially those valued by others, with whom he can have intense new experiences—only to begin to devalue the new women.

EXCESSIVE GUILT, FEAR, OR SHAME LEADING TO SEXUAL AVERSION

Recognizing the Signs

1. Has his avoidance of sex been chronic? Has there ever been a time when he experienced a pleasurable sexual relationship?
2. Is there disgust or extreme aversion, especially to the vagina or to oral sex?
3. Does he come from a strict religious background? Do any other family members have sexual problems?
4. Does he view masturbation as sinful and engage in it rarely, if ever?

5. Is there a possible history of sex abuse of him or other family members? Inappropriate exposure during childhood to coital sex?
6. Does he rarely if ever have erotic dreams, thoughts, or fantasies? Or, if he does, does he immediately try to suppress them?
7. Is he generally fearful and inhibited about his body and nudity? Fearful of handling bodily fluids such as sweat, saliva, semen, or vaginal lubrication?
8. Does he feel disgust, revulsion, or panic in response to sexual stimulation?

What Are the Causes of Extreme Sexual Aversion?

It is currently believed, by Helen Singer Kaplan and other leading sex therapists, that a *quiet avoidance* of sex, due to a lack of interest or low desire, and an *active, phobic aversion* are really two distinctly different entities and stem from different causes.

Frequently the kind of intense, irrational fear that results in sexual aversion extends to other areas that might involve issues of separation, rejection, or criticism. People with sexual phobias may also have a history of other phobias. Although sexual aversion may have multiple causes, most frequently cited among them are having been sexually abused or having had a smothering, overly protective, seductive, or overly critical mother in combination with an absent or aloof father. In the latter case, men frequently doubt their own masculinity and ability to perform and have considerable passivity and basic feelings of inadequacy in other areas of their life as well.

Helping Him Identify His ABCs

To help your man come to terms with any aversion to sex he may feel, first have him list the specific conditions or activating events (*A*s) which he feels upset about and avoids. Next, help him figure out and write down the kinds of irrational beliefs he is maintaining *about* these *A*s. And finally, help him dispute or challenge these irrational beliefs until he arrives at some new, more rational countermessages.

Here is the troubleshooting form worked out by Gail and her twenty-nine-year-old boyfriend, Carl. Carl, who had come from a very puritanical family, had had only a couple of previous sexual relationships and had virtually no sex with Gail.

Troubleshooting Form

Activating Events:

- Gail wants regular sex with me.
- Sex is something my family has always taught me is dirty and sinful.

Self-Defeating Consequences:

- **Emotional:** Anxious; irritated with Gail's sexual needs
- **Behavioral:** Putting Gail off whenever she expresses interest in having sex or talking about why we're *not* having it

Irrational Beliefs:

1. Sex is *too uncomfortable*. I *can't stand* having to face something I've always thought was dirty and evil. If I have sex, I may lose control, and something *terrible* may happen.
2. Gail is a *rotten person* for continuing to "bug me" about sex.
3. This is just the way I am, and I'll *never* be able to change, so I'll just keep avoiding it, and maybe it will go away.

By encouraging Carl to question some of his irrational ideas, Gail and he came up with the following:

Troubleshooting Form (Continued)
Rational Countermessages: 1. Even though sex for me is very uncomfortable, I can push myself and perhaps start with nongenital sex. Even though I might feel anxious, nothing terrible will happen. 2. Just because my father and my religious education taught me that sex was vile doesn't make it true. 3. Just because I'm uptight about sex now doesn't mean I'll never change. If I keep avoiding the problem, it won't go away and will probably keep me from achieving a good healthy relationship with Gail or any other woman.

Tips for You

Early disturbing experiences surrounding sex that result in this degree of inhibition and avoidance are probably not going to be solved for most people without the aid of some professional counseling, preferably by a person trained in sex therapy. A male sexuality group might also help him become less inhibited about sex. The *sensate focus* exercises described in Chapter 9 can provide other good ways for allowing feelings about sex and physical contact to be expressed and dealt with. In Carl's case the dialogue that opened up between Gail and him became a catalyst for his beginning individual therapy. Now he continues to work on these and other issues related to his repressive upbringing and is gradually increasing his sexual contact with Gail. She reports he is "definitely less squeamish and really *there* when we have sex—I used to feel he had taken off for another planet."

AVOIDANCE THAT MAY STEM FROM HOMOSEXUAL INCLINATIONS

In part because we still live in a society that stigmatizes homosexuality, and more recently because of the AIDS crisis, a certain number of men whose main sexual interest is in other men are trying to function as heterosexuals. How do you know if this may be true in your man's case?

He may exhibit many of the same signs as the man carrying sexual aversion from a puritanical or an abusive background. If not willing to acknowledge his inclination, however, he may be extremely difficult to identify. Although he may actually have a fairly strong sexual drive, and masturbate regularly, when a man with homosexual inclinations deals with women only the smallest part of his sexual drive may be operating. If he is gay, there is probably not much you are going to be able to do to inspire his sexual interest, and unless you decide you can live comfortably in a relationship without sex or physical closeness, you're probably best off not pairing with him.

EXTREME FEARS OF INTIMACY

This is one of the biggest complaints expressed by women on the "dating scene." Although some men who fear intimacy do manage eventually to marry, many have only one foot in the nest and maintain a roving eye.

Recognizing the Signs

1. Does he mainly seem to be able to relate to women who are "beneath" him in status, education, or some other way?
2. Does he mainly spend his time with "the boys"?
3. Did he start off in the relationship hot and heavy into sex, only to become, perhaps within a matter of months, relatively disinterested in initiating it with you?
4. Does he seem to lack the familiarity with intimacy that teaches people that they have to endure some uncomfortable or difficult periods in relationships and forgo some of the satisfactions of "the single life" in return for some solid benefits?

5. Has he ever said to you that although he's fond of you and thinks you're terrific, you're not his "ideal woman"?
6. Does he seem to have a fair amount of contempt for women, including his mother?
7. Does he fail to give you much in the way of physical or emotional stroking, rarely hugging or kissing you except when it is time for sex?
8. Does he seem to be highly absorbed in things such as sports, computer games, or his work, but not in you?
9. Does he practically have a panic attack or claustrophobia if you sit down and try to discuss your relationship with him? Turn pale at the mention of commitment?

Although this syndrome can exist to varying degrees in different kinds of men as well as women, it tends to be highly prevalent among the narcissistic personality type discussed on page 194. You probably will not connect with him no matter how much you struggle. Pay particular attention if he's dominating, won't communicate, or feels you're imposing on him if you want him to do things to please you. Your best bet with this kind of man is to leave while you still have your wits about you.

HELPING HIM WITH HIS ANXIETY OVER SEXUAL DYSFUNCTIONS

A substantial number of the men who are avoiding sex may do so not because of lack of desire or arousal, but rather out of anxiety about erections or other aspects of sexual "performance."

This fear leads to a process that Masters and Johnson call *spectatoring,* in which the man—instead of experiencing it as a loose, playful activity—turns sex into a stressful event during which he watches himself like a hawk for any signs of erectile failure. The usual result of this is that he becomes less aroused since his main focus is not on his *pleasurable sensations* but rather on the quality of his erection. And what does he have riding on the quality of his erection? To him it is his self-worth and masculinity. And that's enough to make anyone go limp.

Any woman who has found herself with trouble having orgasms has probably experienced the same situation. The more you tell yourself you "should" be coming, and that there's something wrong with you if you're not, the harder it is to focus on erotic sensations to help you become aroused or to orgasm.

Sadly, his unwillingness to talk about his problem means his ability to do something about it gets cut off at the pass. Most of the time, when people are able to talk about their feelings and behaviors and receive help in dealing with them, their anxiety and feelings of shame tend to decrease, making change possible.

Getting back to the ABCs: It's not "performance" problems at point A that are causing his shame, anxiety, or avoidance; rather it's the *view he takes of them* or his *beliefs* about them. The lower his self-acceptance and frustration tolerance, the higher yours will need to be if you want to help him function better sexually.

Start by talking about his feelings about sex in a relaxed setting, where sexual activity is clearly not on the agenda. Gently ask him how he feels when he finds himself or his penis not responding the way he'd like. Explain to him that these kinds of problems are perfectly normal and that although you can be satisfied by him quite nicely with or without an erection, you'd like to see if there's any way you can be helpful to him since he's shown some concern. Reassure him that by talking about his thoughts and experiences you'll both have a clearer idea of what his "turnoff mechanisms" are. Perhaps together you can develop more relaxed or comfortable feelings about sex. Explain that it's anxiety or feelings of inadequacy that are probably overriding his sexual desire circuits and suggest he try not to focus on his penis, but on things that will help him feel generally relaxed and sensually alive.

You may find it helpful to fill out a troubleshooting form with him. Begin with the *A,* or activating event, that is his particular sexual dysfunction. Then get him to list his self-defeating reactions and finally help him list his irrational beliefs. To help him get in better touch with what he is feeling and thinking, suggest that he try to reexperience his last unpleasant sexual encounter in his mind's eye.

Here is the troubleshooting form worked out by Hank and Sarah, a couple in their late forties.

Troubleshooting Form

Activating Event:

Sarah wants sex with me, and my penis is getting only mildly erect.

Self-Defeating Consequences:

- *Emotional:* Frustrated, anxious, ashamed
- *Behavioral:* Avoiding sexual situations, picking fights

Irrational Beliefs:

1. My penis *should* be harder. I feel like such a wimp because it's not.
2. I can't stand feeling so uncomfortable. What's the use of trying? It's just not going to work.
3. I can't have "real" sex—intercourse—without it. She's just trying to make me feel better when she says she doesn't need intercourse to be sexually satisfied.

Finally, Sarah helped Hank dispute his irrational beliefs by posing the following questions to him:

1. Who says that just because you want it to, your penis *must* get hard?
2. Where's the evidence that when your sex organ is engorged you're a *man,* and when it isn't you're *not?*

Troubleshooting Form

3. Lots of things in life are uncomfortable: who says you *must not be uncomfortable* when things aren't going the way you'd like? Can you *really* not stand it?

4. Tingling and feeling close and having orgasms can all happen without an erection. Who says that that's not "really" sex? Not me!

After Hank responded to the preceding questions, the couple helped develop these countermessages together:

Rational Countermessages:

1. Even though I'd strongly *like* my penis to get hard, there's no universal law that says it *must*.
2. Not getting an erection doesn't make me a wimp: just a man whose penile blood vessels aren't engorged!
3. I'll be somewhat uncomfortable if my penis doesn't get or stay erect. But I won't die of discomfort.
4. My willingness to satisfy Sarah is what counts. She's going to be far happier that I'm willing to please her than if I just keep avoiding sex with her.

Some Other Tips

1. Let him know you really feel good about his willingness to share his feelings with you and to consider other ways of trying to satisfy you.
2. Keep working at not getting too upset if he continues to try to brush you off. No matter how much you try to reassure them, partners with low desire or arousal problems often feel inadequate, yet at the same time resentful of their partner's "demands."
3. Tell him the world won't come to an end, nor will you love him one bit less, if he doesn't get an erection.

4. Suggest that he keep reminding himself: "I have the right to have a sexual problem."
5. Employ some of the techniques referred to in Chapter 9 to help him stop focusing on penetration and to learn to enjoy his whole body and yours, with or without intercourse or even genital contact.
6. Remind him that what you and most sane women really want is a human being who is *connecting* with them, not a superman with an ever-ready penis. Read him the following quote, provided by Bernie Zilbergeld, of one woman's preference in sex:

> I like a man who feels free to be vulnerable, to give up his masculine stereotype, who can be gentle and sensitive and passive, as well as aggressive. . . . A man who can relinquish control of the love-making and allow it to be a shared experience. A man who can tolerate imperfections in himself, his penis, and me. . . .

Getting Him to See a Therapist

Psychotherapists can include clinical psychologists, social workers, and psychiatrists. *Sex therapists* are people who are licensed in one of these professions or in urology, gynecology, or internal medicine but who, in addition, have specialized training in sex therapy. The two main organizations that monitor professional certification in sex therapy—the American Board of Sexology and AASECT—are listed in Chapter 6.

An assessment of any therapist—a general psychotherapist, couples' therapist, or a sex therapist—should include answering these questions:

- How comfortable does the therapist seem with the topic of sex?
- Do you both like him or her as a person?
- Does the therapist behave in an ethical and professional manner?

- Does the therapist give you some kind of practical input, as opposed to just saying "Uh-huh" or "Tell me more about your mother"?

To find a good therapist, follow some of the suggestions already mentioned in Chapter 6.

Most men are particularly resistant to seeing a therapist. But if your partner has serious depression or anger problems, is a substance abuser, was the victim of abuse and this has not been resolved, has long-standing phobias or sexual problems, or is involved in an active extramarital affair, or your marriage is on the brink of dissolving, he's probably not going to get too far without professional help—your best efforts notwithstanding. If he is a substance abuser and staunchly refuses professional help, then suggest he go to Rational Recovery (call **916-621-4374** for information) or AA for a few sessions to try it out while you go to Al Anon for support and ideas. After getting the names of two or three competent therapists, suggest that he at least go and see them for a couple of consultations, then make his decision after he has some actual data.

Be somewhat leery of approaches that spend years going over childhood events without giving you ways to change these patterns in the present or of costly intensive weekends that aim for helping people *feel* better rather than *get* better.

In general your best bet is someone you feel a good connection with, preferably one who specializes in rational-emotive or cognitive behavior therapy—approaches that are relatively time-limited, don't spend excessive time doing an archaeological dig of the past, and have dozens of studies that document their effectiveness. Most sex therapists employ cognitive behavioral and rational-emotive techniques as core ingredients of their therapy.

CHAPTER 8

CONSTRUCTIVELY COMMUNICATING YOUR FEELINGS AND PREFERENCES

"When we wake up in the morning we are fresh. We must go immediately to work. Then when the employer has wrung every bit of usefulness out of us, we are rushed into a crowded bus or thrown into a tangled expressway and told to fight our way home. Once there, at the low point of our energy, we pick up our marriage."
—Richard Lessor

Diane, a thirty-three-year-old law office administrator, has had a grand total of one sexual encounter with her thirty-five-year-old partner Jonathan, a successful real estate broker, during the past three months. Things had been tenuous between them the past year, after a first year-and-a-half idyll that began when they had run gratefully into each other's arms from what each of them described as "horrendous" relationships.

Diane had loved Jonathan's nurturing and sensitivity and was especially touched by how good he was at caring for his six-year-old son on his weekends with him. In addition to the many recreational and cultural interests the couple shared, Jonathan respected Diane's financial and emotional independence, a far cry from his ex-wife's total, clinging dependency.

After living together for some time, however, their physical intimacy as well as their friendship seemed to be drying up. Both of them were growing queasy about their plans to marry. A final, desperate attempt at couples counseling over four months had dramatically improved things, however. A good deal of their anger and hurt had been dispelled, and communication between them was improving. Both were experiencing a distinct thaw and the return of loving and, yes, even sexual feelings.

Now as we sat in session, they reviewed the past weekend. It had been especially good, and the loving feelings that they had thought had dried up were coming back. For the first time in quite a while, Diane felt positive and confident enough to think about approaching Jonathan sexually. However, the minute they arrived home on Sunday evening, he made a beeline for his computer to finish some work he had put off. Though disappointed, Diane decided to apply some of the techniques she had recently learned in therapy and deal with her need for an instant response from Jonathan by calming herself down by reading a book so he would have some time to work.

Forty-five minutes later he came through the living room and in response to her sultry "C'mon over here, honey," said impatiently, "Later—I've got to get my stuff ready for tomorrow." At that Diane exploded.

When they described the next ten minutes to me, I pointed out they could have been used as a model in a handbook on *destructive fighting*. The highlights went something like this:

Diane: You really make me sick. We have a great weekend, and there's finally a chance to have sex and get things back on the right track. But you are just too busy. Frankly, I think you've got some serious sex hang-ups, buster. I'm fed up with this whole relationship. It's never going to go anywhere. We may as well break up.

Jonathan: You're such a selfish princess. When you want to have sex, I'm just supposed to drop everything and jump into bed with you. You always have to have what you want when you want it. You're totally neurotic and impossible: you're getting more like your mother every day.

Diane then ran into the bedroom and slammed the door. Jonathan slept on the couch—badly—and left for work the next morning before Diane woke up.

This story, it turns out, has a happy ending. Rather than becoming the ax that split them apart, the argument and its aftermath became a real turning point in the way they were able to resolve hurts and impasses. By following the basic guidelines in this chapter, they were able to patch things up by themselves the very next day.

We'll return to their story later in this chapter. But first, let's clarify why good communication is so very important in a relationship, and go over some tips on how to make it happen for you.

WHAT'S THE BIG DEAL ABOUT COMMUNICATION?

Intimate communication conjures up images of a candlelit table in a restaurant where two people lean toward each other in intense conversation. Not many people, I think, would complain about being involved in that kind of scenario.

What happens when we extend the concept of communication to include *sharing the day's events, negotiating conflicts, and talking about feelings?* There is a large group of people—many of them male—who experience an aversion, even terror, in response to this kind of intimacy. Some fear it in the same way they fear commitment. Unlike most women, who view communication as a means of strengthening their relationship, many men fear it will erode their relationship—or, possibly, erode *them*.

THE GOAL OF GOOD COMMUNICATION

The fact is, relationships are not sustained by candlelit dinners and moonlight walks; if so, they'd starve to death. Good relationships are nurtured by the kind of intimacy Maggie Scarf speaks of in *Intimate Partners:* "a person's ability to talk about who he really is, and to say what he wants and needs, and to be heard by the intimate partner." Comparing experiences and information at the end of the day, giving each other the kind of positive feedback that helps each feel special and appreciated, respected, and loved; and being able to talk through upset feelings to conclusion are among the most commonly cited ingredients that distinguish functional from dysfunctional relationships.

In a study of 750 couples in conflict, the most frequently given reason for being on the road to divorce was "lack of communication," followed by "constant arguments." When 400 leading psychiatrists were asked why marriages fail, 45 percent of them said that the primary cause of divorce in America was the husband's inability to communicate his feelings; only 9 percent blamed sexual imcompatibility.

It isn't lust, perhaps, that leads people to seek out extramarital relationships so much as it is the need to feel heard, comforted, and understood—to feel that you are with an ally rather than an adversary.

LEARNING TO COMMUNICATE CONSTRUCTIVELY

This chapter will teach you some communication techniques culled from those found to be most effective by psychologists and counselors in helping couples maintain healthy and enduring relationships. I suggest that you first practice these methods in less "loaded" nonsexual situations, then work your way up to areas, such as sex, that are more difficult to talk about.

Assessing Your Nonconstructive Communication Patterns

Does either of you engage in any of the following nonconstructive communication practices when you try to discuss something?

1. *Overgeneralize:* Make "you always" or "you never" statements?
2. *Name-call, or use stereotyping words:* Do you call your partner a "selfish bastard" or "male chauvinist pig," or "totally insensitive," a "nag," or a "hysterical female"?
3. *Keep digging up the past,* or what George Bach calls "playing archaeologist"—especially when what's happened can't be changed?
4. *Collect resentments* for weeks until one day they come out in a giant explosion over a seemingly innocuous trigger?
5. *Use overkill,* such as threatening to divorce him if he doesn't mow the lawn?
6. *Fail to validate or acknowledge each other's feelings or viewpoint*— overriding each other and continuing only to push your own point of view?
7. *Go over the same old arguments and accusations,* with no new information and without stopping to check whether your partner has understood?

8. *Fail to bring up anything positive* about your partner or the nice things he or she may have done—in the past, if not recently?

9. *Try to "guilt-trip" the other,* using maneuvers such as saying the argument is making you feel sick or playing the poor, beleaguered "victim"?

10. *"Kitchen-sink":* Throw too many topics into the hopper at once, failing to distinguish major issues from minor ones, and thus wind up without resolving any of them?

11. *Become overwhelmed by anger, hate, or despair:* Do you yell or scream? Interrupt or "talk over" your partner? Stomp out of the room, throw things, or lapse into heavy, icy silences?

12. *Use the "accusatory you":* "You don't love me" or "You always do this to me" or "You never listen"?

When the focus of an argument is on mutual blaming, couples toss the causes of their unhappiness back and forth like a hot potato, dredging up all their old injuries and everything they dislike about each other. What's more, they *cling to this pattern,* no matter how many dozens of times it hasn't solved anything, rather than try something new.

HOW DO FUNCTIONAL COUPLES COMMUNICATE?

For starters, they *don't* spend most of their time talking in the way Lillian Rubin describes in her 1976 study of blue-collar marriages: *"at* each other, *past* each other, *through* each other—rarely *with* or *to* each other."

When functional couples communicate, they do not necessarily "mince words." Indeed, many are quite forthright and vigorous in stating or arguing for their positions. Instead of getting stuck in communication ruts, however ("You're shouting." "No, I'm not shouting; you are!"), they are able to (1) clearly define the issue and agree they *both* have the problem, (2) stay focused on the *topic* of the discussion, and (3) hear, acknowledge, and attempt to understand each other's position. They see conflicts as challenges that can help strengthen their relationship and provide them *both* with some of what they want, rather than battles where one wins and the other loses.

How do they accomplish this? Here are seven keys to success.

They Manage Their Anger and Other Upset Feelings Effectively

Overwhelmingly the most important factor in maintaining constructive communication is *managing one's own emotions,* especially extreme anger.

Summarizing what we've discussed in Chapters 3, 4, and 7, this means remembering the following:

1. I have the power—no matter how poorly the other person is acting—to regulate how upset I get about his behavior.
2. Even if he doesn't respond the way I like, I can continue to express my concern without either yielding or blaming him if he reacts nastily or doesn't seem to hear my point of view.
3. I will remember that hostility and the need to win or be right sap my valuable energy.

If you often feel yourself on the verge of crumbling, before you next have an important discussion with your mate, you might try using psychologist Susan Forward's creative technique. Picture yourself as a castle. Around the castle, construct walls made of all positive labels about you. Now imagine the castle under siege and your partner's negative labels as arrows being shot at the castle. Picture the negative arrows hitting the protective wall of the castle and falling into the moat—ineffective against the strength of your positive labels. Psychologist Dan Kiley suggests another good imagery technique for dealing with a belligerent man: visualize him as a little boy dressed up like John Wayne but with a gun in one hand and a tattered blanket in the other hand and a pacifier sticking out of his pocket.

They Believe in Assertive Expression

Women and men with good, clear communication believe that:

1. I have the right to express my feelings and needs.
2. My speaking up about my wants and desires does not make me "aggressive" or "castrating" despite what the culture or my mate says.
3. I hope that he or she doesn't get upset or reject me if I say something he does not like; but if the worst happens, I will survive.
4. Her or his minimizing, putting down, or ignoring my needs does not nullify me, or make me worth less. It means that I am being *given* less—as opposed to *being* less. *Self-acceptance* is the best defense. Even if my *mate* doesn't seem to be accepting me, *I* can accept me.

They Clearly Define the Issue and Try to Communicate Succinctly About It

One excellent way of keeping your mate and you on track is to use the following form, which will help keep you focused on your feelings and preferences and away from accusatory *you* statements or character attacks.

Tips for Both of You to Bear in Mind When Delivering Criticism

1. Begin by stating your *feelings* (not your beliefs or thoughts). *"I'm feeling frustrated and hurt that we've been having so little physical contact lately"* (instead of *"I think you're really losing your sex drive"* or *"I feel you don't care about my needs"*).

2. Cite a *recent, specific behavior* and keep it *brief*. *"I'm feeling sad that you haven't initiated sex with me in weeks and have told me 'not tonight' several times when I approach you"* (instead of bringing up a litany of past grievances or predicting a dire future).

3. If possible, *make a specific suggestion* for change. *"I would love it if you would pick one occasion in the next week and surprise me with some sort of sexual treat—even if you're not ravishingly horny yourself."*

4. *State the consequences*, preferably in *positive terms*. *"If you would do this, I would feel really good about our relationship and about your trying to do something that means a lot to me."*

This form may seem somewhat simplistic or formulaic; however, it is likely to increase your chances of being clear about what you want and to help you achieve a dialogue that doesn't leave you feeling drained. If you can, prepare your statement in this form in advance and rehearse it with a friend or into a tape recorder.

They Listen to Each Other

What a quaint idea! But you'd be surprised at how selectively people listen to each other—if at all. Mainly people focus on whatever was said that "pushed a button" in them and tune out the rest. By contrast, women who are successful communicators try to start off with the positive assumption that whatever is being said is something their partner is concerned about and that airing the subject will probably lead to some kind of resolution.

If he says, for example, "I don't feel like having sex because I'm just too tired from trying to make a living, and frankly you just don't turn me on anymore," try to resist the temptation to snipe back, "Big deal—I put in a forty-hour week in the office, plus I do all the housework, and *I'm* still up for sex."

Instead, try to focus on these facts: (1) He's at least talking about why he isn't having sex, and therefore some progress is already being made toward a solution. (2) Although he may not be telling you this *directly,* there is a distinct implication that *he* is having a problem—in this case, for example, his problem is he's not getting as turned on as he used to. And if you listen, you might just hear what some of these problems or fears are. (3) His male programming did not equip him to acknowledge weakness or to be particularly skilled at communicating—especially about sex and relationship problems. The best thing you can do is to listen gently, nod reassuringly, feed back to him what you understood him to have said, and, without attacking, try to elicit what he may not be saying or even be in touch with. For example:

"I'm glad we're taking some time to share our feelings about this. It makes me feel you care, and I feel optimistic that we can deal with it. I appreciate how hard your job is and how beat you are at the end of the day and that maybe it's not as easy for you to get turned as it used to be." *(Pause here.)*

Depending on how he responds, you have several options:

Probing questions:

"What feels the worst about this situation?" *(Then don't get upset at what he says.)*

"Are there any other physical or sexual changes you've noticed lately?"

"Are there some things that I might do to help turn you on?"

"Do you have some ideas for ways we might deal with this?" *(Pause here.)* If he has no suggestions, continue:

Behavioral suggestions:
"How about us setting aside some time to just play around and break the ice? No need for erections, orgasms, or any of that stuff. When would you suggest?"

"Let's take a massage course; I know of one that's being given at the community college. I think it would be a great way for us to help each other unwind."

"I've read that lots of couples who have been together for a while have this problem. There are some really good books, or we could go to a counselor who might be able to suggest some things that could help us. Which would you like to try?"

Nonverbal approaches:
Gently massage the inside of his thigh.
Tickle him.
Reach over and give him a hug and say "I love you" *(but don't press for anything more)*.

⚷ They Try Not to Panic

I'm sure there have been occasions when you're appalled to hear your partner, whom you love and who you thought loved you, say what he's just said. It seems as if a vast canyon is suddenly looming between you and things will never be the same. Successful couples are able to keep at bay that momentary sense of panic that the relationship is over. They do this by remembering:

- I've been in this exact state before with this person, over the same or other issues, and we've survived.
- It may seem that way now, but my mate really isn't a horrible, vile person out to destroy me; just a fallible, confused human being saying some not-very-nice or not-very-smart things.

• Out of some of the most painful and scary discussions we've had have come some of the most important leaps in our relationship.

⚷ They Try to Respond with Positives and, Where Appropriate, with Humor

Try to be optimistic—if it kills you. (It won't.) In a study by psychologists Bruce Forman and D. Stein, nondistressed couples were found to be more likely than distressed couples to engage in more positive verbal and nonverbal behavior, to respond to negative stimuli from the other with positive behavior, and to engage in more problem solving. Nondistressed couples also tend to have a much more accurate picture of their mate's personality characteristics, opinions, and roles. As a result they are able to take certain predictable behaviors—such as their mate's walking out of the room when they were in the middle of telling him about something—with a grain of salt and not get upset by them. "Wisdom," said psychologist William James, "is learning what to overlook."

Use of positive behaviors can include sitting beside him and rubbing his neck when he does something you like or, when in a difficult discussion, saying at some point later on, "I've been feeling a lot better since we finally talked things out, even though it was pretty painful for both of us." Let him hear periodically how much you cherish him.

Humor is often the best bet with those infuriating habits that, after ten years of futile "training" on your part, are still going strong. Having decided your mate's advantages definitely outweigh his disadvantages, you have a choice: you can fume and shout when for the 3,742nd time he interrupts you. Or you can take hold of his hands, look into his eyes, and say with affection, not hostility, "Guess what you just did?" In all likelihood, he'll sheepishly say, "Gee, I thought you were finished," and then let you continue.

☦ They Try to Be Empathic

Empathy means trying to imagine what it feels like to be inside the other person's skin. Probably because of all those years spent taking care of dolls and hundreds of hours spent with their "best" girlfriend talking about relationships, women tend to have an easier time being empathic. Although it has been alleged that empathy is something that may be missing from the male chromosome, it is a skill that both males and females can learn.

How can you help your man increase his capacity for empathy? By demonstrating empathy in your own behavior:

1. *Don't shout and throw out barbs or character-assassinating remarks.* Watch his eyes glaze over and his mind move to another stratosphere when you do.
2. *Use analogies* to help your partner better understand your own emotional feelings. For example, you can explain how you sometimes let your sense of self-worth get tied up with your *relationship's* success, just as he at times lets his sense of self-worth become tied to his job success; and that may be why both of you manage to become so preoccupied and stressed out. Or, you might suggest that his anxiety over having to depend on a boss he feels he can't trust because he keeps putting off the promised raise may be similar to your anxiety about relying on a husband who keeps failing to follow through on his promises to have sex.
3. *Touch him reassuringly while he's talking.* Or say, "Yes, go on . . . I'm listening" or "It's OK to feel that." Smile; hold him; help him feel safe. In turn, let him know the kinds of things he can do that are most helpful to you.
4. *Remember that intimate communication is very painful and hard for him.* Here is some sensitive advice, from a male, on how to help him share his feelings:

Be patient with me. It's hard to explain how incredibly difficult it is for me to express my feelings. I get very uncomfortable and anxious when I think my defenses are being stripped
away. Try to be supportive; go slowly and don't push or try
to figure me out. If you look at my body you'll see I tend to
clutch my hands or tap my foot when I begin to feel tense.
I'm always worried you'll laugh at me or think I'm a weak-
ling, or do something to hurt me if I let down my defenses.
Encourage me, but don't treat me like a child. If I start crying,
don't rush to my rescue: let me work it through myself. Wait
for me to reach out to you. Don't push me or try to convince
me of anything . . . just let me bumble along or even be
arrogant or foolish for a while.

5. *Don't be defensive.* Happily married couples are not so locked
   into defensiveness or attacking attitudes that they can't listen to
   and acknowledge the other's position. Saying a simple thing like
   "You're right—I did screw up" can go a very long way toward
   defusing your partner's anger.

   For example, one couple I know had for weeks been planning
   a date in a special restaurant. When the evening came, the husband was exhausted. His wife was deeply disappointed but said
   only, "Yes, I see you're really tired." He said: "I know you were
   really looking forward to getting out of the house." As a result
   the dialogue got moved into a negotiating mode. They decided
   to watch a film on TV and rebook the dinner reservation for
   Sunday evening. And because this woman did not rigidly cling
   to her romantic dinner scenario, the couple had sex twice that
   weekend.

6. *Some other examples of good use of empathic assertion:*
   Instead of saying,

   > "If you really loved me, you would have managed to find
   > some time this weekend for us to have had sex; you'd think I
   > was asking you to do such an odious thing!"

   Try saying,

   > *"Honey, I know how exhausted you are during the week and how*

many things there are to get caught up on during the weekend. And I know you really love me. But I'm afraid if we don't deal with this issue, we're just going to keep tripping over it, and it will erode our love and friendship. I'd really appreciate your giving it some serious thought; then let's plan on brainstorming some ideas tomorrow night."

Instead of saying,

"How many times have I told you that you shouldn't be late when we're meeting people for dinner? Don't you care about anyone but yourself?"

Try saying,

"*I guess it must seem like I'm asking a lot from you sometimes.* But it's really inconvenient when I have to try to make excuses when you're late. *I realize you don't do it deliberately.* How about my calling you at the office to remind you? I'd really like your cooperation in this. I think you'd wind up being less hassled, and it would create less inconvenience for whomever we're meeting."

7. *Empathize about the difficulty of having upsetting disagreements.* "*I know it's not pleasant to have these disagreements,* and I know I'm not exactly perfect in the way I handle them. But I feel you're being sarcastic now, and it's keeping us from staying focused on the problem so that we can resolve it. It almost seems like you'd rather fight than get along—and I'm seriously concerned about that. I think we have a problem, and it's important for us not to ignore it. And I'd like us to be able to try to share our thoughts and feelings as best we can, even if we disagree."

When he stays with a difficult discussion, say "Thanks for understanding" or "I appreciate your listening."

DIANE AND JONATHAN—"TAKE TWO"

And now, back to Diane and Jonathan, the couple we met at the beginning of this chapter. As you may recall, they were able to talk through "the Sunday night debacle" in a way that made them feel more optimistic about the future of their relationship.

Diane phoned Jonathan the next day at work and said, "I think our relationship is hopeless." He responded, "Well, that was a pretty painful evening. But I think it's important to see conflicts like these as temporary hurdles and not the end of the relationship. I'm really sorry about my lack of consideration and putting you off. And although I can't really talk more right now, I'd like us to set aside some time after dinner to talk about how we can avoid crossing signals so badly next time."

For one thing, this reminder *not to panic or feel hopeless* when there was a major conflict or impasse helped Diane feel much less anxious and more hopeful about their future. Also important was Jonathan's having broken his usual pattern of yelling and accusation, which she had found hard to live with.

After dinner that night, Jonathan explained he had been concerned about preparing for the next day so he could come to bed without feeling distracted. Diane refrained from putting him down for his being so obsessive-compulsive. Instead she suggested that this preoccupation with all the things he "had to do" was what kept him stressed and distracted during the day as well, and that maybe he needed to work out some better ways of handling his overconcern about unfinished tasks and to learn to relax and just "be in the moment."

Jonathan agreed, adding that if he had it to do over again, instead of just saying "later," he would at least have come over and kissed Diane and been more specific, saying something like "How about another fifteen minutes?"

During their session I explored with Jonathan whether any other feelings had come up when Diane had said seductively, "C'mon over here." After a few moments of silence, he acknowledged, "I felt somewhat as though I were being required to perform on command—maybe like I wasn't really in the driver's seat. Though hearing myself, I know that's pretty chauvinistic and not very rational. Also—the last couple of times we had sex I didn't perform too well." I gave him a homework assignment to dispute the ideas that (1) it emasculated him if his partner initiated sex and (2) if his penis didn't spring to attention right away, it was the end of the world. The goal, I emphasized, was to "connect, not erect."

When I asked Diane what she might have done differently, she said she would have reminded herself, "I have the choice not to become hurt and angry." Then she would have approached Jonathan, seductively, and said, "I can't possibly wait any longer for your scrumptious body. I guess you're just going to have to get your stuff ready later or tomorrow morning."

TEN EXCELLENT IMPASSE INTERRUPTERS

Here are several more techniques you might experiment with the next time you feel you're headed for a replay of your same old disastrous script. Keep in mind that these approaches will require practice and that some will work better than others but that you have little to lose in trying to break out of your usual patterns.

1. Write a Humorous Poem

For example:

> Roses are reddish, Violets are bluish,
> Even though you can sometimes be mule-ish and cruel-ish,
> I still love you-ish.

2. Use Puppets to Fight with

This can serve two purposes: to lend some humor and to give some distance to the dialogues you are acting out while highlighting some of the childish elements in each of your behaviors.

Irene and Andrew were on the verge of having a bitter fight over her decision to go on an AIDS fund-raising walk. Rather than go into their usual script, they grabbed their puppets, Doris and Morris. As an opening round, the puppets mocked the fight, taking swipes at each other and saying in childlike voices, "You're a booby." "No, you're a bigger booby." "You're a *super*booby." Then, still using their special voices, they had the following "policy debate":

Doris: Guess you don't want me to be out there with all those liberal political types.

Morris: Guess you're right. *I* want to go canoeing. Aren't I an important enough cause to spend the first nice spring weekend with, you doodoo head?

Doris: Even though you're my favorite doodoo head, this is something that is really important to me. My friend Barry died from AIDS, and I see a lot of people in the hospital suffering from it. This is my way of helping them get money for research and fight for their lives.

Morris: OK, but you still stink. All that notwithstanding, I'm going to very graciously allow you to take me out to a nice dinner afterward.

3. Use Flash Cards

Flash cards such as the ones that follow, used at critical junctures in an argument, can help you make a point that seems to have kept slipping from your mate's memory. Flash cards can create a nice break in tense verbal arguing and make your points in a visually dramatic and more memorable way.

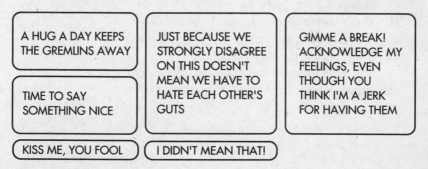

A HUG A DAY KEEPS THE GREMLINS AWAY

TIME TO SAY SOMETHING NICE

KISS ME, YOU FOOL

JUST BECAUSE WE STRONGLY DISAGREE ON THIS DOESN'T MEAN WE HAVE TO HATE EACH OTHER'S GUTS

I DIDN'T MEAN THAT!

GIMME A BREAK! ACKNOWLEDGE MY FEELINGS, EVEN THOUGH YOU THINK I'M A JERK FOR HAVING THEM

4. Periodically Exchange "Wish Lists"

These lists should contain things your partner could do to show affection—giving you a night off while your partner baby-sits, buying flowers or cooking a special meal, or making the bed in the morning. When your partner does something you've long hoped he would, surprise him with an item on his list.

5. Write Your Thoughts and Feelings in a Letter

This can be especially helpful when you're dealing with highly charged issues that have already gotten you stuck in old draining and dysfunctional patterns of arguing. Use as the foundation for your letter the form illustrated on page 214.

6. Sing to Each Other

This is one of my mate's and my favorites, probably because we love musicals and have perfectly matched lousy voices. To the tune of "Tea for Two," for example, we might sing:

Me: Tea, for two, and two for tea,
    I don't leave the room when you're talking,
    But you do it . . . to me.
He: Can't you see, how autistic I can be?
Me: Yes, but I'm going to hate you if you dooo-ooo.
He: I will try . . . my very best,
    But with intimacy skills, I'm not possessed.
Me: How about if . . . I tie you down next time!

7. Use the "to-Me-ness" Principle

This principle, mentioned in Chapter 7, is the all-time best method I've ever encountered for getting away from "There's only one truth here, and it's mine."

Him: "You're a hopeless, hysterical neurotic who nobody but me would ever put up with."

You: "To you I'm a hysterical neurotic; to me I'm an emotionally expressive person trying to collaborate in making our relationship better for both of us. We see me differently."

8. Meet Him Halfway

If he keeps insisting on his point of view, instead of saying "Why can't you understand?" or "You're not listening to me," try "I agree with part of what you say" or "I see your point, but I still think my point also has to be dealt with."

9. Don't Reinforce Sulking

The best way to deal with sulking is probably to ignore it. Or you might try saying "Is there anything I can do to help?" Even if he says, "No," it may make you feel OK about letting it go for now, and he may be more willing to open up later.

10. Set Limits with Your Partner

If he's on an abusive roll, for example, state firmly, calmly, and clearly: "I understand you're very upset at me. But while I don't mind your sharing your feelings and preferences with me, *I am not available for abuse.*" If he continues, state that you are leaving the room since he is having trouble managing his behavior, but that you are willing to resume the dialogue when he's able to discuss things more calmly.

In a society that relegates women to second-class status it is not easy to establish your rights to dignity and respect. When you take a stand like this, don't be surprised if he rebels, perhaps for weeks or even months. But hang in—there is no substitute for continuing to try to get the point across that you are not to be bullied, ignored, or belittled and certainly never to be physically attacked.

A FIVE-WEEK COMMUNICATION PLAN

Even with the best intentions, some of these seemingly simple rules for basic communication can fall quickly by the wayside when a voice is raised or an emotional "button" pushed. How can you and your mate develop some of these skills?

The following is a "mini—home study course" that focuses on one basic skill area each week and can be completed in five weeks. Each skill builds on the next, so that each week you will be practicing that week's tasks while continuing to practice those from previous weeks. Each module is accompanied by specific exercises you can use to build your skills in that area. In the initial stages of this program, I strongly recommend that you do not try to start off with your most emotionally loaded situations such as sex, but rather with moderate- to medium-level problems where your chances for success will be higher.

Week 1: Establish an Agreement to Try a New Communication Approach

Suggested Introduction
"How do you feel about the way our discussions of problems usually go?"
    If he responds with some negative evaluation, suggest: "I've also found

some of our fights painful and difficult, and I sometimes feel like just throwing in the towel. But I've just come across some terrific suggestions for how to help take some of the long-windedness and pain out of couples' communication. How do you feel about giving it a try? We'll need maybe twenty minutes or so, a couple of times a week."

Exercise 1
Alternate in completing the following sentence: "What I find hard to deal with in discussions with you is _____."

Follow these rules:
- Each person gets to make two statements.
- Comment about the *behavior;* don't attack the person.
- Make your statements as succinct as possible.
- The other person is to write down what he or she heard you say.

When both lists are complete, you each read to your mate your notes on what your mate would love to see changed; your mate neutrally corrects anything you heard incorrectly.

For example:

Tom: What I understand is that you find it hardest to talk to me when I talk in a loud voice, when I give you one-word answers or say, "I don't know." Is that right?

Mary: Yes, except it isn't the loud voice by itself—it's when your voice gets loud and you're also leaning toward me in a way that frightens me.

Mary: What I understood from you is that you find it hardest to talk to me when I speak in a whining voice, and also when I try to talk to you when you're watching TV. Is that right?

Tom: Yeah, I guess so.

Exercise 2
Draw up a tentative "communication contract." Ultimately it will be typed up, with copies available to both of you. You can refer to it

before you start discussing a sticky topic and when communication starts to snag. Refer to the suggestions in this chapter for ideas.

Remember: In the course of following any of these exercises, as well as when you're discussing actual problems, continue to use constructive techniques yourself—*no matter how badly the other person may be acting.*

Week 2: Practicing "I" Messages and Active Listening

Suggested Introduction
"*This week we're each supposed to practice stating our feelings about something specific we don't like in the other's behavior and what we wish the other would do differently. Then we're supposed to practice feeding back what we heard—like last time but with a specific problem. And I know this is going to be hard for both of us, but for now we're definitely not supposed to get into any debates—just communicate and listen. Willing to try?*"

Exercise 1
Taking turns, read aloud the examples of nonconstructive communication patterns on pages 210–211.

Exercise 2
One at a time, express a specific complaint, after which the other person simply reflects back what she or he understood to be the essence of what was said. Last, the person making the complaint is to correct any misunderstandings. (Note: Try not to be too picky. It's important that your partner be able to summarize your points as empathically as possible—not repeat verbatim what you said.) For example:

Mary: When you keep buying expensive gifts for your son, I feel frustrated and concerned. What I wish you would do is work more on your guilt about having left the marriage, and on thinking through the long-range effects on your son and us if you continue to give him whatever he asks for.

Tom: What I heard you say is that you're jealous of my son and think I buy things for him just because I feel guilty. [Compare this to what an unconstructive answer would look like: "You've got a lot of nerve telling me what to do with my money."]

Mary: I guess it's possible at times I feel jealous; but what I was trying to convey was that I think your spending so much money on your son may create problems for him down the line, when he sees he won't always be able to get everything he wants; and it may create problems for us, if we aren't able to put away more money for both our kids' education. [Note: She doesn't get defensive about Tom's attacking statement.] What was your understanding of what I just said?

Tom: *(Somewhat sarcastically)* You're worried about him getting spoiled and about my spending all our money on him. Do I have it right, teacher?

Mary: Yeah, that's pretty much on the mark. OK—it's your turn to tell me something that I do that you don't like.

Tom: I feel pissed off when you interrupt me while I'm watching an important game on TV.

Mary: What I understand you to be saying is that you feel especially negative about me—angry and wishing you weren't married to me—when I interrupt your watching a game on TV. Am I accurate so far?

Tom: Yeah, except when I said, "pissed off," it doesn't mean I didn't want to be married to you. Only that I wish you'd stop bugging me!

Mary: What I'm not clear about is what I can do if I need to talk to you soon and the game won't be over for quite a while. It would really help me out a lot if you could come up with some alternative. How about just throwing out one or two ideas?

Tom: I dunno—there you go, bugging me again!

Mary: How about, if you're involved in a game, giving me a specific time when we can talk—and then sticking to it?

Tom: All right—I'll try.

Week 3: Problem-Solving Procedures

Exercise 1
Take turns reading aloud the following suggestions.

1. When you're having an important discussion, pick a time that's agreeable to both of you (e.g., "There's something it's important for us to discuss. Is now a good time?"). If the other person balks, request that she or he suggest a specific alternative time.
2. Before you get together, you each ask yourself what's really bothering you. How do you feel about it? What might you have contributed to the problem, and what might you be able to contribute to its solution? What specific thing(s) would you like your partner to do?
3. Remember that differences in desire, as well as other differences, stand a good chance of being worked out when both partners are determined to make the time and effort to brainstorm options and make necessary adjustments in their behavior.
4. Schedule a regular couple's meeting once a week and stick to it. It's an excellent way to prevent issues from piling up until they explode, and also of discussing in advance difficult situations or events that may be coming up.

Exercise 2
Define a specific problem to be solved along with its related long-term goal. An example:

Problem: Develop a mutually agreeable plan for having some one-on-one time each week for talking or touching.

General goal: To help diminish dissatisfaction in the relationship (Mary feels disconnected; Tom feels Mary is always bugging him about it); and to try a new approach to see if we can both achieve a warmer and better "connection," emotionally and/or physically.

Exercise 3
Take turns reading aloud the following procedures for brainstorming solutions.

1. Brainstorm as many possible options for solving a specific problem as possible—however farfetched they seem—and write them down without comment, especially without anger or attacking. If your partner's suggestion is unclear, ask clarifying questions.
2. Ask each other, "If you were me, how would you resolve this issue?"
3. State to your partner, "You know what *my* position is. Now what would *I* have to do to get you to accept *my* position?"
4. Take some time before making a decision if additional information is needed; if so, divide responsibilities for collecting it from people, books, or other sources.
5. Narrow down the options and try to calculate the pros and cons, risks and opportunities of each of the options, including both partner's feelings about them.
6. Try to argue logically for your preferred solutions by giving reasons for and against, rather than attacking the other person or his position.
7. Be willing to concede a point or make a trade-off and be gracious about accepting the final compromises.
8. Plan a review at the end of a week, or a month, or three months to assess how the chosen solution worked in achieving your goal and to consider possible revisions, if necessary.

Week 4: Getting Past Impasses

Suggested Introduction
"You know how we have certain emergency procedures if the fire alarm goes off? Let's try to see if we can figure out some sort of emergency

procedures to follow if things look like they're getting out of control between us."

Exercise 1
Read the following list of impasse-resolving techniques, checking off the ones that might be helpful to each of you and, where appropriate, "customizing" them to better suit your own personalities.

1. *Take ten minutes out and go into separate rooms. Then, try your best to put yourself in your partner's shoes and see the problem from his perspective.* Be prepared, when you return, to communicate that you see the validity of your partner's perspective—without adding "yes, but. . . ."
   For example:

   Mary: I guess you're feeling overwhelmed with pressures and are thinking, I'm married to this self-centered person who instead of appreciating my pressures and all the comforts my income is providing just wants more, more, more. And instead of leaving me alone to have some peace and quiet when I come home, she is always pressuring me to "talk" or "show more affection" or a hundred other things that I just can't do.

   Tom: I guess you sometimes feel taken for granted or that you're just the maid around here. And you probably just want what I guess most women want: more affection, more touching, being able to talk about things that happened during the day. You're probably especially frustrated because you're always putting out for the kids and me, and for your staff at work, and don't feel you get much back for yourself.

2. *Ask each other, "What can we do to make things better?"* Then try your best to answer as specifically as possible. For example:

> *Tom:* I guess when I come home I could hug you and ask you how your day went.
>
> *Mary:* I could attempt not to have any heavy discussions or intrude on your space for at least the first hour and a half that you're home.

3. *Tape the argument.* Then listen to it *separately*, each writing down at least two things you and your partner could do next time to make your communication more constructive.

4. *Work out some signal in advance,* such as tugging on your right ear or holding up a card that says "oops," to remind the other person when he or she is defaulting on a previously agreed-on promise, such as keeping each communication to a maximum of three minutes.

5. *Change the surroundings and activity.* For example, agree to go for a walk in the park and enjoy the sunshine, take a merry-go-round ride, or go to the beach. Then talk only about the scenery and don't mull over your anger.

6. *For fifteen minutes, switch to a topic that will remind you of a time when you felt close and optimistic.* For example, talk about a wonderful trip you took together, including details on what made it so pleasant. Or ask each other to recall a time you did something the other really appreciated or was especially proud of.

7. *Hold or hug or touch each other. Give each other reassurance,* even if it doesn't at the moment feel particularly "authentic." Let your mate know that you do love and care for him, that you want to have a good relationship. Work out the kinds of statements that will be most likely to help the other person reduce his or her anger/anxiety/hurt/depression, such as:

   "I care about you."

   "I am very committed to you and to this relationship."

   "I know this feels unpleasant . . . but I really think we can get through this and work it out."

Week 5: Make a "Behavioral Exchange Contract"

One of the all-time best ways to help motivate your partner to change something you dislike is to agree to change a behavior of yours that particularly bothers him.

Rona and Nick had just finished their thirty-ninth battle in the past year about how cool and aloof he seemed to her each evening, and how he thought the house was in such shambles.

"Let's make a deal," Rona suggested to Nick following a session with me in which I had explained behavioral exchange contracts. "For the next two weeks I will commit myself to making sure the bed and the dining room table are cleared by the time you get home. If I promise to do this, can you commit to a fifteen-minute snuggle session at least twice a week?"

The following rules need to be clearly spelled out and agreed on to maximize the chances of success with your contracts.

1. *Each of you will continue to hold to your commitment even if the other person defaults.* "You didn't do yours, so I'm not going to do mine" will just put you back where you started.
2. *Each choose a maximum of two or three specific, measurable behaviors to work on.*
3. *Do not pick too large an increase over the current level of the behavior.* For example, if your mate has done just about no cuddling at all the past few weeks, don't go for five cuddling sessions in one week; go for one or two. Better to pick a small step and succeed than too high a goal, fail, and wind up feeling frustrated or angry.
4. *Let each other know how very pleased or appreciative you are* when something positive is done.
5. *Sign and date the agreement* and make a copy so you'll each have one. Then look at your contract at least once a day to remind yourself.

Warren and Andrea's Contract

Each of us, being of sound mind and wishing to enhance the State of our Union, agrees to do the following. We will each continue to make our best efforts even if we feel the other is defaulting. We will discuss the results in 14 days.

Warren	**Andrea**
1. I will refrain from exploding or getting defensive if Andrea criticizes me and try to feed back to her what I understand her to be saying. 2. I will take full charge of the kids two nights a week (helping them with their baths, homework, getting them fed and to bed).	1. On at least three occasions this week, I will express affection to Warren or tell him I really appreciate something he's done and I will refrain from criticizing him for "the small stuff." 2. I will cook a special meal that I know Warren really likes two nights a week.
Signed: _____ (date)	Signed: _____ (date)

SOME FINAL TIPS

What are your four best bets for maintaining a healthy and happy relationship—both in and out of bed?

1. Be mutually willing to recognize your partner's rights to express feelings openly and honestly.
2. Be flexible in negotiating conflict. If you don't bend, you'll break.
3. Express appreciation of your partner's efforts and struggles.
4. Try to maintain a sense of perspective and humor.

CHAPTER 9

HOW TO GET
THE "CHEMISTRY"
HEATED UP

"What's good in bed is the same thing as what's been good out of bed: honesty, imagination, a little mischief, and a lot of kindness."

—Eleanor Perry

"I don't know," Darlene said skeptically when I suggested she might be able to get some sort of sex life going again with her husband, Tony.

"Whenever *I* try to initiate it, he says he's not in the mood. And if I wait for him to get in the mood and initiate it—well, I could wait until I'm blue in the face. It takes two to tango," she sighed, "and he just isn't dancing."

"I agree that he's probably not going to be suddenly swept away by sexual desire," I responded. "You'll probably need to help him develop his desire capacities through some mental and physical exercises, much as an exercise program at a gym builds muscles. Your first step will be to help get the 'pilot light' in his brain turned on, to get him motivated to embark on this new sensuous voyage. The next step will be for you both to discover what kinds of stimulation most turn you on, and to share this with each other verbally and then incorporate these kinds of stimulation into your love play.

Your credentials? First, you've done a lot of good work on yourself. You've learned to accept yourself as a sexual person whether or not he manages to connect with you physically. You've expanded your own sensuality by becoming more fully auto-erotic or just thinking of yourself in a more positive way. You've learned to control your hurt and anger when he acts like a creep, and to feel less anxious, guilty, or depressed if he's critical or rejecting.

In addition, you've made progress in helping him:

- become more self-accepting;
- take as good care of his psyche and body as he does of his car;
- reduce stress through cognitive and behavioral relaxation procedures;
- reduce low frustration tolerance and anger by trying to view things as hassles, rather than horrors; and
- learn about sex—such as how falloffs in sexual interest and functioning happen to millions of people, and that doesn't make them— or him—a whit less worthwhile.

And, finally, you've tried to help improve the interactions between the two of you by:

- keeping your communications with him upbeat;
- where problem confrontations occur, discussing your feelings and preferences as calmly and succinctly as possible;
- using better approaches to resolve disagreements; and
- increasing positive one-on-one experiences in nonsexual areas.

Although there are never any guarantees of success—especially if you happen to be dealing with a fairly rigid or disturbed partner— your chances for making some progress with him in the area of physical intimacy and sensuality are much improved by the time you've reached this point in my program. And whatever happens, you will have the satisfaction of knowing you gave it your very best efforts.

"LET'S GET PHYSICAL" MONTH

Here is the Let's-Get-Physical-in-a-New-Way Project that I laid out for Darlene.

This compendium of activities draws on creative procedures used successfully by couples I have worked with and from the work of pioneering sex therapists such as Masters and Johnson, Bernie Zilbergeld, Helen Singer Kaplan, and Albert Ellis. Although the goal is to help you learn more about each other's pleasure zones, its aim is not to make sexual and sensual activity into a "work" situation. Rather these exercises are designed to instill an upbeat feeling and sense of playfulness into your physical relationship. They will be especially helpful if he's worried about any aspect of his ability to "perform" during intercourse. Most men are surprised and delighted to discover the joys of non-goal-directed sex, a highly sensuous experience focusing not so much on the genitals but on the entire body-mind experience.

Introducing Him to the Notion

Pick a good setting and time to talk about your idea for a "Let's Get Physical" Month. Bring up the subject when he's in a somewhat relaxed, positive mood.

You might open the subject like this:

"You know, I've been thinking about sexuality and sensuality and how, with so much crammed into our lives and our being so used to each other, we've let it fall by the wayside. What I think would really be relaxing and fun is if we made this month "Let's Get Physical" Month. I think it would be great to start fresh—sort of like Adam and Eve—and touch and play and see how we can expand the ways we can get pleasure from our bodies. How does that sound to you?"

If he seems even mildly curious, try to enlist his agreement on the following guidelines.

"Let's Get Physical Month" Guidelines

1. "There's no way we can "fail" or "lose" at this. All we've got to do is play—that is, we just experiment and find out what feels good. If we wind up with two or three new ways of making our bodies feel good, it's well worth it."
2. "We both commit ourselves to setting aside the time—at least an hour a week. Otherwise, you know what's likely to happen— we just won't get around it it!"
3. "Even though sometimes we may feel a bit uncomfortable or silly, we're really going to try to forget other worries and get involved in what makes our bodies feel nice. Doing anything new physically is always somewhat uncomfortable until you've done it a few times."
4. "And, guess what? No intercourse for the month. Intercourse is like eating delicious chocolate cake: it's greatly enjoyable, but suddenly it's gone. We can always get back to it later, if we want. The idea is to explore our *other* erogenous zones and just get more comfortable being physical with each other—without any other pressures. Then we have the rest of our lives to do nice stuff to each other's body, including intercourse. That doesn't sound too bad, does it?"

To seal the bargain, make two photocopies of the following contract on nice paper, read them together aloud, and then cosign them.

"Let's Get Physical" Contract

We, the undersigned, having gotten into somewhat of a rut as far as our sensuous life is concerned, do hereby agree to devote the following four weeks _____ (dates) to Getting Physical: to exploring our erogenous zones and sparking up our sex life.

Toward this end, each of us agrees to cooperate in the following:

1. We shall set up regular times, in advance, write them in our appointment books, and stick to them—even if we really "just don't feel like it." (It may actually revive us!)
2. We shall both help in setting up a nice location and [if applicable] in farming out the kids.
3. We shall each take responsibility for maintaining our own "physical equipment" in good condition: properly fed and reasonably relaxed.
4. We shall stick with doing the specific activity for the "session," no matter how silly we might feel. If any balking occurs, the balker is to share fully the feelings he or she is experiencing.
5. We shall agree to listen carefully to each other in order to learn more about what turns us on or off, neither passing judgment nor upsetting ourselves about what we hear.

Here's to our mutual pleasure! And to our learning to get more comfortable with each other sensually, and sexually, and discovering the best ways to make our bodies feel good. (And we hereby relinquish the myth that if couples are not automatically and spontaneously turned on to each other, it's useless to try to do anything about it!)

Signed:

_____   _____

_____   _____
Date   Date

There will be seven sessions over the one-month period. Each session's experiments will involve both a verbal and a physical component.

Session 1 (45 Minutes)

Equipment: Massage oil, pencil, and paper. Note: Don't use body lotion or baby oil, which is not particularly good for massages.

Physical Activity: Learning Ways of Touching that Feel Good (15 Minutes)

To begin: Close your eyes and take a few slow, deep breaths together and, as you exhale, say "C-A-L-M" or the mantra "O-M-M," letting the vibrations of the sound fill your inner core. Set a timer for five minutes.

One of you begins by warming some massage oil in his or her hands and then slowly, gently stroking the other's hands and forearms, *going no higher than the elbow.* There is no "right way" to do this exercise, no goal other than enjoying and becoming aware of physical sensations.

Experiment with gentle, light strokes of the fingertips and different kinds of kneading of the muscles. Enjoy the texture of the skin, the contours and suppleness of the muscle. Imagine you're playing a beautiful musical instrument and exploring the range of sounds it can produce. Try to clear your mind of distracting thoughts and anxieties. Just experience the good feelings that are there, and the nuances between what feels especially good and what feels uncomfortable. Wiggle your finger if something becomes too irritating. Don't talk during the massage. When the timer goes off, the person being massaged describes first the things he felt and what he liked; then what he didn't like or what felt especially uncomfortable. The other listens actively, asking any clarifying questions after the feedback is finished. Then reverse the entire procedure, including the postmassage feedback, with the masseuse now becoming the "massagee."

Not only will this exercise give you more information on the kinds of touching that feel good, but it will also make you both more comfortable and secure with touching each other, not only as a prelude to sex but as something pleasurable and relaxing in and of itself. You are encouraged to try all the "touching" exercises for at least four sessions, to get conditioned to relating physically without any need to perform or reach a certain goal. Most people who do them report that they are fun and real eye-openers.

Organ-between-the-Ears Activity: Distinguishing between Sexual Myths and Facts (15 Minutes)

To begin: Separately each of you is to answer the following questions. Jot down your answers, then alternately share them aloud. The listener is to be as nonjudgmental and neutral as possible. Clarifying questions are permissible; offensive challenges or defensive reactions are not.

1. To me, sexually "normal" means _____
_____

   To me, sexually "abnormal" means _____
_____

2. I sometimes feel under pressure to have orgasms/erections.
☐ No ☐ Yes
(Explain.) _____

3. Sex is not really complete if it doesn't include intercourse.
☐ Disagree ☐ Agree (Explain.) _____

4. I ☐ do ☐ do not think it's OK to have fantasies about other people when you're having sex with your mate.

5. A session of sex can't be very good if only one person is really aroused. ☐ Disagree ☐ Agree (Explain.) _____

6. It spoils things if you have to tell your partner what to do to help you get more turned on. ☐ Disagree ☐ Agree (Explain.) _
_____

After you have both shared your answers to all six questions (either verbally or by exchanging papers), alternate in reading aloud the following "Myths vs. Facts" list to help clear up any misinformation that may be getting in the way of your having a better sex life.

The Myths vs. the Facts

Myth #1:
You need to be automatically aroused by your partner to have sex.

Fact: Sexual excitement—whether it's with yourself or with a partner—is created and enhanced by (1) the presence of good physical stimulation (fondling, touching, rubbing, kissing) and possible erotic mental imagery and (2) the absence of negative emotions or self-talk or external distractions. If you're telling yourself before or during sex, "This isn't working" or "This is boring" or you're failing to focus on your sensory input—*that* is what is interfering with your arousal.

Myth #2:
Sex should happen spontaneously—not be scheduled.

Fact: If sex with your partner happens spontaneously, fine. But usually in the course of a busy life it doesn't. "Simultaneous arousal" is almost as unlikely as simultaneous orgasm. Anything worth doing is worth scheduling—especially things that require some time and space and freedom from distractions. We schedule activities all the time, from tennis games and plays to grease jobs on our cars. Surely sex is just as important to our physical and mental well-being—not to mention our relationship!—as these other activities.

Myth #3:
When you're used to somebody, and he or she is like your sibling or best friend, you can't get turned on.

Fact: Baloney! This is true only if you lack imagination and initiative. It's a natural part of most relationships' evolution for people to become habituated—namely, to find that the initial thrills have subsided. But despite your being used to your partner, you *can* still get turned on. We're used to babies . . . to sunsets . . . to home runs—but we can still get turned on by them the thousandth time we've seen them.

Myth #4:
Intercourse (i.e., penetration of the vagina by the penis) is the "real thing." Anything else is second-class or "foreplay" and doesn't really count as sex.

Fact: We all have fingers, tongues, toes, skin, ears, and lots of erogenous zones. Sexual behavior is any behavior that involves intimate physical contact or the sharing of body parts, which arouses or is intended to arouse erotic feelings. It need not involve orgasm or orgasms to be enjoyable. Intercourse does *not* equal sex—that's a very narrow definition. It's merely *one of many forms* of sexual expression. We can get moments of physical contact and sensuality when we snuggle, hug, or hold hands. As for more erotic sex, intercourse and orgasm are options, but they are in no way essential. In fact the emphasis on them is what frequently contributes to sexual dysfunction, with the man trying desperately to slow down his orgasm and the woman hurrying to orgasm faster. Perhaps it would be better if sex were called *physical relations,* which has a broader implication and could include all the various factors of physical communication between human beings.

Myth #5:
Lovemaking cannot be particularly satisfying if only one person is turned on.

Fact: If only one person is turned on, that person can have a quite pleasurable time. And if that person's partner isn't resentful, the potential is there for getting some satisfaction out of pleasing the other person and nurturing the relationship—whether or not either winds up having an orgasm. It is perfectly acceptable for one person to stimulate the other without becoming particularly aroused: it signals neither the absence of love nor the existence of a sexual problem. Lovemaking is a way of *sharing love*. Because there are so many ways of sharing love, every lovemaking session can be seen as a success—for *both* partners.

Myth #6:
It's artificial or silly to experiment and try out new things.

Fact: Among the best ways to keep life fresh and exciting are taking risks and trying new things. These can include new foods, hobbies, or sex practices. Just as a willingness to experiment with cooking recipes can keep meals from becoming routine, so can experimenting with new sexual practices and places to touch change pedestrian sex into *Cordon Bleu sex*. If only one out of ten of your physical experiments produces some nice sensations or experiences—great! Eventually couples who experiment find a few good ways of producing especially delicious sensations and largely stay with these—with occasional forays into fantasy scenarios or other special twice-a-year treats. By expanding the ways the body can be "played," you can then adapt your sex life to keep it fresh and exciting. It's a heck of a lot more sensible than the old expedient of trading in the relationship to get better sex, only to wind up coming smack up against the same problems.

Myth #7:
When a woman "takes the lead" or is assertive, a man can't enjoy sex—it's emasculating.

Fact: Research by Abraham Maslow and others indicates that between men and women who are more flexible and freer to be active as well as passive, sex becomes more varied and enjoyable. However, if a man tells himself, "This is unnatural and unmanly" or "It's awful if I'm not in control or ready to respond the moment she initiates things"; or if *she's* telling herself, "I'm being too aggressive," these thoughts can lead to inhibition or anxiety, and hence to *decreased* sexual variation and enjoyment.

Myth #8:
If your partner is overweight or has wrinkles or is not that attractive, you can't really get turned on.

Fact: Millions of men and women do. They're busy focusing on good stimulation and erotic thoughts, not telling themselves, "Yechh . . . how disgusting" or "I must have someone who looks like my sexual ideal in order to be turned on." Just because it may be easier to get turned on by someone gorgeous or with a perfect body doesn't mean that these are the only conditions under which you can get aroused.

Myth #9:
You should not have lustful thoughts or have sexual fantasies about people other than your mate. It's abnormal, and it's cheating.

Fact: A sexual response can be triggered by a wide variety of sexual stimuli, including touch, smell, sight, thought, fantasy, or just about anything that has sexual significance for you. Surveys show that from one-half to as many as three-quarters of men and women use fantasies, and they significantly enhance their sexual experiences. Fantasies are movies of the mind. They are among the *very best ways* to get the brain tuned to its sex channel and the sexual juices flowing. Although many fantasies, like dreams, may seem bizarre, that does not make them necessarily pathological. As for seeing them as cheating, what's *really* cheating is to deprive your partner of sex, especially when she or he badly wants to make contact, just because you're not automatically turned on to her!

Taking a few "fantasy breaks" during the week can allow you to excite your erotic imagination and keep your sexual drive active. If you run out of ideas, trying reading the letters to the editor from *Penthouse Forum* or an erotic book or see an erotic film. If you and your mate are not into sharing fantasies, then keep the details to yourself. They are a low-budget source of private pleasure and safe sex.

Myth #10:
You shouldn't have to tell your partner what makes you feel good; you shouldn't have to touch yourself during sex.

Fact: A lot of men believe they should be able to produce their own arousal, including their erection, as well as their partner's excitement, and that if they have to ask you for help or touch themselves, it means they're weak or inadequate. (Note how many are reluctant to ask for directions when they're lost!) Our brains are hooked up to our nerve endings. Mind reading is a highly *ineffective* practice to get the sexual circuits charged up. The secret of good sex is to be as specific as possible in sharing likes and dislikes, without criticism or judgment—and then to keep experimenting. *Knowing exactly how your mate most likes to be touched is the best aphrodisiac.* Once you've learned the kind of stimulation that drives your partner wild, use it to the full! As for touching yourself during sex, it can be of tremendous value to men and women both in arousal and in helping them over the orgasmic threshold.

After going over this section, write down the three myths each of you has most strongly held. Next, write down all the ways in which each myth has caused *difficulties* for you, giving specific illustrations from your past. Finally, list all the ways that *giving up* the myth will benefit you. Periodically read these new beliefs out loud to reinforce them.

Session 2 (60 Minutes)

Equipment: Massage oil and clean feet

Physical Activity: Footsies and Thighsies
To begin: Close your eyes and take a few slow, deep breaths together while saying to yourselves "C-A-L-M" or "O-M-M-M," letting the sound resonate through your body. Set a timer for seven
minutes per person. Then, coat your hands with massage oil and
begin gently massaging the other person's toes and feet—stroking,
kneading, enjoying the different touches, experimenting. The "massagee" relaxes, with eyes closed; no talking. Remember: there's no
right or wrong way to do this. You're simply experimenting with
ways of making each other's body feel good, and with increasing
your feelings of comfort and pleasure in touching and being touched.

Work your way slowly up the calves, to the knees, and finally to
the thighs. (Don't cheat—do not touch anything above the thighs.)
The massagee then gives you feedback—first on what felt particularly good physically and emotionally, then on what didn't feel good.
If you are not sure what really "hit the spot" for your partner, have
him or her demonstrate it on you.

Now reverse roles.

*Organ-Between-the-Ears Activity: Sharing Fantasies and
Feelings* (20 Minutes)
To begin: You each write down your answers to the following
questions, without looking at each other's notes. When you've both
finished, exchange papers and read each other's answers to yourself;
then discuss. Asking clarifying questions is fine; e.g., "Do you like
your bottom stroked gently or firmly?" Defensive or offensive responses and snickering at the other person's answers are not allowed. Listen, absorb, and learn; it's all in a very good cause! Once
you've learned what your partner's biggest turn-ons are, you are in
the best possible position to know how to light his fire.

1. My favorite sexual or sensual experience with you was when (describe in as much detail as possible): _____

2. Three wonderful things you could do that could turn me on or improve sex for me are (kinds of touching, talking, positions, etc.):

_____

3. The best way for me to orgasm is (describe in as much detail as possible): _____

4. Two things that I find sexually frustrating in our relationship are:

_____

5. A fantasy I might like to act out with you is (write out a detailed scenario, including what each of you is doing, feeling, hearing, tasting): _____

_____

6. Two things I am afraid might happen if I have sex more regularly with you are: _____

_____

7. The thing I'm most embarrassed to tell you about is: _____

_____

(Examples could include that you haven't been having orgasms for the past eleven years; that you'd like to be stimulated anally; that you've felt inadequate about your oral sex skills).

8. One of the most erotic or sensuous experiences I ever had was:

_____

What made it good was _____

9. One of the worst sexual experiences I ever had was: _____
What made it bad was: _____

Physical Activity: Assertiveness Exercise
Tell your partner another part of your body that you'd like touched or massaged and the details of the way you'd like it done. If you

feel uncomfortable at this point saying it aloud, whisper it or write it on a piece of paper. Your partner then massages you there for two or three minutes. Afterward, discuss how it felt, focusing on the positives. Then switch.

Session 3 (60 Minutes)

Equipment: Massage oil, showered and nude body

Physical Activity: Full-Body (Almost) Massage
One of the most outstanding contributions to pleasureful sex has been what Masters and Johnson call "sensate focus," an approach designed to free people of the idea that sex equals intercourse and instead to promote their focusing on feeling good all over. Here's how you do it.

Make sure you've set aside at least an hour of quiet, uninterrupted time. Take a relaxing bath or shower and create a sensuous environment of soft lights or candles, perhaps with background music or incense. A firm pad on the floor is usually better than a bed, which is too soft. With a clear contract that the experience is not to end in intercourse, one of you at a time is to lie down, nude, relaxing the entire body as much as possible while the other person explores the entire body except for breasts and genitals. Start with the head, tenderly and sensitively caressing and massaging the back of the head, ears, neck. Go slowly down your partner's back and sides, the arms, the buttocks and insides of the thighs, the legs, the feet, the toes.

When you've finished one side, gently turn your partner over and touch, stroke, and massage the front of the body from head to toe, *excluding the nipples and genitals*. The massagee is simply to concentrate on feelings, without worrying whether the masseuse is getting bored or tired and is to signal the masseuse only if something feels distinctly uncomfortable. Then switch roles, again experimenting with different kinds of strokes, rhythms, and pressure.

After both of you have been "pleasured," verbally share with each other what felt especially nice, along with any other feelings or thoughts that came up for each of you.

As in the previous pleasuring exercises, the "giving" partner is providing pleasure to the "receiver," while at the same time developing her or his own pleasure in touching. Another advantage of this exercise is that it helps both of you develop the flexibility and comfort to move beyond traditional gender roles (active, initiating male vs. passive female). If your partner seems impatient or uncomfortable with the passivity of his role, encourage him to let go, relax, and just enjoy receiving.

This exercise can be done on as many occasions as you wish, either in conjunction with genital sex or as a treat in and of itself.

A nice way to end the pleasuring exercises (or at times instead of them) is to lie quietly together, enjoying the delicious sensations, listening to some gentle music and touching hands or fingertips. Or, if you're so inclined, you may just want to snuggle in each other's arms or lie "spooned" together or cradle your partner's head in your lap, stroking his hair. Enjoy the tenderness, the sensuality, the relaxation. And no intercourse. It's very important to begin to establish touching and cuddling as ends in themselves, and not merely as foreplay or afterplay.

Organ-Between-the-Ears-Exercise: Getting in Touch with Touching

If you're not too mellowed out to talk at this point, do the following exercise, developed by my colleague Polly Kellogg.

Take a deep breath, close your eyes, and relax. Then, starting with your childhood, think back to nonsexual ways of touching you have enjoyed. Did you ever curl up on someone's lap when you were tired, lay your head on someone's shoulder or tummy, give or receive back rubs? Have a playful wrestle or pillow fight? Have you ever felt upset and cried on someone's shoulder, hugged someone, maybe stroked his or her face or hair—or wanted to but held back? After each of you has had a chance to get in touch with some of these feelings and memories, share them with each other, nonjudgmentally.

Much of sex is similar to early infancy, when the child, through kissing, hugging, and touching, learns about the world and establishes his or her earliest connections to people. (Maybe this is why so many people talk "baby talk" when they are having sex.) Male socialization and/or early experiences with nonnurturing or abusive parents, however, can condition people to derive not pleasure but fear from this kind of closeness. If either you or your partner has had such negative experiences, try to talk about them; then listen, hold, and support your partner, in whatever way needed.

Regularly take time in your life to get back to the child in each of you: to tease each other, tickle each other with flowers, roll in the grass together, have playful pillow fights, snuggle, be silly. Even parodies of children's exuberant play can give you a high. To catalyze the process, keep soft stuffed animals around—they'll help regress you faster than anything I know!

Session 4 (60 Minutes)

Equipment: Massage oil and "accessories" (such as feathers, satin sheets, strawberries)

Physical Activity: Sexual Massage
The goal of this pleasure session is to discover what gives each of you genital pleasure and arousal—but *not* to "go for orgasm."

The accessories you choose to bring to your session can be ones that you or your partner has mentioned in the previous sexual sharing discussions or your old favorites.

> A wonderful source for erotic "accessories," including such items as Kama Sutra Oil of Love, erotic books, massage videos, and a vast array of vibrators and other sex toys, is Eve's Garden. Call (800) 848-3837 (or 212-757-8651 in New York) for a mail-order catalog.

Start by doing as much general body caressing as is needed to begin to arouse your partner, drawing from what you've learned so far about erogenous zones. Keep it teasing and nonpressured, each spending approximately fifteen minutes on the other. First use your fingers and later on your lips or other "accessories." He might play gently with your breasts, nipples, vulva; then move back to another part of your body you like having caressed, such as your earlobe, breasts, or thighs, returning once again to your vulva.

When his turn comes, you might also want to alternate genital caressing with stimulating other erotic parts of the body. Always try to use a teasing, rather than a driving-for-orgasm, kind of stimulation. Try not to talk; instead, let each other know what feels good by saying things like "Ummm," "Oh, yes!" or "Ahhhhh."

Erections and orgasms are *not* the goal; it's simply to experience the pleasure of caressing and being caressed and of helping your partner feel good, freed from pressures to perform and "fear of failure."

Is There a Vibrator in the House? (If Not, There Should Be!)

Although the affection and human interaction that the two of you share cannot, of course, be replaced by this "machine," vibrators are a *great* adjunct to sexual enjoyment; a woman and her partner need never worry about her having an orgasm with one around. Since some men feel the presence of a vibrator means they can't "do the job" properly, it's important to talk this through together.

Electric vibrators are generally far superior to the battery-operated variety. Once you've acquired one, you'll probably need to experiment for a few sessions to find the right "touch." Having discovered its talents, however (not the least of which is its ability to vibrate at sixty cycles per second), you'll want one for both home and travel as an adjunct to partner sex as well as for "solo" use.

> ## Is There a Vibrator in the House? (If Not, There Should Be!) (Continued)
>
> Betty Dodson reports on the vibrator experience of one of the women in her Bodysex workshops who reached her first orgasm at age 48. Intercourse is foreplay for her, and after he comes, she has a vibrator orgasm while they kiss and hug. Both she and her husband feel they are having a second sexual honeymoon.

Organ-Between-the-Ears Exercise: Sexual Massage "Debriefing" (15 Minutes)

Discuss what the sexual massage exercise felt like for each of you. Include what felt especially relaxing or arousing, and what felt physically uncomfortable. Also talk about any emotions, positive or negative, that the exercise evoked, such as "I started feeling all warm and relaxed. Then I suddenly got anxious thinking, my penis should be responding more—if I can't get excited in this kind of situation, is there any hope?"

Listen carefully to each other, counteracting any tendency to feel hurt or angry or discouraged. If something positive is expressed, respond enthusiastically. If he says, "That just didn't do very much for me at all," ask him if he thinks there might have been any distractions going on in his head or any feelings that were interfering with his just going with his senses.

Session 5 (60 Minutes)

Equipment: Massage oil or Astroglide, an over-the-counter, close-to-natural lubricant.

Although there are few people who still believe masturbation will make hair grow on their palms, it remains for large numbers of people—including couples who have been together for many years—the ultimate taboo subject, shrouded in shame and mystery. One of my clients asked her boyfriend with whom she'd been having wild sex for two years if he ever masturbated. Flushing beet-red, he responded indignantly, "That's an *awfully* personal question!"

Why are we talking about masturbation when we've got a partner? What's the point? For one thing, it frees you from overdependence on your partner's availability and mood. What's more, for most people it is the most reliable way to orgasm. Women who masturbate regularly reach orgasm over 95 percent of the time; while in partner sex, the figure drops substantially.

People who are skillful at self-stimulation tend to be more comfortable with their own bodies and knowledgeable about the kinds of stimulation that produce the best arousal. When you are able to focus attention exclusively on your own sensations, your nervous system can tell you where the "itch" is and what corrective action for your hand to take to relieve it. Your partner does not have this direct hook-up to your nervous system.

Being knowledgeable about your own sexual "buttons" can be a tremendous boon in partner sex. Rather than your partner's having to "guess" at the kind of stimulation you need at the moment, you can provide him with this information, thus sparing him considerable frustration and allowing greater flexibility in your sexual repertoire. A woman, for example, who can get *extra stimulation* during intercourse is far more likely to orgasm than a woman who has only the "look, Ma, no hands" kind of intercourse that stimulates the vaginal walls but for many women does not provide sufficient arousal to bring them to the point of orgasm. It is estimated that as many as 70 percent of women need direct clitoral stimulation while having intercourse to reach orgasm consistently. Similarly, if a man's penis and other erogenous zones are stimulated by his partner's hands or mouth, he may more easily be able to achieve erection and/or orgasm, with or without intercourse. Sometimes no hands, or two hands, can work just fine; at others, having all four hands involved can be sensational.

Surprisingly, millions of men and women have never really taken the time to show their partners how they like their genitals touched. This session will provide you with a wonderful opportunity to do a thorough job of it.

Organ-Between-the-Ears Exercise: Sharing Masturbation Histories (20 Minutes)

Alternate, with your partner, discussing the following questions:

1. When did you first masturbate? How did you feel?
2. When did you first discuss masturbation with anyone? How did you feel?
3. Share with your partner what leads up to your deciding to masturbate. What "preparations," if any, do you make before you begin? Are there any "accessories" you typically use, such as erotic books, magazines, vibrators, or videos?
4. Are there kinds of touching you would like to give yourself or have your partner give you on a more regular basis?
5. Talk about how you felt discussing this and tell each other what was most interesting about what you learned about yourself and your partner.

Physical Exercise: Masturbating Together (30 to 45 Minutes)

To do this exercise, create a relaxed space with phones turned off and kids farmed out or sound asleep. If you feel comfortable enough, do the exercise in the same room, facing away from each other; then, once you're "warmed up," lie together. If stimulating yourself in front of your partner is something you're just plain too uncomfortable with for now, then do it simultaneously in separate rooms. Another possibility is to start masturbating while you are in separate rooms; then join each other in the same room (possibly facing in opposite directions) while continuing to masturbate to orgasm. Still another variation would be to start masturbating yourself, then switch to the other one until each of you has climaxed.

Try actively to arouse yourself and keep pushing any distracting thoughts out of your mind. Let your body enjoy the ebb and flow of sensuous feelings, freed from any time pressures. When you start feeling very aroused, you may want to tease yourself by temporarily switching from your genital area to other parts of your body. If you start feeling uncomfortably tense, stop and take a few slow, deep breaths; it will bring more oxygen to your muscles and give you an overall relaxed feeling.

As you watch each other masturbate, you will probably learn more about each other's sexual triggers than you could from reading a dozen sex manuals.

Organ-Between-the-Ears Exercise: Masturbation "Debriefing" (15 Minutes)

Sometime after your "simultaneous masturbation" session, discuss with your partner what each of you finds particularly effective and pleasurable. Tell your partner specifically how you like to be stimulated, such as "I like a gentle, teasing stroke at first—then a more vigorous one as I get closer to orgasm." Feel free to ask each other questions; for example, "What was the thing that finally helped you let go and explode?"

Discuss, too, any of the things that might have been going on that may have been blocking your pleasure. Were you feeling anxious or self-conscious? Guilty? Hopeless about your sexual abilities? Embarrassed about anything?

Session 6 (45 to 60 Minutes)

Physical Exercise: Stimulating Each Other (45 Minutes)

Do this only after you have both become reasonably comfortable with having your partner watch you, and have learned the kind of stimulation that each of you likes best. Choose a position that is most comfortable for each of you. Something that works well is for the person being focused on to sit between the partner's legs with her back toward him, allowing each of you to fairly easily reach your partner's genitals and for the person being masturbated to help guide your fingers. It also may help reduce the possibility of distraction and self-consciousness since you will not be looking directly at each other. You can also experiment with other positions. Keep in mind that all of these activities can become part of a rich, expanded sex life; they are not merely one-shot exercises.

Help guide your partner's hands or give a brief verbal tip or two; encourage your partner periodically to check out if your finger or tongue is in the right place or you're going too fast or too slow. Experiment with teasing each other, building up several times to high levels of arousal, then backing off momentarily. You can even "play doctor," that is, examine your partner's genitals, looking carefully at the different parts and helping each other identify them by name.

It's crucial, if you want to improve your sexual relationship, that you learn to ask for what you want and exchange information on what's pleasurable and what's not. Showing each other things you like in a sexual encounter and expressing preferences to each other is not attacking or demanding: it's honest, adult communication.

Organ-Between-the-Ears Exercise: Stimulating Each Other "Debriefing" (10 to 15 Minutes)

Afterward, discuss your feelings with your partner: what felt good as well as what felt uncomfortable. Then share with each other helpful suggestions for things that might be good to try next time. For example: "I'd love it if you could grip my penis fairly firmly near the base with one hand and use your other hand, with lots of lubrication, as a sort of ring and slide it up and down my penis." Or, "I think it would be helpful if I could signal you at the point I need continuous, fast stimulation and you seem to be slowing down."

After trying this several times, you will almost certainly become more relaxed and confident, enjoying your partner's enjoyment of himself as well as learning many new ways of stimulating each other. One of the biggest boons of integrating masturbation into your sex life will be that you now have a great way to have sex together when only one of you is in the mood for sex. Either one can hold the other while masturbating, or you can masturbate your partner, while still having the warmth and connection of a shared sensual experience.

"We've gotten *so* much better at touching each other's body," one couple reported. "It's amazing how much you can learn by simply getting some feedback. Now we love to watch each other and sometimes do it together."

Session 7 (45 Minutes)

Physical Exercise: Using Your Head (and Mouth!) (45 Minutes)

Oral sexual stimulation is a very natural practice that has been carried on since ancient times. It is especially effective because the mouth, lips, and tongue contain a rich supply of sensory nerve endings, and saliva provides excellent lubrication. Oral sex can be the main act, or a prelude or postlude to intercourse. And skillful use of the tongue can especially be a boon to men, who need never worry about having an excellent means with which to satisfy their mate.

Begin by taking a relaxing shower or bath—separately or together—taking particular care to get your entire body squeaky clean. The "pleasuree" lies in a comfortable position, focusing only on his or her own sexual/sensual sensations. As each of you takes your turn, remember that your best key to success is to be relaxed and experimental and willing to stimulate not only your partner's genitals, but the surrounding erogenous zones as well. You can also switch from time to time to kissing or touching other areas, then resume genital stimulation. This kind of experimentation—combined with good, specific feedback—should easily fill the bill as a totally satisfying sensual experience, whether each partner orgasms or not.

Although oral sex may or may not be your or his favorite cup of tea, once you learn how to pleasure each other, you may find that both of you derive a lot of pleasure from your *partner's* intense pleasure.

YOUR SEXUAL REBIRTH: BEGINNING A NEW ERA OF "EXPANDED SENSUALITY"

If you continue to practice the various emotional, attitudinal, and behavioral skills described in this book, and if neither you nor your partner remains overly disturbed about the problem, things will almost certainly improve significantly on the sexuality/sensuality fronts.

By now you have both:

- become more flexible about the rigid conditions that you've believed *must* occur for sex to happen;
- challenged the old narrow definition of sex as intercourse and replaced it with a more playful notion of sex compatible with humans' broader erotic possibilities;
- learned more about the good sensations your body and your partner's can obtain through experimentation with a wide variety of sensual experiences;
- learned how to monitor and challenge thoughts that create anxiety and block arousal; and
- improved your ability to communicate comfortably what you and your partner would like sexually.

Putting It All Together

Sex can now be as varied as you make it: not always gourmet sex, but highly satisfying—a source of love, stress reduction, sensuality, fun, or various combinations of these. It needs never be a "test" or an obligation; the Eskimos' word for intercourse is "laughing together."

Sometimes your sexual experiences together may consist of a three-hour "orgy" involving whipped cream and eight of the most exotic activities from Alex Comfort's *Joy of Sex*. At other times a "quickie" or a "meat and potatoes" experience can be highly satisfying. Sex need never become routine or chronically dull as long as your brains and goodwill and sensory nerve endings hold out.

One sex therapist observed that people's memories of pleasant sexual experiences seem to fall into three general categories: (1) tenderness; (2) unexpected; and (3) transgression—that is, something more on the exotic side. The various sensate focus experiences described in the beginning of the chapter address the tenderness and intimacy climate. The remainder of the chapter will detail ways to creatively expand both your "spontaneous" and "exotic" sexual experiences.

General "Rules"

• Although you don't have to pick the perfect time, don't pick the worst time. Especially good times might be when he's feeling some positive spurt, such as after some success or good news, or at points in the day when he's minimally stressed or tired.
• Be playful and cuddling even when you're not involved in genital sex, making sure to communicate how much you value him.
• Try making overtures once or twice, but if it's very clear he's not interested, back off—without hurt or anger. Even stud bulls have their off days. Go off and do something else that's involving and don't personalize his reluctance! You are not responsible for his lack of sexual desire.

SOME "FIRE-LIGHTING" TECHNIQUES

1. Gently, teasingly stroke an erogenous zone. Lightly massage the inside of his palms and arm; gently knead the inside of his thighs; run your finger over some of his other erogenous zones. All of these can usually be done with clothes on, as well as unclothed. They can be done when you're snuggling together watching TV or passing in the kitchen.
2. While hugging him, slowly and teasingly rotate your pubic bone against his groin, and perhaps give him a light squeeze on his derriere.
3. Suck gently on his chin, his fingers, or his ear.
4. Massage the back of his neck.
5. Stroke his entire body, from his forehead to his toes.
6. Keep a male and a female figurine on the mantel. Whoever

feels like having sex lays the figurine on its side. If the other agrees, sometime during the evening the other figurine is laid down too.

7. Make an erotic telephone call to your partner at work or leave him a note, such as "Hot flesh will take you soon to new fantasies."

8. If he wakes up with an erection, strike while the iron is hot.

9. Playfully wrestle on the floor or couch or bed until you feel some physiological arousal—even deep breathing counts—then rechannel it into a sexual encounter through some of the preceding kinds of teasing/touching.

10. Greet him at the door nude or in a sexy outfit or surprise him by coming into a room dressed in some see-through lingerie. Have some oysters and champagne or other sexy foods handy.

11. Put on some music and get him away from the TV—so you can dance slowly and sensuously with lowered lights, as you used to during courtship.

12. Take a bath together, with frothy bubbles that hide what's below the surface—so you can surprise each other by touching unsuspecting body parts. Or take a shower together in a darkened bathroom (making sure you know where things are beforehand so that it's safe).

13. Tell him that you love to look at and rub your hands over his wonderful body or bury your nose in his fuzzy chest. Buy him some satin shorts.

14. Talk about a favorite fantasy, read passages from an erotic book, or watch an erotic film together.

15. Exercise to a videotape and then fall into bed while your bodies are still tingly.

16. Give each other back rubs.

17. Kiss or suck each other's lips while concentrating on the memories of your first passionate kisses together.

Ways to Enhance Your "Quickies"

1. Occasionally change your usual location. Possibilities include a rug, a sofa, over the back of the chair, in front of the fireplace, a secluded beach or meadow.
2. Switch your usual roles, with one of you taking charge of the whole scenario, from initiating to ending the encounter. The other is passively responsive and receptive. It's a good way to get out of ingrained active-passive, male-female roles.
3. Wear blindfolds to bed and pretend you're adolescents with raging hormones just discovering sex.
4. Kneel next to him and slowly massage his most erogenous zones, letting him enjoy the ebb and flow of erotic buildup. (Then switch!)
5. Fantasize while you're making love and encourage your partner to do so as well. At the point of orgasm, you can switch off the fantasy and just focus on the delicious feelings you and your partner are experiencing together.
6. Lie together and let every part of you fill the crevices of every part of him.
7. Touch every orifice of each other's body with your nose, fingers, toes, breasts—including the often-overlooked but highly sensitive ones. Or blow gently on erotic areas of each other's body.
8. Take a shower together and massage each other all over with soapy hands.

One of the simplest and best ways for a couple to heighten arousal and increase the intensity of orgasms is to tease each other. Teasing, the slow seductive gathering of pleasure, is an easily accessible "nonprescription" aphrodisiac that will enliven almost any sexual relationship. You can add an element of surprise by bringing your partner to high levels of arousal, then pausing to build up sexual tension before resuming intense stimulation.

Plan "Gourmet Specials"

1. *Agree on a sexual fantasy you'd like to try enacting.* One person then takes charge of setting up the scene and bringing in any required "props." Build up the suspense by making whispered references to it several days in advance.

2. *Alternate setting up a special "exotic" session every month or two.* One of you, for example, could arrange for body paints and a discardable sheet and plastic cloth. Another week, your mate might get an erotic video to be played at a special weekend he's arranged at a romantic hotel.

3. *Share sexual fantasies without acting them out.* "I'll tell you one of mine if you tell me one of yours" can be arousing, fun, and bring you closer as well as help increase your sexual comfort and freedom from guilt. Fantasies are harmless images in our heads and are probably one of the best and safest aphrodisiacs around.

4. *Set a "theme of the month."* Make one month "Everything but Intercourse" month, another "Playing Doctor Month," making a habit of periodically bringing variety and freshness into your sex life.

5. *Have an orgy for two.* Make sure your phones are turned off and your kids shipped out for several hours. Pack in enough food and beverages to keep you going for several hours. Getting out of bed only to go to the toilet or to change the music, and with a bottle of massage oil and several erotic books next to you in case you run short of ideas, play. Be as inventive, as passive, as active, as relaxed as you wish. Talk, laugh, tease; explore each other's bodies. Try licking your partner all over or having sex in the shower. Have rough-and-tumble times interspersed with tender-and-relational times.

   Experiment with delaying orgasms as long as possible, moving together slowly and signaling your partner if orgasm seems imminent, then stopping your movement temporarily until your arousal level subsides somewhat. Try sitting facing each other during intercourse, if you can manage it: it provides marvelous opportunities for slow, sensuous intercourse.

6. *Play relaxing, sensuous music.* Many of the "New Age" audiotapes now available in bookstores, music stores, and health food stores provide just the right atmosphere.

7. *Pack a picnic basket with champagne* and take it to bed or to a beautiful, secluded setting, along with blanket or foam mat. Even if there is not enough privacy for sex, you can still have a marvelously sensuous time.

8. *Keep a grab bag handy with slips of paper suggesting sex ideas*—from your own repertoire or from such books as Alex Comfort's *New Joy of Sex.* If sex starts waning or getting dull, pick one at random and try it out.

9. *Write a scenario for the best sexual experience you can imagine,* and have your mate do so as well. Collaborate on a "script" and play it out. You can each "rehearse" in advance so that you can easily switch into character when you're ready to play the scene.

WHAT TO DO IF HE HAS PROBLEMS WITH ERECTIONS OR EARLY OR RETARDED EJACULATION

If you've done many of the sensate focus and other self-help exercises in this book, by now you will likely have made some real progress in discovering that sex can be highly enjoyable—with or without regular erections. If he still wants to improve his erectile capacity, however, sit down and have a frank discussion about ways the two of you can work on it together. The most effective techniques for dealing with erectile and ejaculation problems are fully described in Helen Singer Kaplan's *Illustrated Manual of Sex Therapy, How to Overcome Premature Ejaculation,* and Bernie Zilbergeld's *Male Sexuality.*

How to Help Him with His "Performance Anxiety"

Occasional erectile failures—a lot more common than the common cold—should not be a cause for much concern. But how can you communicate this to *him*?

An especially helpful technique for dealing with performance anxiety that you can teach your partner is *rational-emotive imagery*. Several times a week he is to close his eyes and imagine having sex with you, with his penis not erect [or ejaculating too quickly or slowly.] He is then to imagine his partner (you) getting disappointed or even irritable and himself feeling like a dud. Then, keeping the same "performance problem" in his mind's eye, he is to change his feelings from shame or anxiety to disappointment or mild frustration.

This exercise provides a sort of "stress inoculation" so that when he is in the actual situation his emotional resilience is more likely. The effective ingredient in changing the disturbed emotional reaction to a more appropriate one is, once again, rational thinking. The thoughts most often reported by men as successful in reducing performance anxiety include: "This is uncomfortable, but my worth as a human being does not ride on the size of my penis." "Where is it writ I must always be engorged in exactly the way I'd prefer to be?" Other helpful coping statements can include "Relax" or "I'm just going to concentrate on my feelings of pleasure and closeness and the dozens of other nice things we can do to each other's bodies—and scrap intercourse for this session." Suggest to your mate that he write at least five rational coping statements on an index card, and refer to them regularly.

Even if he has trouble getting or maintaining erections a significant percentage of the time, you can both probably live with this. But make sure he knows how to use his fingers, toes, tongue, and thighs to help give you pleasure and that you are also willing to do some of the things he needs to help him get aroused or in other ways be sensually gratified. Skillfully combining the pleasures of the mind and the physical senses gives your physical relationship the potential for being marvelously pleasurable.

What to Do If His Erectile Problems Are Organically Based

Although until about ten years ago it was widely accepted that the majority of erectile problems were purely psychogenic, it is currently thought that up to 40 or 50 percent of them may be organically based—that is, caused by diseases or the use of drugs.

When, because of an organically based condition, erectile capacity is not sufficient for penetration, and a man still wishes to have the option of intercourse, several possible treatment options are now available. These include two kinds of penile implants (semirigid and inflatable), penile revascularization (a procedure akin to arterial bypass), and injection of papaverine or phentolamine into the side of the penis. Most recently, a finding that defects in the nitric oxide system of the penis may account for 7 to 8 million of the impotence cases among American men was reported by urology professor Dr. Jacob Rajfer in *The New England Journal of Medicine*. It is expected that this important finding may eventually pave the way to developing better methods for treating erectile problems.

None of these treatments should be considered without careful diagnosis by one or more physicians and thorough education as to the risks of each of the procedures.

As for aphrodisiacs, the U.S. Food and Drug Administration prohibits the sale of any over-the-counter products purported to arouse or increase sexual desire because of lack of adequate data to establish the safety and effectiveness of any of them.

HOW TO BE SEXUALLY ASSERTIVE

Now let's try out some of the communication skills you learned in Chapter 8 in a variety of sexual situations.

Initiating Sex

You're in bed with your partner at 11:00 P.M. and feel like having some physical contact. Your partner gives you a kiss on the cheek, says "Good night," and turns his back to you, as he has for the past three weeks.

Some possible responses:

- Stroke his body for a few seconds, then back off if he either ignores you or says "I've got to get to sleep."
- Say "I'd like to borrow your body; ten minutes should be all I need. Erection is optional—I'd love just to make out with you. I'm sure ten minutes less sleep won't hurt."

Possible response if he still refuses:

- "OK, sweetheart—but rest assured I'm going to be after your hot little body tomorrow night at 10:00. Or you can surprise me—that would be fun too!"

It's Sunday afternoon. Your partner is sprawled on the couch in his running clothes, with the sports section, damp with sweat after a three-mile run. You sit next to him and playfully run your hand over his thigh. He freezes, then says, "C'mon—can't you see I just need to collapse?"

Possible response:

- Slip him a note that says, "You have a date in the shower in half an hour; clothes optional."

Dealing with His Anxiety About Erections

You're in bed, beginning to have sex, but your partner is having problems becoming aroused. He says impatiently, "Look, I'm just not in the mood."

Janet L. Wolfe / 269

Possible response:

- "You mean to tell me you're going to let "that guy" decide whether or not we're going to make love? Imagine letting him push you around like that! Let's forget about him and just roll around and have some fun!"
- "I've got an idea. How about seeing what you can do with my body for the next ten or fifteen minutes? Then, if there's anything you have a yen for that I could do for you—feel free!"

If he continues to be overfocused on his erection, ask him:

- "What do you suppose would happen if you just forgot about your penis for the evening? Pretend it's on vacation."

Handling His Procrastination over Sex

He's promised that you would definitely have sex; but, like his promises to pick up the dry cleaning, he's already defaulted, your gentle reminders notwithstanding. You're beginning to feel frustrated and resentful.

After working on your self-talk, you might approach him and say:

- "I need your help with something. Is this a good time to talk? I know you're pretty overworked and distracted these days and probably would just like to be left alone. But there's something that's really important to me, and that is having some physical contact time together every once in a while. It feels good, and goes a long way toward helping me feel warm and appreciated and connected to you. Any suggestions on how we can deal with this problem?"

If he continues to complain of his fatigue:

- "Yes, I can understand that. But tactile stimulation and aerobic activity can help relieve fatigue. Let's test it out."

Dealing with "You Can't Force It"

He says, "I just don't feel any chemistry anymore. You can't force it if it's not there."

Possible response:

- "Says who? Even though neither of us may feel particularly lustful, let's see what happens if we do a little experimenting. We might be surprised! Even if only one of us gets turned on—well, one out of two isn't bad! Besides, I've got some really hot sexual fantasies going that I'd like to try out." Then don't tell him what they are until he's entwined with you.

Asking for Some Special Stimulation:

- "I would just love it if sometime I could just lie back and have you make love to every part of my body."
- "Sometimes when you're stimulating me, you stop just when I'm almost ready to come. I'd really like it if, when I'm starting to explode, you would keep up the pace for a little while longer, until I let you know to stop."
- "How about you just lie there with your arms around me, and me and my vibrator will do all the rest."

Once you and your partner are able to talk openly about sex, you will have opened up a new world of intimacy and togetherness that will have a positive effect on the rest of your life as well.

IF YOU'VE TRIED EVERYTHING, AND HE'S STILL RESPONDING LIKE A DEAD FISH

What are you to do if you've reduced your hurt and anger, tried your best to get your partner to have some fairly regular sexual/ sensual encounters, and he's still resisting sex as if it were the plague?

- Do not revert to blaming yourself or being angry at him. He's got a problem—let's face it.
- Strongly encourage him either to see a therapist alone or to go to a couples or sex therapist with you to work on the problems. Explain firmly that you're not willing to keep pushing this under the rug. If he continues to see sex as something you do only with "whores" and not with his wife or the mother of his kids, he probably has a fairly deep-seated problem. Similarly, if he's withholding sex because of anger or misogyny, is chronically depressed, or has a substance abuse problem, he is likely to continue to be a pretty poor partner, both sexually and nonsexually.

CONCLUSION

We have the capacity to break lovemaking out of a rigid, routine, orgasm-focused ordeal into a loose, playful experience to which both partners can look forward. To do so, you will need to free yourselves from the formulaic notion that sex must always lead to intercourse and from the pressure to perform. Also, you will each need to assume some responsibility for your own sexual pleasure, each asking the other for what is wanted and exchanging information about what is pleasurable and what is not. A third important ingredient is being open in acknowledging your anxiety when it starts to interfere with pleasure.

Making it a priority to carve out periods of time when you are together physically and emotionally is crucial. "We always make some time each week for one-on-one intimacy," confided one of the busiest but most loving couples I know. "If necessary, we postpone the laundry or cancel our tennis date or call in the grandparents or a baby-sitter. It's hard, and we have to keep reminding ourselves that it's important, but it works. A few years ago, when we just passed each other coming and going and fell into bed exhausted each night, we were ready for the divorce courts. But we're just fine now, even though the house isn't quite as orderly as it used to be!"

This couple went on to explain that they had to teach the kids not to interrupt them when they were in the bedroom with the door closed; and they even added a lock on their door for extra peace of mind. They also explained to their youngsters that although some of the noises they sometimes heard from the bedroom might sound like someone was being hurt, "it's actually pleasure— our way of expressing love to each other." And none of this planning precludes spontaneous sex: "We still manage to grab those moments when we can."

Another couple, in which the husband had erection problems because of his need to be on hypertensive medication, has wonderful sex because "we got off our 'penis focus' and learned a lot about the dozens of other wonderful things you can do in sex. I miss the fact that I no longer have the ability to fly at 'full mast,'" he said, "but we're having more delicious times than ever—even when one or both of us doesn't come!"

CHAPTER 10

HOW TO BE HAPPY THOUGH HORNY

"Mind, not body, makes lasting wedlock."
—Publilius Syrus, *Sententiae*, 43 B.C.

THREE WOMEN'S SOLUTIONS

Christie

Christie and Scott's marriage had been about as traditional and uncomplicated as apple pie. With apple pie, however, you never quite know what's going on under the crust until it's pierced. When their son went off to college, leaving only their sixteen-year-old daughter at home, forty-six-year-old Scott accepted a promotion that required several days a month of traveling.

Christie described their relationship up to this point as one in which "we got along OK. Maybe we got into fights occasionally, but they usually blew over pretty fast, and I guess you'd say we had an average sex life—not sensational, but OK. We made love maybe once or twice a week for the past several years; it was usually before we fell asleep and pretty quick."

For the first year after his promotion Scott seemed energized by his new job responsibilities, and when he came home from his trips he even seemed a bit more affectionate. Gradually, however, he began to become moody and withdrawn, sexually and emotionally. When Christie tried to figure out what was happening, Scott responded, "I guess I'm not sure about our relationship. Maybe with the kids growing up, there's not all that much left between us." When pressed as to whether there was "anyone else," Scott reluctantly confessed that he had been regularly seeing a young woman on his out-of-town trips, but that it had ended since she had found someone who was "marriage material."

Appalled and frightened, Christie came in to see me, confessing she'd never seen a therapist but was having a hard time getting a grip on the situation. Although she was open to seeing me together with her husband eventually, for now she wanted the therapy to herself to sort things out.

In the course of sorting things out it emerged that Christie, on the surface, had been "the perfect wife." Despite holding a four-day-a-week nursing job for the past eleven years, she cooked, did the lioness's share of the household work, deferred to her husband's wishes, and kept herself physically fit and attractive. Underneath this well-functioning persona, however, lay a somewhat rigid person—fearful of confrontations, upset by disorder, and rather out of touch with her feelings—which now, to her surprise and embarrassment, came pouring out.

Four months of her active participation in combination individual and group therapy produced some rather dramatic changes. The group and I encouraged her to stop blaming herself for her husband's withdrawal and to open up more with us and him about some of the dreams and desires that were submerged during her nineteen years of marriage. Initially this unleashed a certain amount of anger, largely directed toward Scott, at how unhelpful he had been with the house and kids while she had "juggled everyone's needs but my own." She also began to read about women's issues and sheepishly admitted one day that she and Scott had been following their script like Ma and Pa Kettle and that she now saw how destructive it had been to their relationship. She had, however, known no other way to be at the time.

She especially worked at becoming less angry and more appropriately assertive with her husband. Although still deeply hurt by the affair, she encouraged him to open up about some of the feelings he'd had about their marriage and the dreams he had for the future. She let go of a good deal of her compulsiveness about household neatness and social and family events. She strongly urged Scott to see a therapist and provided him with two names. He reluctantly saw one once, claimed "the guy said I was fine," and never returned. He was willing to see me for occasional couples sessions with Christie when (at my urging) she explained to him that I needed to hear his side.

Over a period of several months, his depression and confusion over the future of the marriage generally abated. Their communication improved, and there was a new spark in their relationship as they realized their kids' transition to adulthood had a plus side: it freed them up to try out some new things. The last time I spoke to them, they had just returned from a ballroom dancing weekend and were planning their first trip to Europe. Sex had become much more experimental, as well as more loving, something Scott had thought he would find only with a new woman. Scott is having some discomfort in adjusting to Christie's new sexual assertiveness, asking me "What did you do to her? She's getting to be too much for me!" He's still insistent on being the initiator most of the time, turning down her overtures with "Not now" or "I'm too tired"; but he is struggling with trying to adjust to the new shift in their roles. Christie feels slightly impatient with having to restrain herself but is highly positive about the many constructive changes that have occurred in herself as well as in her marriage.

Rhoda

When last we left her in Chapter 7, Rhoda was struggling to catch up on the debts her husband, Brian, had accumulated, and she was much more aware of how disturbed he was. After four couples sessions Brian disappeared during the one-week trial separation he and Rhoda had agreed to, returning with a complicated story about how he had gone to the country for a long "platonic" weekend with a former female classmate and another couple. He then failed to show up for their next couples session; on a hunch Rhoda went to his favorite bar and found him there.

Rhoda spent the next three weeks assessing the pros and cons of staying with him, finally concluding that he seemed too heavily locked into feeling sorry for himself; and his breaches of faith every time she had "given him another chance" decided her against putting any more energy into the relationship. Sad that things had not worked out and apprehensive about "getting back into that whole dating scene again," she nonetheless felt that at least now she had the possibility of finding someone who could be a responsible mate and co-parent.

Lorna

Thirty-four-year-old Lorna and her forty-year-old husband, Joe, had an exciting relationship—sexually and in every other way—during the year and a half when they "commuter-dated" three times a month between St. Louis and California. Six months after they married and moved in together, he all but stopped having sex with her and declined her repeated overtures. When their daughter was born a year and a half later, she was engrossed enough in being a new parent to be temporarily diverted from her physical longings for Joe. By the time the baby was two, however, she was growing increasingly frustrated, sexually and emotionally.

Because Joe was a loving husband and involved father and had worked hard to kick his addiction to alcohol, Lorna was not about to leave him. He acknowledged, too, that the problem with sex had nothing to do with her and promised to commit himself to having sex with her at least once a week, if she would first be willing to watch a porn video with him to help him get in the mood. Although she had largely recovered from her hurt at his sexual rejection of her, she felt disheartened at the thought that "he needs pictures of other women to turn him on."

When he also acknowledged, attempting to be as honest as possible, that he occasionally went to massage parlors and "peep shows" and masturbated there, she became furious—especially when she found out it cost him approximately $150 a month out of their tight budget.

After calming herself down and reminding herself of the many positives in their relationship, she explored with him what it was about having sex with "slutty women" that made him prefer it over having sex with a wife he supposedly loved. He responded, "For one thing, it's different and totally removed from everyday life—a place I go to unwind—like some men do at the gym, I guess." The other reason, he said, was that sex, in his mind, was still something you did with "sluts," not clean-cut women like Lorna.

Because Lorna was eventually able to listen without significant hurt or anger, the two of them were able to create a dialogue and continue to work on the problem. Although Joe has stopped going to massage parlors and instead puts the money into a weekend fund for both of them, he does not yet feel ready to have sex more often with Lorna. (He has had problems getting erections several times when he has tried.) However, he has agreed to hold her whenever she wants to use her vibrator, and they sometimes give each other massages. Although still frustrated about their sexual situation, Lorna gets her physical stimulation where she can and has learned to indulge in extended masturbation sessions. She has also begun to work part-time and has resumed her painting, both of which provide her with stimulating outlets. And she continues to feel optimistic that

Joe will gradually get unhooked from his "whore fantasies" and develop a more expanded sexual repertoire as they go through more of the exercises listed in Chapter 9.

TO HANG IN OR TO GET OUT?
THAT IS THE QUESTION

How long does one "suffer the slings and arrows of outrageous fortune"—in this case, stay with a man who won't connect with you sexually no matter what you try? Outrageous fortune may have its slings and arrows, but it's up to you to regulate the amount of *suffering* you experience.

You may or may not succeed in influencing your mate to connect with you sexually or to change other behaviors. Once you've tried your best to communicate your wants and preferences and have balanced the pros and cons of the relationship, the bottom-line question is:

If I never get these things I'd like to have from my spouse, can I live with that, without making myself miserable and unhappy?

It's extremely difficult to clarify your priorities in a relationship and to decide what you can and cannot live with. A good way to begin the evaluation process is to return to the checklist on pages 66–67 and review your mate's strengths versus his weaknesses.

Then answer the following set of questions, designed to help you achieve a clear assessment of the relationship "package" you currently have.

1. Are you friends? Would you still seek each other out should you cease to be primary partners?
2. Do you expect him to fill the emptiness in you? Are you afraid to leave out of fear of being alone?
3. Does each of you believe in your own worth and value?
4. Do you feel you have developed the ability to achieve a balance

among being able to be with each other, to stand up against each other, and to be solitary?

5. Do you like the way you are when you're with him? Does he bring out the worst in you or the best in you?
6. Would you still try to develop a relationship with him if you were meeting him for the first time?
7. Would you want to be in a relationship with *yourself*? If not, what should you continue to work on?
8. Are you *both* putting energy into keeping this relationship healthy?

How does sex fit into the scheme of things? Only you can assess that. On sex educator Dr. Sol Gordon's list of "The Ten Most Important Ingredients of a Mature Relationship," sex is relegated to *ninth* place under the heading of "Passion, including, but not limited to, a healthy sex life."

Here are the eight items he places *before* sex:

1. *Intimacy:* closeness and the ability to truly love and care for each other
2. *A sense of humor:* willingness to laugh at oneself and the world at large
3. *Honest communication:* openness and good listening skills
4. *A common sense of mission and purpose:* shared ethical and/or spiritual goals
5. *Equality:* a conscious sense of the essential importance of respect for each other as partners and shared responsibility in career, leisure, child rearing, and life-style choices
6. *A sense of adventure:* a desire to keep the relationship fresh; discovering new and interesting ways of expressing affection for each other
7. *Shared experience:* an ever-growing repository of mutual undertakings, private conversations, and shared thoughts on issues and events
8. *Respect for the other person's feelings and wishes:* the willingness to delay one's own short-term desires [on behalf of your spouse]

in the knowledge that a similar willingness will exist on the part of the other person at a later time.

Some women want to have a full connection that is psychological, intellectual, emotional, *and* physical. This generally takes a fair amount of effort both to find and to maintain. If that's what you want, however—go for it!

Others have decided they have most of the ingredients they want. And because they accept the fact that no relationship is perfect and have developed the capacity to tolerate emotionally what theirs lacks, they have decided to stick with it.

Still others, having failed to achieve a mature and accepting relationship with *themselves,* are either hanging on to deeply flawed men out of terror of being alone, or have been unable to work out a relationship with well-adjusted men out of their inability to deal with hurt and low frustration tolerance when flaws appeared.

One woman whose sex life was practically nonexistent, but who is still happily hanging in, said: "The most important thing is that we love each other deeply and continue to grow together. Sure, I'd love to have a hot sex life; but we've discussed it and come to terms with it, and I no longer feel hurt and rejected."

WHEN IT'S PROBABLY TIME TO STOP TRYING TO DRAW BLOOD FROM A STONE

Are you with a man who still won't connect with you sexually, affectionately, or in practically any other important way after you've exhausted all the methods in this book? How do you know if you have one of these PNEs (Probably Not Educables)?

Did you feel your heart and your hopes sink as you read any of the lists of desirable relationship qualities? If he remains narcissistically self-absorbed, allergic to intimacy and communication, and unwilling to be responsive to your wants or to negotiate to conclusions, chances are—even if you had the lustiest sex in the world and achieved an unusually high degree of frustration tolerance—you'll probably continue to have an unpleasant and unfulfilling relationship.

If he's in need of massive emotional education, social skills training, tenderness expression practice, a personality transplant, or some antidepressant medication—*and isn't willing to do anything about it*—he's Probably Not Educable. And as painful as it might be in the short run, you're probably going to be better off in the long run if you move on.

A far more difficult decision to make would be whether or not to leave someone with whom you have a solid and loving relationship, but with whom you have to put yourself through hoops to enjoy sex and sensuality—or one whose virtues are legion and whose flaws are tolerable, but who just doesn't fire you up.

With either of these scenarios, if you are considering calling it quits and seeking out the whole package—romance, passion, plus all the other ingredients of a mature relationship—here is some important advice:

1. *Don't hang on to a seriously flawed person because you think you'll never find anyone* and must thus live miserably ever after. A lot of women look for a strong man to depend on because they feel ineffectual and unable to operate on their own. Instead, work on giving your all to enjoying other aspects of your life and to being as happy as you can with or without a man.

2. *The grass is not necessarily greener on the other side*. Often that handsome couple you see walking arm in arm may be siblings, friends, or at the denouement of a soon-to-end three-day-long sexual fling. Even that man you see affectionately holding his wife around the waist may—once in bed—be technically inept and not very interested in sex.

3. *The so-called "single life" is not lonelier than a bad marriage*. "At least now I can do something about it [loneliness]," one woman said. "When you're single and things are bad—tomorrow's an-

other day. When you're married and things are bad—tomorrow is the same day." More and more research is showing higher rates of happiness among single women than among married women. Something is not necessarily better than nothing.

4. *Do not commit to mate number two while "madly" in love.* Romantic relationships can be exciting but volatile. If you put all your eggs in the romance basket you could wind up with nothing.

5. *You will not die from temporary—or even permanent—lack of partner sex.* All of us have survived this situation at one time or another. Not only has no one ever died from it, but many in fact have flourished, producing poetry and paintings and gardens and bestowing many services on humanity and the planet.

IF YOU DECIDE TO STAY: HOW TO REDESIGN YOUR LIFE TO GET YOUR PASSION NEEDS MET

> ". . . the human need for sex is made to bear the burden of all our bodily starvation for contact and sensation, all our creative starvation, all our need for social contact, and even our need to find a meaning in our lives."
> —Deirdre English and Barbara Ehrenreich

If, despite the flaws in your relationship, you decide that its advantages definitely outweigh the disadvantages, resolve right now not to feel deprived or victimized. Remember that no one is going to make your life good for you. It's up to you to find alternatives for creating the passion and sensuality and other things your mate seems unable to provide.

Exercise: Think back to your more satisfying sexual and sensual experiences and "scenes"—either with your present partner or previous ones. Close your eyes and imagine as many details as possible of the setting and the elements about it that were most pleasurable; then jot them down.

Next, after you've jotted these down, list *alternative* ways you could achieve some of them.

Many of our most "romantic moments"—walking on moonlit beaches, dining by candlelight on sensuous foods—become associated with having a man to share them with. Is it necessarily he who evokes the emotional fullness and sensory pleasure? Or are these feelings largely stimulated by the experience itself, with a "halo" effect carried over to him? Is a solo for unaccompanied cello any less beautiful than a duet?

How many of us allow ourselves to feel the same kind of feelings when alone? Or with women friends or platonic male friends? Too many women, alas, seem to rate all these sensory experiences as somehow lacking unless there is a man to share them with.

Many women to whom I have given the preceding "homework" assignment have reported that at first they were mainly aware of a longing to share these experiences with someone. Once they got into it, however, a whole new world opened up to them.

In the process, they arrived at the point where they saw that not only would life not be intolerably lonely and unhappy without their mate if they were in dead-end relationships, but in fact they might actually *enjoy* themselves, whether or not they decided to pursue another relationship.

The following table was generated by one of my women's groups in response to the "homework" on how to get their passion needs met in ways other than partner sex. The left column contains the women's list of "needs" that sex serves for them; the right column contains alternate ways of getting many of these same elements.

The Needs that Sex Serves for Me	Alternative Ways I Could Get These Needs Met
A sense of being suspended in time or transported to another world	Spend some time in a quiet, comfortable space. Listen to some "New Age" music. Walk on the beach at sunset.
The feelings of having every orifice filled and exploding with pleasure	Do gourmet masturbation with a small dildo. Then use your mind, your fingers, your vibrator (or all of the above) to drive yourself sexually out of your mind.
Rocking back and forth as though riding on gentle waves	Float in a warm pool or tub.
Every part of my body tingling	Get a massage. Rub yourself all over with a loofah sponge.
Feeling loved and cherished	Spend time with friends who love you and treat you well. Buy yourself flowers or a present periodically, such as beautiful lingerie or linens. Dictate some self-loving self-affirmations into a tape recorder and periodically play it.
Laughing and playing like a child, without shame or self-consciousness	With a group of friends, find a secluded spot where you can romp in the grass or leaves; roll down hills; rub flowers over each other. Play silly games.
Feeling of being inside a soft, warm cocoon with no worldly pressures	Spend some time in a sauna or some other quiet, gentle place.

A feeling of intense connection with the cosmos	Spend time quietly enjoying nature.
Enjoying oral sensuousness	Suck on a sensuous food, such as a tangerine or a liquid-cherry-center chocolate. Or pair up with a friend and feed each other with your eyes closed.
Feeling as though the other person's soul and mine had become one	Spend a lovely, relaxing day with a close friend. At the end of it, sit quietly together and enjoy your feelings of deep connectedness.

This exercise can be extremely helpful for men to do as well.

Living Life with Passion

You can have a passionate life under extreme sexual restraint or even without sex—as was the case with Emily Dickinson, the Brontë sisters, and Virginia Woolf. There are many ways to get your juices flowing, to connect with others, and to feel good. Here are some of the best ones.

Enjoying Long-Term Friendships
While lovers (and even husbands) may come and go, best friends often last forever. Among the nicest things about close friends is that they know quickly what you are feeling and accept you no matter what. Despite the source of comfort, affection, understanding, and connection they provide, many women accord their friendships much less importance than love relationships with men and especially less importance than marriage—even though the friendships may often be of higher quality than their spouse or lover relationship. Studies comparing people's friendships with those of

their spouses and lovers have shown fairly consistently that while love relationships will typically have higher levels of fascination, exclusiveness, and sexual desire and greater depths of caring about the other person, they also have a greater potential for distress, ambivalence, conflict, and mutual criticism.

Whether or not you are mated, having at least two close women friends with whom you can share the secret corners of yourself— your worries, dreams, and joys—is pure gold. Ironically, what is perceived by a lot of men as "kaffeeklatsching" among women consists in fact of profound discussions and analyses of central problems in our social structure.

In addition to having many of the same advantages of close female friendships, women find that platonic relationships with *male* friends, including those who are gay, often provide another dimension: the subtleties of sexual attraction, even though not acted out. Also, these friends can serve as a sounding board when you want a "male point of view."

With friends you can celebrate the occasions of your life, be they landmark birthdays, your first orgasm or promotion—even menopause!

Achieving Natural Highs

One of the very best ways to increase life's pleasure is to enjoy nature. Go for a woodland hike or a walk alone on the beach; take in the sun, the moon, the birds, the sky. Increase your sense of relatedness to all living things, your feeling of being a part of the cosmos. As you do these things, say to yourself: "I am a feeling, breathing work of nature; I am a complete and whole person."

Being in an unspoiled natural setting is a transcendent experience that can help us feel connected with all living things, not to mention the whole universe. Can sex and religion give us a greater feeling than that?

Being in nature is also a golden opportunity to appreciate your body. Instead of worrying how large your thighs are or how thick your ankles are, enjoy the kiss of the sun and wind on your skin or the way your leg muscles ripple as they propel you along.

Spending Time Alone

Former congresswoman Shirley Chisholm once said that if she could choose anybody in the world to take to a desert island, she would take herself.

Taking time to have privacy for yourself—that is, being *with* yourself as opposed to being "alone"—is one of the best ways to get to know yourself well and to become a whole, independent person.

Use solitude as an opportunity to engage in that lifelong voyage toward discovering as much beauty, happiness, and experience as you can. Read a historical novel and see the themes of love and power threading back through time. Find a lovely natural spot, sit in a scented bath, or go to a quiet, comfortable space in your own home where you can relax and listen to music, read, or meditate, free from any distractions. Just as the sensate pleasures outlined in Chapter 9 are an excellent route to discovering what makes your body feel good, these "psyche-focusing" sessions can be your means for discovering what pleases, stimulates, or relaxes your mind and soul.

Developing Vital, Absorbing Interests

> "I can always be distracted by love, but
> eventually I get horny for my creativity."
> —Gilda Radner

Women's owning their own sexuality is to me a metaphor for empowerment, going out to participate as fully and actively as possible in the activities available to them on the planet. Not surprisingly, a common occurrence noted by many therapists who have conducted groups for nonorgasmic women is that by the end of the group the women are glowing and confident. "They clean up their relationships, change their hairdos, go back to school. They feel better about themselves, and their partners and their kids and the people they work with feel better about them, too," says Toni Ayres, who ran some of these pioneering groups at the University of California Medical Center.

One woman who felt very strongly about the relationship between the sex drive and the drive to live successfully was Mae West. She believed that those with the strongest sex drive also had the strongest passion for their chosen careers and for just about everything else in life. "Sex energy is in everything you do," she said. "The greater your sexual energy, the greater your creative energy. That's why I always abstained from sex when I was working, to save all my energy for my work."

Develop your own list of things you enjoy—or think you might enjoy—doing. Then start doing them. If you run out of ideas, look at the list in Chapter 7 (pages 158–164) of ways to cultivate *joie de vivre*.

Writer Jane O'Reilly summed up some of the joys of being unpartnered in a recent article: "I float about these days in my own bubble of psychic space that I can fill up and furnish and shape as I wish."

Gourmet Masturbation

If you want a tender, imaginative, sensuous, and skillful lover for those times when your partner is not available, one of your very best resources is . . . *you*. The pure pleasure you can receive from the joy and richness of loving yourself is something that you can have access to as long as you're alive.

Feel the touch of your body through your fingertips. Lie on your stomach and move your derriere against silken sheets, imagining dozens of fingertips gently stroking you. Lie on your back and stroke your face, your breasts, the insides of your thighs, at times using scented massage oil. Take your time, being playful, dropping back, spacing out, teasing yourself. Focus your mind on erotic thoughts and the pleasurable feelings of your skin tingling and your body pulsating. Imagine yourself surrounded by an erotic "aura." For additional inspiration in the fantasy realm, try Lonnie Barbach's wonderful book of women's sexual fantasies, *Erotic Interludes*, or Nancy Friday's books, *My Secret Garden* and *Forbidden Flowers*. For a truly wild and wonderful treat, get yourself a shower massager to play with in the bathtub.

Many women at first protest, "But it's just not the same as being with a partner." Self-loving can, however, be quite delicious. Women who allow full range to their erotic imagination and are willing to play their bodies like beautiful instruments report that some of their masturbation sessions are actually far more exciting than many of their partner experiences have been. Just remember Woody Allen's wonderful advice in *Annie Hall:* "Don't knock masturbation—it's sex with someone I love."

At the peak of sexual ecstasy most people find they are able to abandon themselves and let go of reality. "In a really good orgasm," as Dr. Helen Singer Kaplan put it in an interview, "the woman doesn't know who she is, where she is, or how she got there. She just goes on that trip."

Babs took advantage of her husband's being out of town to unplug her phone and have an orgy for one. Beginning with caviar, cognac, and soft music, she moved to a long perfumed bath and thence, clad in a silky peignoir, to her candlelit bedroom. There she engaged in two hours of reading erotica, teasing herself, and having a total of five orgasms before she fell off to sleep, exhausted but tingling with pleasure.

Massages, Saunas, and Exercise
The laying on of hands need not necessarily be done by a sex partner to be pleasurable and relaxing. Professional massages or saunas on a regular basis are marvelous ways to make your body relaxed and mellow—as can a nice back rub by a friend.

Running, bicycling, aerobic dancing, and playing a vigorous game of volleyball are also excellent ways of helping charge you up and get your endorphins going and even, at times, provide transcendent moments.

Other Passion Preservers

Ginny went on a "girls' ski weekend," enriched by two glorious evenings by the fire with her four dearest friends, snuggled up close together on pillows with their arms around each other or their heads in each other's lap, giggling themselves silly while sipping wine and sampling sensuous snacks each of them had brought. There was no sex in any traditional sense among the friends, but the flow of warmth and friendship between their bodies and their souls was the kind of treat it seems American women rarely allow themselves to have with anyone but animals, young children, or sex partners.

Arlene, whose extremely low-sexed husband would probably be happy if he never had sex again, regularly plans "sexless orgies" with him during which they create sensuous environments and lie together in each other's arms, listening to music by candlelight, only occasionally accompanied by genital sex. They joke about someday writing a book called *The Joys of Cuddling*.

Over the past few years forty-five-year-old Geri has achieved a high level of fulfillment. Now in her second marriage, she has put together her own "package," one that provides what she had unsuccessfully tried to get in her first marriage.

She spends approximately six companionable hours with her mate each week, including a couple of dinners together and a fifteen-minute or so chat before he goes off to bed, plus several hours of doing chores or socializing on the weekend. They have partner sex approximately once every month or two, and she has marvelous "self-loving" sessions several times a month.

But there's a lot else going on in her life. She has a sense of doing her job well, frequently enjoys talking on the phone with friends, and pursues a variety of stimulating activities. She loves the independence that her marriage gives her.

Social historian Shere Hite reports in *Women and Love* that many married women are making a new sort of arrangement by developing a home-based marriage. They are doing what men have always done—making marriage their home base and going outside for friends, entertainment, etc. This is one way that marriage can work for a lot of women, especially those longing for a deeper emotional contact with their husbands than may be possible.

You can create a full, rich life even though you don't share all you'd like to with a man. Psychologist Charlotte Kasl rewrites the pathetic endings of two familiar stories, with the women passionately alive and well:

> Anna Karenina reports that she is feeling less obsessed and paranoid about the Count's abandoning her. She has taken up writing and is making friends so she won't be so dependent on him. Juliet decides to put the brakes on her infatuation with Romeo, realizing it is a bit melodramatic to think of killing herself if they couldn't be together.

You, too, have the opportunity to rewrite your own script. You will probably be surprised to find your life happier and more full of passion than you might ever have thought possible.

SEXUAL SUPPLEMENTATION

In case you thought I'd never get around to it, I do, in fact, have a few thoughts to offer you about the "*A* word"—an affair, having sex with someone other than your mate. Current estimates suggest that anywhere from 25 percent to 70 percent of women have had extramarital affairs. How do they decide to do it? Sometimes it's spur of the moment. You're out of town, at a convention. People are mingling at meetings and cocktail parties. One thing leads to another—usually it's a onetime shot, but sometimes it's "same time next year" at the next convention. At other times it happens between people who have almost daily contact. And sometimes women's "supplements" are their best friend.

Some Cautions

We've already seen how sex is sometimes used to shore up a sagging ego; to reassure oneself that one can still function sexually and is desirable; to serve to punish a partner; or to achieve relaxation or a "buzz."

Earlier in this chapter we discussed other ways you can fulfill these needs. Many people, however, want "sex or nothing." Let's look at some of the potential advantages and disadvantages of having sex with someone other than your mate.

First, here are some of the disadvantages and risks:

1. If you're angry at your mate, you may lose the opportunity to try to deal with the problems, since you are off spending time with the other person.
2. If there's a sexual problem, you don't get a chance to work it out. On more than one occasion I've seen couples ostensibly for marriage counseling or sex therapy, only to find when I interviewed them separately that one was having an active outside relationship and wasn't motivated to work things out at all.
3. If you're having the relationship to make yourself feel more worthwhile or desirable, you may not make the changes necessary to increase your self-acceptance permanently.
4. You may be going for short-term thrills and in the long run lose the relationship with your spouse. If the spouse learns of the outside relationship, potential exists for a good deal of emotional pain among the people and families involved.
5. You may acquire a sexually transmitted disease—including AIDS.
6. You may become so caught up in a web of lies that you become alienated from yourself.

To Supplement or Not to Supplement?

To have an extramarital relationship or not is a decision each person must make according to the dictates of his or her value system, and also an assessment of the short- and long-term pros and cons.

There are many healthy, thriving marriages where one or both partners may have had sex with others, sometimes with positive results. We've all heard more than one story of a couple in whom the painful discovery of "an affair" heralded the dawn of a bright new era in their relationship and a sense of renewed commitment. There are even couples who know about the other's outside relationship though they don't necessarily discuss the details with their spouse. In the event that you do decide to have a supplemental relationship, it would better be conducted with sensitivity to the potential effects on your spouse and a determination not to allow the outside relationship to draw time, love, sex, or affection from your primary one.

Some Women's Experiences

One woman, married for eight years, said this of her three-year love affair with a former business colleague: "It gave me something special to look forward to each week. And it wasn't just the sex: it was having someone out there who called to see how my day was, to have fun with—to make me feel appreciated. Sure, the sex was very nice. But I'm not sure how much of that came just from having a couple of hours off by ourselves, free from our 'normal' lives. There's a lot more time just to lie quietly holding each other, and somehow it seems easier to be more experimental without having kids in the next room."

Other typical comments are:

"It was the one time I didn't feel like a drudge. Normally I come home from the office, throw together dinner, and manage the household with little help from my husband. Then I get criticized if I ever just want to take time out for myself and take a class."

"It was an adventure. The timing was right, and it just happened. And though it was quite a lovely evening, and the guy was very sexy, he's not anyone I could imagine living with in a million years! I have sex with my husband a lot less frequently than I'd like—but he's an incredibly sane, sensitive, and caring guy. And let's face it: there aren't many of *those* around!"

"There was a period of two or three years when I was so turned on to sex, and my husband was such an unimaginative lover, that I couldn't get enough of it. I think I've somewhat gotten it out of my system, though. At this point I'm pretty involved with my work and family, have managed to rev up sex somewhat with my husband, and I have absolutely no desire to go through the lying and other hassles involved in trying to have outside flings."

One woman put it succinctly: "These affairs have saved my marriage."

Is It Worth It?

Every woman's situation is different. Many of the purposes sexual supplementation serves can be met through developing an appreciation of oneself and one's sensuality apart from others, finding enjoyment and passion in many aspects of life, and doing your best to improve the emotional and physical connection with your mate.

Good relationships require a high degree of trust and commitment, and for most people (though not all), having outside relationships may undermine this.

Learning to make a life together with another person, in love, commitment, and tenderness, remains one of our greatest challenges. A good rational philosophy, combined with a lot of goodwill and willingness to keep creatively searching for solutions, is your best bet to help you succeed.

SUGGESTIONS FOR
FURTHER READING

DEVELOPING SELF-ACCEPTANCE

For women:

Friedman, Sonya. *Men Are Just Desserts: How Learning to Be a Woman with a Life of Your Own Can Enrich the Life You Share with a Man.* New York: Warner Books, 1984.

Kasl, Charlotte Davis. *Women, Sex, and Addiction: A Search for Love and Power.* New York: Ticknor and Fields, 1989.

Russianoff, Penelope. *Why Do I Think I Am Nothing without a Man?* New York: Bantam Books, 1985.

Steinem, Gloria. *Revolution from Within: A Book of Self-Esteem.* Boston: Little, Brown & Company, 1992.

Walker, Alice. *In Search of Our Mother's Gardens.* New York: Harcourt, Brace, Jovanovich, 1982.

For men:

Farrell, Warren. *The Liberated Man: Freeing Men and Their Relationships with Women.* New York: Berkley Books, 1992.

Goldberg, Herb. *The Hazards of Being Male: Surviving the Myth of Masculine Privilege.* New York: Signet, 1976.

Naifeh, Steven, and Gregory Smith. *Why Can't Men Open Up?* New York: Clarkson Potter, 1984.

Changing Men (4 issues/year). A magazine covering gender, sex, and political issues. 306 N. Brooks St., Madison, WI 53715.

For both:

Burns, David D. *Feeling Good: The New Mood Therapy.* New York: Signet, 1981

Ellis, Albert. *How to Stubbornly Refuse to Make Yourself Miserable About*

Anything—Yes, Anything! New York: Lyle Stuart/Carol Communications, 1988.

Russianoff, Penelope. *When Am I Going to Be Happy? How to Break the Emotional Bad Habits that Make You Miserable.* New York: Bantam, 1988.

IMPROVING YOUR RELATIONSHIPS

Ellis, Albert. *Anger: How to Live With and Without It.* New York: Citadel/Carol Communications, 1977.

———. *How to Live With a Neurotic.* N. Hollywood, CA: Wilshire Books.

———. *Twenty-Two Ways to Brighten Up Your Love Life* and *Conquering Low Frustration Tolerance* (Audiotapes). Institute for Rational-Emotive Therapy, 45 East 65th Street, New York, NY 10021.

Goldstine, Daniel et al. *The Dance-Away Lover.* New York: Ballantine, 1977.

Gordon, Sol. *Why Love Is Not Enough.* Holbrook, Mass: Bob Adams, Inc., 1988.

Hite, Shere. *Women and Love: A Cultural Revolution in Progress.* New York: St. Martin's Press, 1989.

Jakubowski, Patricia, and Art Lange. *The Assertive Option: Your Rights and Responsibilities.* Champaign, IL: Research Press, 1978.

Lazarus, Arnold. *Marital Myths.* San Luis Obispo, CA: Impact, 1985.

Rose, Phyllis. *Parallel Lives: Five Victorian Marriages.* New York: Vintage Books, 1984.

Tannen, Deborah. *You Just Don't Understand: Women and Men in Conversation.* New York: Ballantine Books, 1991.

SEXUALITY

Men's:

Hite, Shere. *The Hite Report on Male Sexuality: How Men Feel about Love, Sex, and Relationships.* New York: Ballantine Books, 1987.

Zilbergeld, Bernie. *The New Male Sexuality: A Guide to Sexual Fulfillment.* New York: Bantam, 1992.

Women's:

Barbach, Lonnie. *For Yourself: The Fulfillment of Female Sexuality.* New York: New American Library/Dutton, 1976.

Boston Women's Health Collective. *The New Our Bodies, Ourselves.* New York: Simon and Schuster, 1984.

Dodson, Betty. *Sex for One: The Joy of Selfloving.* New York: Crown, 1992.

Hite, Shere. *The Hite Report: A Nationwide Study of Female Sexuality.* New York: Dell, 1987.

Both:

Reinisch, June M. *The Kinsey Institute New Report on Sex*. New York: St. Martin's Press, 1990.

SEXUAL ENHANCEMENT

Books of Fantasies:

Barbach, Lonnie (ed.) *Erotic Interludes*. New York: Harper & Row, 1987.
Friday, Nancy. *My Secret Garden*. New York: Trident Press, 1973.
———. *Forbidden Flowers*. New York: Pocket Books, 1975.
Nin, Anais. *Delta of Venus*. New York: Bantam Books, 1978.

General:

Comfort, Alex. *The New Joy of Sex (A Gourmet Guide for Lovemaking for the Nineties)*. New York: Crown, 1991.
Dodson, Betty. *Sex for One: The Joy of Selfloving*. New York: Crown, 1992.
"J." *The Sensuous Woman*. New York: Dell, 1970.
Sex After 50 (Videotape). Narrated by Lonnie Barbach. Sensitive and uplifting. Available from Better Sex Video Service, Suite 3635, 3600 Park Central Blvd. North, Pompano Beach, FL 33064. (800) 866-1000.
Sex Over Forty (monthly newsletter). Up-to-date and informative. Available from Sex Over Forty, P.O. Box 1600, Chapel Hill, NC 27515. (800) 334-5474.
Stubbs, Kenneth Ray, with Louise-Andree Saulnier. *Erotic Massage: The Touch of Love*. Larkspur, CA: Secret Garden, 1989.

SEX THERAPY

Kaplan, Helen Singer. *The Illustrated Manual of Sex Therapy*. New York: Brunner/Mazel, 1987.
———. *PE: How to Overcome Premature Ejaculation*. New York: Brunner/Mazel, 1989.

BIBLIOGRAPHY

Acton, William. *Functions and Disorders of the Reproductive Organs*. London: J & A Churchill, 1871.

Anthony, Susan B. In Ellen Dubois, ed., *The Stanton-Anthony Reader*. New York: Schocken Books, 1981.

Ayres, Toni. As quoted in "Sex 101: Continuing Education." *Ms. Magazine*, Aug. 1976, p. 22.

Bach, George R. and Peter Wyden. *The Intimate Enemy: How to Fight Fair in Love and Marriage*. New York: William Morrow & Co., 1969.

Barbach, Lonnie G., ed. *Erotic Interludes: Tales Told by Women*. New York: Harper & Row, 1986.

———. *For Yourself: The Fulfillment of Female Sexuality*. New York: Doubleday and Co., 1975.

Bernard, Jessie. *The Future of Marriage*. New Haven: Yale University Press, 1982.

Blood, R.O. and D.M. Wolfe. *Husbands and Wives: The Dynamics of Married Living*. New York: Free Press, 1960.

Bly, Robert. *Iron John: A Book About Men*. Reading, MA: Addison-Wesley, 1990.

Booth, Alan and John N. Edwards. "The Cessation of Marital Intercourse." *American Journal of Psychiatry*, vol. 133, no. 11, Nov. 1976, pp. 1333–1336.

Botwin, Carol, with Jerome L. Fine. *The Love Crisis*. New York: Doubleday and Co., 1979, p. 251.

Brannon, Robert. "No Sissy Stuff: The Stigma of Anything Vaguely Feminine." In Deborah David and Robert Brannon, eds. *The Forty-nine Percent Majority*. Reading, MA: Addison-Wesley, 1976.

Butler, Robert, and Myrna Lewis. *Sex After 60*. Boston: G.K. Hall, 1977.

Chodorow, Nancy. *The Reproduction of Mothering*. Berkeley: University of California Press, 1978.

Comfort, Alex. *The New Joy of Sex*. New York: Crown, 1991.

Cuber, John F. "The Natural History of Sex in Marriage." *Medical Aspects of Human Sexuality*, July 9, 1975, pp. 51–75.

de Beauvoir, Simone. *The Second Sex*. New York: Alfred A. Knopf, 1952.

deHardt, Delores. "Can a Feminist Therapist Facilitate a Client's Heterosexual Relationships." In L.B. Rosewater and L. Walker, eds., *The Handbook of Feminist Therapy*. New York: Springer, 1985.

Dodson, Betty. *Sex for One: The Joy of Selfloving*. New York: Crown, 1992.

Ellis, Albert. *The Intelligent Woman's Guide to Dating and Mating*. New York: Lyle Stuart, Inc., 1979.

English, Deirdre and Barbara Ehrenreich. "The Politics of Sexual Freedom." *Issues in Radical Therapy*, vol. 2, no. 3, 1974, pp. 15–17.

Farrell, Warren. *The Liberated Man*. New York: Random House, 1974, p. 32.

Forman, Bruce and D. Stein. "Perceptions of Behavior Exchange Patterns in Distressed and Non-Distressed Couples." *Psychotherapy Bulletin*, vol. 24, no. 2, 1989, pp. 11–14.

Forward, Susan. *Men Who Hate Women and the Women Who Love Them*. New York: Bantam Books, 1987.

Frank, Ellen, Carol Anderson, and Debra Rubinstein. "Frequency of Sexual Dysfunction in 'Normal' Couples." *New England Journal of Medicine*, vol. 299, no. 3, pp. 111–115.

Friday, Nancy. *Forbidden Flowers*. New York: Pocket Books, 1975.

———. *My Secret Garden*. New York: Pocket Books, 1973.

Gilligan, Carol. *In a Different Voice*. Cambridge, MA: Harvard University Press, 1982.

Goldberg, Herb. *The Hazards of Being Male*. New York: Signet, 1977.

Goldstine, Daniel, Katherine Larner, Shirley Zuckerman, and Hilary Goldstine. *The Dance-Away Lover*. New York: Ballantine Books, 1977.

Goleman, Daniel. "Chemistry of Sexual Desire Yields Its Elusive Secrets." *New York Times*, Oct 18, 1988, p. C1.

———. "Marriage: Research Reveals Ingredients of Happiness." *New York Times*, April 16, 1985, p. C1.

———. "Men at 65: New Findings on Well-being." *New York Times* Jan. 16, 1990, p. C1.

Gordon, Sol. *Why Love Is Not Enough*. Holbrook, Mass: Bob Adams, Inc., 1988.

Gottman, John M. and R. W. Levinson. "The Social Psychophysiology of Marriage." In P. Roller and M.A. Fitzpatrick, eds., *Perspectives on Marital Intercourse*. New York: Taylor & Francis, 1988, pp. 182–200.

Harris, Marvin. "Why Men Dominate Women." *New York Times Sunday Magazine*, Nov. 13, 1977, pp. 46–123.

Harrison, Barbara G. "What Men Want from Love and Marriage." *McCall's*, Aug. 1981, pp. 26–32.

Hite, Shere. *The Hite Report on Male Sexuality*. New York: Alfred A. Knopf, 1981.

———. *Women and Love: A Cultural Revolution in Progress*. New York: Alfred A. Knopf, 1987.

Jong, Erica. *Fear of Flying*. New York: Holt, Rinehart and Winston, 1973, p. 9.

Kaplan, Helen S. *Illustrated Manual of Sex Therapy*. New York: Quadrangle/New York Times Book Co., 1975.

Kaplan, Helen S., M.D., and Clifford J. Sager. "Sexual Patterns at Different Ages." *Medical Aspects of Human Sexuality*, June 1971, pp. 10–23.

Kasl, Charlotte. *Women, Sex and Addiction*. New York: Ticknor & Fields, 1989.

Kenn, Sam. *Fire in the Belly: On Being a Man*. New York: Bantam Books, 1991.

Kellogg, Polly. Women's Sexuality Workshop conducted at the Institute for Rational Living, New York, 1973.

Kelley, Harold H., E. Bersheid, A. Christensen, J.H. Harvey, T.L. Huston, G. Levinger, E. McClintock, L.A. Peplau, and D. R. Peterson, *Close Relationships*. New York: W.H. Freeman & Co., 1983.

Kernberg, Otto F. "Further Contributions to the Treatment of Narcissistic Personalities." *International Journal of Psychoanalysis*, vol. 55, 1974, pp. 215–240.

Kiley, Dan. *What to Do When He Won't Change*. New York: Fawcett Crest, 1987.

Kinsey, Alfred C., Wardell P. Pomeroy, and Clyde E. Martin. *Sexual Behavior in the Human Male*. Philadelphia: Saunders, 1948.

Kolodny, Robert C., and William H. Masters, Robert M. Kolodner, and Gelson Toro. "Depression of Plasma Testosterone Levels after Chronic Intensive Marihuana Use." *New England Journal of Medicine*, vol. 290, April 18, 1974, pp. 872–874.

Lauer, Jeannette and Robert Lauer. "Marriages Made to Last." *Psychology Today*, June 1985, pp. 22–26.

Lessor, Richard. *Love and Marriage and Trading Stamps: On the Care and Feeding of Marriage*. Chicago: Argus Press, 1971.

Levinson, R., and John Gottman. "Physiological Affective Predictors of Change in Relationship Satisfaction." *Journal of Personality and Social Psychology*, vol. 49, 1985, pp. 85–94.

Lief, H. "What's New in Sex Research? Inhibited Desire." *Medical Aspects of Human Sexuality*, vol. 2, no. 7, July 1977, pp. 944–94.

LoPiccolo, Joseph, and Jerry Friedman. "Broad-Spectrum Treatment of Low Sexual Desire." In S. Leiblum and R. Rosen, eds., *Sexual Desire Disorders*. New York: Guilford Press, 1988, p. 112.

Maccoby, Eleanor E. "Gender and Relationships: A Developmental Account." *American Psychologist*, vol. 45, no. 4, April 1990, pp. 513–520.

Maslow, Abraham. "Self-Esteem (Dominance-Feeling) and Sexuality in Women." *Journal of Social Psychology*, vol. 16, pp. 259–294.

Masters, William H., Virginia C. Johnson, and Robert C. Kolodny. *Masters and Johnson on Sex and Human Loving*. Boston: Little, Brown, 1988.

Men's Health Survey. In Karen Peterson, "What Men Like in a Lover." *USA Today*, Aug. 25, 1988.

Miller, Jean Baker. *Toward a New Psychology of Women*. Boston: Beacon Press, 1976.

Montagu, Ashley. In Philip Berman, ed., *The Courage of Conviction*. New York: Ballantine Books, 1986, pp. 180–181.

National Opinion Research Center Survey. In Tom W. Smith, "Adult Sexual Behavior in 1989: Number of Partners, Frequency of Intercourse and Risk of Aids." *Family Planning Perspectives*, vol. 23, no. 3, May/June 1991, pp. 102–107.

O'Leary, Virginia. "Sex Makes a Difference: Attributes for Emotional Cause." American Psychological Association Symposium. Washington, D.C.: Aug. 13, 1988.

O'Reilly, Jane. "A Different Rapture: Note on the Romance of a Lifetime." *Lear's*, March 1989.

Perry, Eleanor, contributing author. "How's Your Sex Life?" *MS. Magazine*, Nov. 1976, pp. 82ff.

Pietropinto, A., and J. Simenauer. *Not Tonight Dear: How to Reawaken Your Sexual Desire*. New York: Doubleday and Co., 1990.

Pillay, A. P., and Albert Ellis. "Is the Vaginal Orgasm a Myth?" *Sex, Society and the Individual*. Bombay: International Journal of Sexology Press, 1953.

Publilius Syrus. *Sententiae*. 43 BC.

Rajfer, Jacob, William J. Aronson, Peggy A. Bush, Frederick J. Dorey, and Louis J. Ignarro. "Nitric Oxide as a Mediator of Relaxation of the Corpus Cavernosum in Response to Nonadrenergic, Noncholinergic Neurotransmission." *New England Journal of Medicine*, Jan. 9, 1992, pp. 90–94.

Rose, Phyllis. *Parallel Lives*. New York: Alfred A. Knopf, 1983, p. 168.

Rubin, Lillian B. *Worlds of Pain: Life in the Working Class Family*. New York: Basic Books, 1976.

Russianoff, Penelope. *Why Do I Think I Am Nothing Without a Man?* New York: Bantam Books, 1982.

Sands, Melissa. "Your Man Got Away—But His Spirit Still Haunts You." *New Woman*, May 1984, pp. 116–118.

Scarf, Maggie. *Intimate Partners*. New York: Ballantine Books, 1987.

Schiavi, Raul C. "Nocturnal Penile Tumescence in the Evaluation of Erectile Disorders: A Critical Review." *Journal of Sex & Marital Therapy*, vol. 14, no. 2, Summer 1988, pp. 83–94.

Shaver, Phillip and Jonathan Freedman. "Your Pursuit of Happiness." *Psychology Today*, Aug. 1976, pp. 26–32.

Sills, Judith. *How to Stop Looking for Someone Perfect and Find Someone to Love*. New York: St. Martin's Press, 1984.

Sloan, Don, and Lillian Africano. "Female Sexual Dysfunction." *Forum: The Journal of Human Relations*. New York: Forum International, 1978.

Starr, Bernard D. and Marcella D. Weiner. *The Starr-Weiner Report on Sex and Sexuality in the Mature Years*. New York: Stein and Day, 1981.

Stearns, Peter N. *Be a Man!: Males in Modern Society.* New York: Holmes & Meier, 1979.

Tannen, Deborah. *You Just Don't Understand: Women and Men in Conversation.* New York: William Morrow & Co, 1990.

Tavris, Carol, and Susan Sadd. *The Redbook Report on Female Sexuality.* New York: Delacorte Press, 1977.

Vaillant, George E. and Caroline O. Vaillant, "Natural History of Male Psychological Health, X: Work as a Predictor of Positive Mental Health." *The American Journal of Psychiatry,* vol. 138, no. 11, Nov. 1981. pp. 1433–1440.

Waldron, I. "Why Do Women Live Longer than Men?" *Journal of Human Stress,* vol. 2, 1976, pp. 1–13.

Wallis, Claudia. "Back off Buddy." *Time,* Oct. 12, 1987, pp. 68–73.

Zilbergeld, Bernie. *Male Sexuality.* New York: Bantam Books, 1978, p. 239.

Zilbergeld, Bernie and Carol R. Ellison. "Desire Discrepancies and Arousal Problems in Sex Therapy." In S. R. Leiblum and L.A. Pervin, eds., *Principles and Practice of Sex Therapy.* New York: Guilford Press, 1980.

FOR THE BEST IN PAPERBACKS, LOOK FOR THE

In every corner of the world, on every subject under the sun, Penguin represents quality and variety—the very best in publishing today.

For complete information about books available from Penguin—including Pelicans, Puffins, Peregrines, and Penguin Classics—and how to order them, write to us at the appropriate address below. Please note that for copyright reasons the selection of books varies from country to country.

In the United Kingdom: For a complete list of books available from Penguin in the U.K., please write to *Dept E.P., Penguin Books Ltd, Harmondsworth, Middlesex, UB7 0DA.*

In the United States: For a complete list of books available from Penguin in the U.S., please write to *Dept BA, Penguin,* Box 120, Bergenfield, New Jersey 07621-0120.

In Canada: For a complete list of books available from Penguin in Canada, please write to *Penguin Books Canada Ltd, 10 Alcorn Avenue, Suite 300, Toronto, Ontario, Canada M4V 3B2.*

In Australia: For a complete list of books available from Penguin in Australia, please write to the *Marketing Department, Penguin Books Ltd, P.O. Box 257, Ringwood, Victoria 3134.*

In New Zealand: For a complete list of books available from Penguin in New Zealand, please write to the *Marketing Department, Penguin Books (NZ) Ltd, Private Bag, Takapuna, Auckland 9.*

In India: For a complete list of books available from Penguin, please write to *Penguin Overseas Ltd, 706 Eros Apartments, 56 Nehru Place, New Delhi, 110019.*

In Holland: For a complete list of books available from Penguin in Holland, please write to *Penguin Books Nederland B.V., Postbus 195, NL-1380AD Weesp, Netherlands.*

In Germany: For a complete list of books available from Penguin, please write to *Penguin Books Ltd, Friedrichstrasse 10-12, D-6000 Frankfurt Main 1, Federal Republic of Germany.*

In Spain: For a complete list of books available from Penguin in Spain, please write to *Longman, Penguin España, Calle San Nicolas 15, E-28013 Madrid, Spain.*

In Japan: For a complete list of books available from Penguin in Japan, please write to *Longman Penguin Japan Co Ltd, Yamaguchi Building, 2-12-9 Kanda Jimbocho, Chiyoda-Ku, Tokyo 101, Japan.*

FOR THE BEST IN HEALTH BOOKS, LOOK FOR THE 🐧

☐ **ADDICTIVE DRINKING**
   The Road to Recovery for Problem Drinkers and Those Who Love Them
   Clark Vaughan

A recovered addictive drinker himself, Clark Vaughan leads you through the disagreement and confusion concerning addiction treatment and answers questions no counselor could answer before.

318 pages   *ISBN: 0-14-006969-0*

☐ **MENOPAUSE**
   Rosetta Reitz

Growing out of Rosetta Reitz's own search for answers, this book tells how to deal positively with all the physical and psychological changes that menopause brings.   *276 pages*   *ISBN: 0-14-005120-1*

☐ **NO MORE MENSTRUAL CRAMPS AND OTHER GOOD NEWS**
   Penny Wise Budoff, M.D.

The one essential health guide for women of all ages, *No More Menstrual Cramps* reports that menstrual pain has a specific physical cause and that safe, non-narcotic remedies are available.

312 pages   *ISBN: 0-14-005938-5*